## Praise for "This Is the Life"

"Using the finely-tuned skills of a detective, Clinton resident and historian Leslie Perrin Wilson has taken the clues found in a pocket diary, added valuable context, and created a meticulously detailed profile of Jennie McLeod, a life-long Clinton resident who came of age during the World War I era. The resulting book provides a 'written snapshot' of the early adult years of a young woman living within and reacting to the norms of her time. By bringing Jennie's story to the fore, Wilson offers an insightful peek into the history of this Massachusetts mill town and elevates the lives of countless similar unknown women of the time. This is a 'must read' for those with high interest in primary source material, social history, and women's studies."

**Heather Lennon**
Chairperson of the Lancaster Historical Commission (Lancaster, Massachusetts),
President of the Lancaster Historical Society

"Jennie McLeod, a young resident of the Massachusetts mill town of Clinton, graduates from Smith College and enters womanhood and working life on the eve of America's entry into World War I. What did Jennie think about? Who were her friends and influences? How did she get around? Have fun? Earn money? And how did she capture it all in her little diary? Wilson's commentary sets the diary against the arc of Jennie's life and the background of family, hometown, college, and national events. Travel along, via train, streetcar, 1915 Ford, and Jennie's own words. It's a great ride!"

**Jayne Gordon**
Public Historian

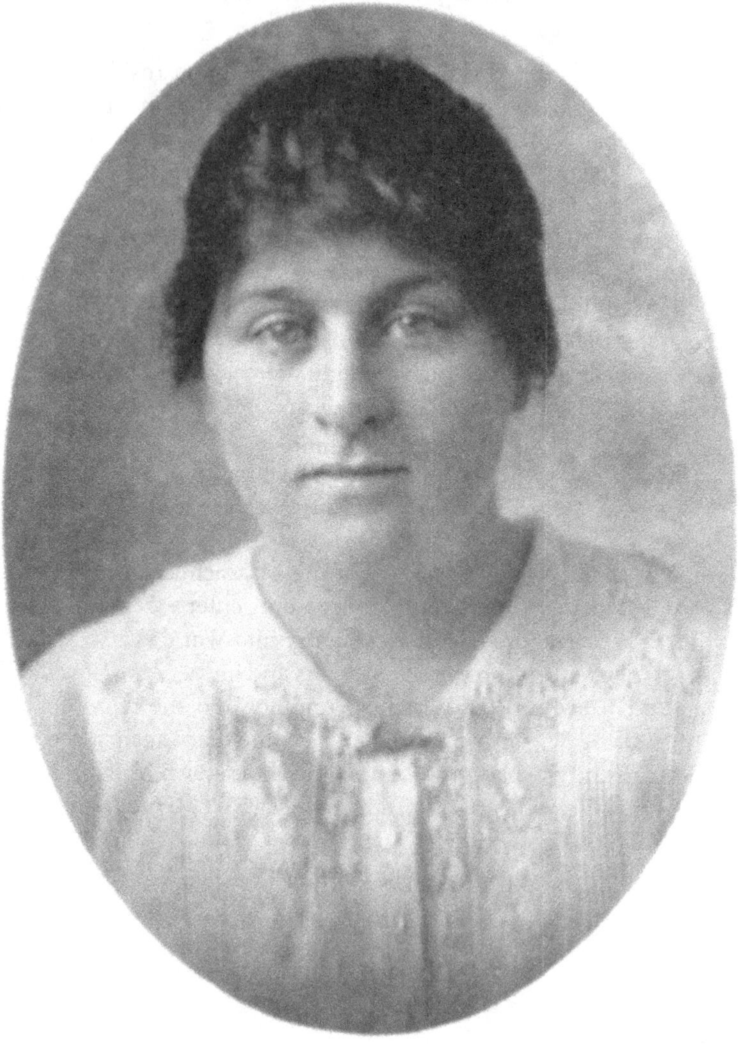

# "This Is the Life"

*The Diary*
of
## Jennie McLeod

edited, with introduction, by
## Leslie Perrin Wilson

Copyright © 2020, Leslie Perrin Wilson

All rights reserved. No part of this book may be reproduced, stored in a retrieval system, or transmitted in any form, or by any means, electronic, mechanical, photocopying, recording or otherwise; without prior written permission of the author, other than those quotes or material attributed to another source.

Moonglade Press
Publishing New Works by Uncommon Voices
www.moongladepress.com

Distributed by IngramSpark

ISBN: 978-0-9987639-8-9
Library of Congress Control Number: 2020925542

Printed in the U.S.A.

*For Pat and Jocelyn*

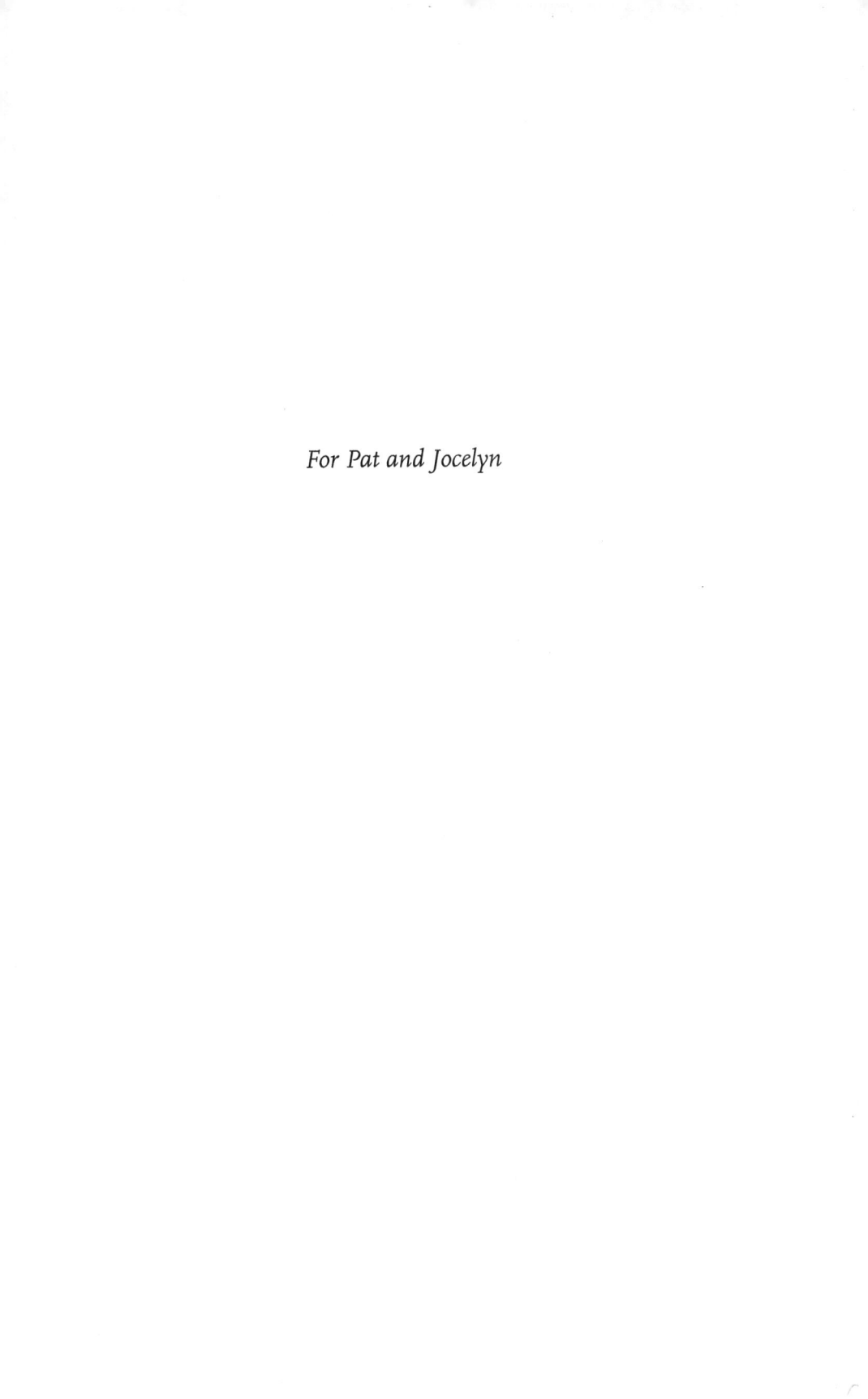

# CONTENTS

- 2 Illustrations
- 3 Preface
- 9 Introduction
    - 9 The Diary at a Glance
    - 13 Jennie's Themes
    - 16 Hometown Context
    - 32 Jennie in Her Family
    - 48 The Education of Jennie McLeod
    - 66 The Bigger Picture—World War
    - 75 Reform Unfolding—The Suffrage Movement
    - 79 Jennie's Life, Going Forward
- 103 The Diary
    - 104 Note on Transcription and Annotation
- 106 Annotated Transcript
    - 106 1914
    - 182 1915
    - 258 1916
    - 284 1917
    - 293 1918
    - 294 Memoranda (financial records)
- 296 Acknowledgments
- 298 Sources

# ILLUSTRATIONS

All illustrations come from sources in the author's collection, unless otherwise specified.

Cover design based on the binding of Jennie McLeod's diary

Frontispiece: Jennie McLeod, December 11, 1914, from Smith College *1915 Class Book* (yearbook)

- 8 First page of Jennie McLeod's diary
- 17 High Street, Clinton, looking south, ca. 1915 (postcard image)
- 19 Lancaster Mills, Clinton (postcard image)
- 22 Wachusett Dam, power station, and fountain (postcard image)
- 38 244 Water Street, Clinton, June 2020. Photograph by the author
- 49 Clinton High School, intersection of Chestnut and Union Streets (postcard image)
- 54 College Hall, Smith College, Northampton (postcard image)
- 84 Ellen K. Stevens, from Clinton High School *Memorabilia* (yearbook), 1922. Courtesy Clinton Historical Society
- 116 Main Street, Northampton, ca. 1905-1910 (postcard image)
- 124 Christine L. Beck, from 1915 Wellesley College *Legenda* (yearbook)
- 137 High Street, Holyoke, ca. 1910 (postcard image)
- 143 High Street, Clinton, looking north, ca. 1905 (postcard image)
- 150 Clinton Town Hall, ca. 1910 (postcard image)
- 166 Hockanum Ferry, Northampton to Hadley (postcard image)
- 184 John M. Greene Hall, Smith College (postcard image)
- 211 Summit of Mount Tom, Holyoke (postcard image)
- 227 Paragon Park, Nantasket Beach, showing roller coaster (postcard image)
- 234 Mildred Hutchinson (Hutch), from Smith College *1915 Class Book* (yearbook)
- 245 Carolyn W. Sprague, from Smith College *1915 Class Book* (yearbook)
- 277 Main Street, Worcester, ca. 1912 (postcard image)

## PREFACE

FOR THIRTY YEARS, MY HUSBAND AND I LIVED AND RAISED OUR FAMILY in a renovated nineteenth-century district schoolhouse in Lancaster, Massachusetts. As a professional curator and local historian, I delighted in viewing the past through the window our antique house opened. Digging into its story opened my eyes to the documentary riches available locally, introduced me to members of the town's historical community, and made me feel connected in a personal way to earlier inhabitants of our home. In 2011, when changing circumstances prompted a move to a two-family house, we rejoiced at finding a new home in neighboring Clinton that met our practical requirements and simultaneously offered me the opportunity to explore the long narrative of another old building.

We moved into the stately and well-preserved Italianate Victorian at 244 Water Street in October of that year. Almost immediately, I began searching for documentation relating to those who had occupied our home before we took possession. I discovered that the house was built in 1878 and first inhabited by Erastus P. Whittaker, or Whitaker (an overseer at the nearby woolen mill), and his wife Betsey. Over the following months, I consulted print, manuscript, and electronic records and communicated with local people to gather information about former owners. It turned out that in the one-hundred and thirty-plus years since its construction, only three families had owned the home before us.

Along the way, I found that local plumber George McLeod had purchased the house in 1916. The McLeod family lived there into the 1990s. After George McLeod died in 1936, his oldest daughter Jennie C. McLeod was subsequently identified in the federal census as the head of the 244 Water Street household.

One day in January 2013, after the rush of Thanksgiving, Christmas, and New Year's had passed, I returned to house history, the pursuit of which had languished during the holiday season. Plugging the names of people I knew had lived at 244 Water Street into the Google search box and adding "Clinton, Massachusetts" to increase the likelihood of meaningful search results, I was intrigued when the name "Jennie C. McLeod" brought up the website of a Canadian book and manuscript dealer. M. Benjamin Katz was offering for sale what he described as the "1914-1917 original manuscript diary of the life and times of a pre World War I Smith College student." As I read his listing for the item and poked around on the Internet for corroborating evidence, it became clear that the Jennie McLeod of the diary was, indeed, the Jennie McLeod who had lived in my house from 1916 until her death in 1968. I had not anticipated unearthing archival gold among the possible outcomes of my exploration.

Alas, the asking price for the diary was more than I could justify spending casually, so I made note of the information available in the dealer's description and reluctantly clicked back to the Google search box. I later mentioned my discovery to my husband, who was not overly excited about the possible purchase of a high-ticket item that I did not, by any standard, actually need. I did my best to put the diary out of my mind.

But I was unsuccessful in the attempt. Over the subsequent weeks,

PREFACE

I periodically rechecked for the listing, half-hoping and half-dreading that someone else—Smith College, perhaps?—might have decided to scoop it up. Each time I looked, there it was, still waiting to be bought. I suppressed the acquisitive instinct for a full six months before admitting to myself that the diary was emblazoned with my name. I have had considerable experience in transcribing and contextualizing manuscript material—including a woman's diary of the 1830s—for publication. Moreover, the association of the little leather-bound volume with our house was compelling. Ultimately, I gave in. After some negotiation about price, I made the purchase.

It was thrilling to experience the tangible connection with the past that holding and reading Jennie McLeod's diary for the first time created. I longed to transcribe the whole and to make sense of it for an audience of interested readers. After all, what is the point of acquiring a piece of the documentary record unless the final result is its greater accessibility to others for whom it possesses potential meaning and value? But the reality of a demanding full-time job prevented me from plunging into the work required to achieve that end. Forced to put the diary aside for the moment, I vowed to make it my first retirement project. July 26, 2019 was my final day as Curator of the William Munroe Special Collections of the Concord Free Public Library. Immediately thereafter, I set about making good on my resolution.

Someone once asked me whether Jennie McLeod was consequential enough to warrant a close study of her diary. But the assumption that only well-known figures merit attention discounts the importance of ordinary lives in illuminating social history, both local and broader. Jennie McLeod was no superstar of history or literature. The scope of her story is modest in comparison with that of Abigail Adams, for instance, or Margaret Fuller, or Laura Ingalls Wilder, or Eleanor Roosevelt. Whatever the diary's writer may have lacked in celebrity, however, her daily

PREFACE

jottings organically captured the world she occupied—both in college in Northampton and at home in Clinton—and allow the contemporary reader an informed, empathetic understanding of it.

You may be drawn to Jennie McLeod's diary specifically for what it can tell you about women's history and women's education in the Progressive Era, or more specifically about Smith College life at the time. Or perhaps you are drawn by the history of Clinton, Massachusetts, on the eve of America's involvement in World War I, or McLeod genealogy and family history, or the concept of community, or even by the story of one local structure of respectable age. I delight in the fact that there may be something here for readers of many stripes, whether driven by research interest, town pride, nostalgia, or simple curiosity. At the same time, I hope that those who take up the diary for what they hope to find in it will suspend personal mission long enough to appreciate, on its own terms, the portrait embedded within of one young woman's life and time.

In Clinton, as in many other places, women's stories remain relatively underdocumented and underexplored. To be sure, men played the dominant roles in founding and managing the local mills and in building the Wachusett Dam and Reservoir—both aspects of town history closely identified with Clinton's sense of itself. But history at all levels is richer and more nuanced than the traditionally credited version suggests.

Although undertaken as a private record, Jennie McLeod's diary reflects a woman's vantage point on matters small and large relating to the social fabric of Clinton and the world beyond. Moreover, the fact that it is unpretentious and intelligent gives it added value, as does knowledge of the diarist's ultimate transformation into a strong and competent woman in a period when men were typically in charge in both home and workplace. Whether she was "important" as that term is

PREFACE

commonly understood is irrelevant. Embrace and respect her diary for what it is, not for who she was or was not, and enjoy it.

*Leslie Perrin Wilson*
*244 Water Street*
*Clinton, Massachusetts*
*September 12, 2020*

## JANUARY 1

19 1/4 Th. New Year's party at Mildred's Alpha Club and friends. Delightful reunion. Dr Jordan called in the afternoon. Hope to keep this 5 yr without fail

19/5 F. Not a resolution. Spent morning and afternoon on Road Dept. accounts. Typewrote dept letter to Finance Comm. in the evening

19/6 Sa. Cooked and sewed in the morning and ironed and tatted in the afternoon. Anna and Marg came down to supper. Marg late as usual. Grand reunion

19/7 mon. New Year resolution — To keep my diary regularly henceforth — Wrote remaining thank you notes. Read The Contagion of Character & Spanish reader

19

First page of Jennie McLeod's diary

# INTRODUCTION

## The Diary at a Glance

JENNIE MCLEOD'S FIVE-YEAR DIARY IS HEIR TO THE POCKET DIARY volumes popular in America from the 1850s.[1] This compact and highly portable product enjoyed a steady market demand.[2] Blank pocket diaries with lined pages could be purchased from stationers and booksellers and were often given as Christmas or New Years' presents, particularly to women and girls.[3] Jennie McLeod's diary may have been a present from a family member or a friend, but the volume itself offers no evidence beyond the fact that the first entry in it was made on January 1, 1914.

In the nineteenth century, diary-keeping was promoted in print as an appropriate pursuit for the middle and upper classes, and diary publishers targeted an educated clientele.[4] For those who aspired to self-improvement, the discipline necessary to make regular entries

---

[1] Molly McCarthy, "A Pocketful of Days: Pocket Diaries and Daily Record Keeping among Nineteenth-Century New England Women," *The New England Quarterly*, Vol. 73, No. 2 (June 2000), 275, 281.
[2] Ibid., 280.
[3] Ibid., 278-79.
[4] Ibid., 284.

offered additional appeal.⁵ Jennie McLeod was a literate and well-read middle-class girl. Her view of diary-keeping may have been colored by these historical associations with the activity.

Jennie's diary measures approximately three and a half inches wide by five and seven-eighths inches high (front cover) by seven-eighths inches deep (book block)—in fact, small enough to fit into a pocket. It is bound in blue Morocco leather, stamped in gold on the front "A Line A Day," with an ornamental fleuron stamped in gold below the lettering. The edges are gilt, the back cover unadorned.

Printed in black and red, the title page of the diary reads *Ward's "A Line A Day" Book. A Condensed, Comparative Record for Five Years. "Nulla dies sine linea." (No day without a line.) Trademark Ward's Stationery Boston*. The volume was copyrighted in 1892 by the Ward Company. The prefatory note following the title page is headed in red ink, with the text in black and the first printed letter a hanging capital "Y" in red. Overall, the decorative touches used to ornament the volume appear intended to camouflage its mass production.

Each page of the diary proper is printed with a heading for a day of the year ("January 1," "January 2," and so on). Below the headers, each page is divided into five sections, each section printed with the first two digits of a year ("19"), the remaining two digits left blank for completion by the diarist. Each of the five sections on a page contains four lines for a manuscript entry. The diary entries for a single date over five years would thus follow one another on a page, retrospectively offering a kind of bird's-eye view.

As publishers of printed, lined, commercial pocket diaries emphasized, the predefined entry length permitted by the allotted space minimized the burden of journalizing. The Samuel Ward Company of

---

5   Ibid., 285.

Boston—publisher of Jennie's diary—observed in the printed preface to the little volume that while diarists had "neither the time nor the inclination, possibly, to keep a full diary," jotting down a line or two daily would still provide a "record of events, incidents, joys, sorrows, successes, failures, things accomplished, things attempted," making the book "of the greatest value in after years." The pocket diary thus offered a fast track to achieving the benefits of more open-ended specimens of the genre.

On the front free endpaper of the volume is inscribed in ink: "Jennie C. McLeod / 117 Pearl St. / Clinton, Mass."—the second of two Pearl Street homes where the McLeods lived, and the Clinton address where Jennie recorded most of her diary entries. She wrote later diary entries at 244 Water Street, where the family moved in 1916.

In a reasonably legible manuscript hand, Jennie recorded diary entries without fail in 1914 and neglected only two—for June 21 and 22—in 1915. She was less faithful in 1916, when she made regular entries for January and February but began sloughing off in March, ultimately leaving blank the lined space for well over two hundred days. In 1917, Jennie wrote fairly regularly in January, less so in February, and ceased altogether for the rest of the year beginning on February 28. Finally, in 1918 she made a single entry on April 18. Her five-year diary is thus really a full record of two years—1914 and 1915—with intermittent later additions.

Printed pocket diaries traditionally featured pages at the end for recording debits and credits—personal, household, or business-related.[6] In keeping with this convention, Jennie used the "Memoranda" section at the end of her diary to list receipts and expenses for two Clinton organizations with which she was involved—the Junior Chautauqua and the Clinton Chamber of Commerce.

---

6    Ibid., 275.

Jennie's inability to sustain momentum beyond two years was not for lack of intent. She tried hard to stay on task. On January 1, 1914, her first entry in the volume, she wrote optimistically, "Hope to keep this 5 yr without fail." Fourteen months later, in her entry for March 5, 1915, she revealed she had neglected to record entries for a week and was making good by filling them in retroactively. She commented on how little she could "recall of the days doings—Moral don't delay diary 1 wk." In November 1915, five months after her graduation from Smith College in Northampton, Massachusetts, she lapsed again, writing on November 23, "Wrote to Anna, made up diary bathed & retired." Her entry for July 2, 1916, discloses yet another attempt to recover after backsliding—"Inspected house, ate, talked, made up diary." Struggling to keep her daily record going, she resolved on New Year's Day in 1917, "To keep my diary regularly henceforth."

That the diarist lost impetus at the end of 1915 reflects her diary's role as transitional in bridging the gap between girlhood and adulthood. It allowed her to memorialize and ultimately to leave behind concerns that absorbed her for a time and shaped the mature woman she became.

The value of Jennie's diary-keeping for her was rooted in its capacity to capture events as they happened. In the words of nineteenth-century French novelist George Sand, "Writing a journal implies that one has ceased to think of the future and has decided to live wholly in the present."[7] As a college student, Jennie's major responsibilities consisted of successfully completing her studies and enjoying the intellectual and social smorgasbord available at Smith—a suspended state that afforded her the luxury of focusing on the details of the moment. But once she graduated, serious consideration of her own life going forward and of

---

7   As quoted in Mary Jane Moffat and Charlotte Painter, *Revelations: Diaries of Women* (New York: Vintage Books, 1975), 15-16.

unfolding events in the larger world would soon engage her attention.

Significantly, three times during her college career (May 28, 1914, January 29, 1915, and May 7, 1915), Jennie was moved by seemingly pedestrian occurrences to exclaim in her diary, "This is the life"—a revelation that she approached the volume as a means of embracing her life as it presented itself. After her college graduation, the phrase does not appear again. Jennie graduated from Smith in 1915. By the close of that year, her diary had largely served its purpose. From that point on, she was engaged in sorting out what relationship, work, and personal fulfillment would look like in her future.

## Jennie's Themes

WHAT DID JENNIE MCLEOD WRITE ABOUT IN HER POCKET DIARY? The volume offers a snapshot of what mattered to her both at home in Clinton, where she spent college vacations and to which she returned permanently following graduation, and in Northampton during the academic year.

Many of the diary entries Jennie made in Clinton center on her immediate family—her mother, father, and four younger siblings—and her interactions with them. She was especially close to her father, George McLeod. Her local friends troop through the diary, as well. Among the most important of these was her Clinton High School classmate Christine L. Beck (they graduated with the Class of 1911). Christine was a student at Wellesley College while Jennie was at Smith.

Jennie's working life, both before and after graduation, also forms a diary topic. She wrote up public lectures for the *Clinton Daily Item*, kept her father's plumbing store, performed office work for the Clinton Road Commission (of which George McLeod was a member and sometime chair), and helped out in the insurance office of Miss Ellen K. Stevens, which Jennie would later take over and run under her own name. She also made money by tutoring and substitute teaching in Clinton and elsewhere.

Social life, lectures, entertainment, church activities, local politics, and celebrations in Clinton feature prominently in the diary. Because Jennie McLeod frequented downtown shops and stores, business in Clinton also has a place. And Jennie's sustained drive to maintain a thinking life and to improve upon her capabilities and skills form a recurrent diary theme after her graduation from college and return to her hometown.

Academics and the social experience—topics of universal interest to college students—fill the diary entries Jennie made at Smith. She commented on classes, lectures, and labs; exams, quizzes, and papers; hunkering down in the library; faculty, staff, and speakers from beyond the college (for instance, Booker T. Washington, who spoke about the Tuskegee Normal and Industrial Institute on January 11, 1914)[8]; club activities (Jennie was a member of Colloquium, a departmental club at the college)[9]; musical and dramatic events (among them a performance by virtuoso violinist Fritz Kreisler on January 14, 1914); sports; college rituals and traditions (chapel, step singing, Mountain Day, Ivy Day, Rally Day, and prom); residential life at 17 Belmont Avenue during the 1913-1914 academic year and in Gillett in 1914-1915;[10] formal and informal social occasions (teas, ice

---

8   *Smith College Weekly*, January 14, 1914, as cited in Alexander S. Leidholdt, *Battling Nell: The Life of Southern Journalist Cornelia Battle Lewis, 1893-1956* (Baton Rouge: Louisiana State University Press, 2009), 32.
9   Smith College, *1915 Class Book* (Northampton, Massachusetts: The College, 1915), 90.
10  Jennie's residence during the 1913-1914 school year is documented in *Bulletin of Smith College; Catalogue, 1913-1914* (Northampton, Massachusetts: The College, 1913), 123, and during 1914-1915 in *Bulletin of Smith College; Catalogue, 1914-1915* (Northampton: The College, 1914), 156.

cream parties, Welsh rarebit parties); housemates and friends; trips to Northampton stores and eateries; area amusements; and the books she read.

Compact by definition, pocket diaries did not offer scope for the extensive analysis of daily events or for deep introspection. From time to time, Jennie McLeod pushed the physical limits of her diary by inserting an extra line or two between what she wrote on the printed lines. But such improvisation did not really encourage significantly longer entries.

Nevertheless, Jennie was capable of expressing strong emotion without waste of words. On January 30, 1914, she wrote plaintively, "My twenty-first birthday and without question the unhappiest day of my life." This is a striking statement for a young woman not much inclined to self-dramatization. Although she did not explicitly identify the reason for her unhappiness in that entry, she had written of homesickness the previous day. On June 14, 1915 (the day before her commencement), she again communicated the loneliness triggered by the absence of family, "Cried myself to sleep because the family aren't coming."

Jennie broached serious subjects like religion obliquely rather than head-on and she only intermittently made note of matters of regional and national significance. She was aware of events in the news, but kept them in the background of her diary. She wrote in passing on March 17, 1914 of the burning of College Hall at Wellesley College—a major event in the history of that institution—and, on April 19 and 21, 1914, of the Tampico Affair and the impending United States occupation of Veracruz. Her restraint in reportage is particularly apparent in her references to the ongoing war in Europe (which would eventually directly touch the McLeod family) and to the fight for women's suffrage, which Jennie worked to advance.

Overall, the tone of Jennie McLeod's diary reflects her demeanor as those who remember her characterize it—forthright, frank, matter-of-fact, and brisk.[11] In addition, her writing conveys a sense of humor and a capacity for wry self-deprecation. Her occasional archness and use of slang give her away as a smart modern girl, comfortable with popular culture. (For example, she repeatedly played on the title of the 1909 hit song "I Love, I Love, I Love My Wife, But Oh! You Kid," exclaiming on August 23, 1914, for instance, after a visit to the amusement park at Revere Beach, "Oh you roller coaster."[12]) Moreover, her diary entries radiate a basic optimism about moving forward.

There is no denying that Jennie's daily jottings are sometimes cryptic. To some extent, this arises from the format of the preprinted diary volume. It is difficult to spell things out fully when given only four lines to do so. But it also reflects the important fact that it simply was not necessary for her to elaborate on what she wrote. She was, in effect, her own audience. Maintaining her diary for her present and future self, she took for granted that she would understand elliptical comments and references in later reading it.

## Hometown Context

DURING THE PERIOD JENNIE MCLEOD KEPT HER DIARY, HER HOMETOWN was riding the tail end of a wave of prosperity, growth, and optimism that had started to build momentum a hundred years earlier. Clinton

---

11 Personal interview with Robert and Judith McLeod, September 20, 2019.
12 According to Jody Rosen, "Oh! You Kid" "captured the zeitgeist ... of the times. It incited countless newspaper editorials, fulminating sermons by preachers, and at least one fatal shooting"—Jody Rosen, "'Oh! You Kid!' How a sexed-up viral hit from the summer of '09—1909—changed American Pop Music Forever," *Slate* (June 2, 2014), www.slate.com/articles/arts/culturebox/2014/06/sex_and_pop_the_forgotten_1909_hit_that_introduced_adultery_to_american.html (accessed October 1, 2019).

P7439   High Street, Looking South, Clinton, Mass.

High Street, Clinton, looking south, ca. 1915

as Jennie knew it was, indeed, "a child of the nineteenth century and a product of the Industrial Revolution."[13]

Located in central Massachusetts, Clinton was originally part of agricultural Lancaster, the oldest town in Worcester County, incorporated in 1653. In 1850, Clinton became the last of Lancaster's daughter towns to separate from the mother town to become a distinct municipality.[14]

The topography of the area that became Clinton—in particular, the Nashua River and several good-sized brooks—endowed it with water power and the capacity to support manufacture. Relying on these attributes, John Prescott—a seventeenth-century founder of Lancast-

---

[13]  Waldo T. Davis, "Clinton at the Turn of the Century, 1900-1910," *Clinton Centennial Volume, 1850-1950: The Story of Clinton, Massachusetts* ... (Clinton: The Town, copyright 1951), 25.

[14]  *Towns of the Nashaway Plantation* (Hudson, Massachusetts: Lancaster League of Historical Societies, 1976).

er—had established a gristmill, a sawmill, and his homestead in the southern part of town (later Clinton), not far from where the house at 244 Water Street stands today.[15]

The Industrial Revolution came to Clinton early in the nineteenth century, when David Poignand and Samuel Plant established a cotton mill on the factory system in the place where Prescott had operated his mills.[16] The vicinity subsequently became known as Factory Village. The natural advantages of the area later attracted other entrepreneurs who hoped to capitalize on the burgeoning textile industry.

Born in West Boylston, Massachusetts, brothers Erastus and Horatio Bigelow rented mill property in what is now Clinton, and installed a power loom, designed by Erastus for the complicated process of manufacturing coach lace (livery lace for carriage and coach trim). In 1838, the brothers formed the Clinton Company, named for the Clinton House, a New York hotel favored by Erastus.[17] Factory Village was soon dubbed Clintonville, whence came the name formally given the new town when it was established as a separate entity in 1850.[18]

Clintonville was some distance from the administrative center of Lancaster, making it difficult for village residents to get to town meetings. The character and needs of dynamic Clintonville did not mesh with those of Lancaster, and once manufacture took hold, irreconcilable differences evolved. The population of the area grew along with manufacture, as did the need for better roads and the desire for control over schools and municipal services. Separation from the mother town was inevitable, if not entirely congenial.[19]

---

15   Andrew E. Ford, *History of the Origin of the Town of Clinton, Massachusetts, 1653-1865* (Clinton: Press of W.J. Coulter, *Courant* Office, 1896), 40-44.
16   Ibid., 139-61.
17   Ibid., 192-252.
18   *Towns of the Nashaway Plantation*, 157.
19   Ford, 269-83.

LANCASTER MILLS, CLINTON, MASS.

Lancaster Mills, Clinton

The Bigelows achieved success and boosted the profile and economy of their adopted home by branching out into multiple industrial enterprises. The inventive Erastus had earlier developed a loom for weaving a new type of counterpane (coverlet or quilt). His managerial brother Horatio served as agent for what became the Lancaster Quilt Company in 1848. In 1844, Erastus and Horatio were both involved in the establishment of the Lancaster Mills, which employed improvements by Erastus in the weaving of gingham fabric.[20] From 1839, Erastus worked at perfecting a power loom to weave two-ply ingrain carpeting in quantity. The Bigelow Carpet Company was incorporated in 1854.[21] Erastus and Horatio Bigelow were also original directors of the Clinton Wire

---
20  Ibid., 219-20.
21  Ibid., 244.

Cloth Company (manufacturer of screening, netting, fencing, and other wire products) when it was incorporated in 1856.[22]

Three major nineteenth-century operations in which the Bigelows were key still dominated the local economy in the early twentieth century. The Lancaster Mills, Bigelow Carpet Company, and Clinton Wire Cloth Company employed thousands and drew a swell of immigrants to work and live in Clinton. The mills provided work for independent tradesmen and contractors, too. As a plumber, Jennie's father George McLeod—a Scottish immigrant who moved from Boston to Clinton around 1893—benefited directly from the building boom associated with Clinton's growth as a center of manufacture.

The local mills offered opportunity for outsiders looking to improve the material circumstances of their lives. In the nineteenth century, many had come from elsewhere in Massachusetts, from New Hampshire, Vermont, and Maine, from northern New York, and from beyond the United States (Nova Scotia, New Brunswick, England, Ireland, Scotland, and Germany).[23] The three big local mills, along with some smaller manufacturing operations, attracted these groups both before and after 1900.[24] Other ethnicities—Italians, Greeks, and Poles—came as immigrants in the early twentieth century.[25] The Italians, in particular, came to work on the construction of the Wachusett Dam and Reservoir, a labor-intensive feat of public engineering.[26]

In 1915, Clinton's population was a robust 13,192, up by just 87 from 1905.[27] This reflected a marked decline in growth as compared with the

---

22   Ibid., 344.
23   Davis, 25.
24   Ibid.
25   Ibid., 26.
26   Ibid., 32-34.
27   Commonwealth of Massachusetts, *The Decennial Census, 1915. Taken Under the Direction of Charles F. Gettemy, Director of the Bureau of Statistics* (Boston: Wright and Potter Printing Co., 1918), 54.

increase of more than 1,600 between 1895 and 1905.[28] Although local people were not yet ready to accept the fact, the town's population and economic expansion were leveling off. Notwithstanding, the continued productivity of the mills and the ethnic diversity of the people who worked in them distinguished Clinton from its close neighbors. The population of Lancaster in 1915 was just 2,587 (a fifth the size of Clinton's), and the numbers were much smaller for Sterling (1,403), Harvard (1,104), Boylston (783), and Bolton (768).[29] Of the 6,128 people fourteen years or older employed in Clinton, 4,311—more than three-quarters of the total—worked in manufacturing and the "mechanical industries."[30] The influence of the mills on the town was profound.

While Jennie McLeod was growing up, Clinton had long since ceased to be predominantly Anglo-Saxon Yankee in its makeup. In 1915, a full one-third of its population was foreign-born.[31] However, although the town was characterized by ethnic diversity, its welcoming embrace did not extend across the racial divide. Of its 13,192 residents in 1915, only six—.045%—were identified in the 1915 Massachusetts decennial census as "colored."[32] It is likely that before Jennie went off to Smith College, she did not have much interaction with people of color.

Clinton was as denominationally diverse as it was ethnically heterogeneous. By the 1910s, its population included Congregationalists, Baptists, Methodists, Catholics, Unitarians, German Congregationalists, Christian Scientists, Free Methodists, Episcopalians, Presbyterians,

---

28   Commonwealth of Massachusetts, *Census of Massachusetts: 1895. Prepared Under the Direction of Horace G. Wadlin, Chief of the Bureau of Statistics of Labor. Volume I. Population and Social Statistics* (Boston: Wright & Potter Printing Co., 1896), 82.
29   *The Decennial Census*, 1915, 47.
30   Ibid.
31   Ibid., 202.
32   Ibid.

Wachusett Dam, power station, and fountain

Lutherans, Greek Orthodox, and Jews.[33] The McLeods were active members of the First Congregational Church through the period reflected in Jennie's diary, but Jennie later became an Episcopalian.

Although local people had long prided themselves on the cordiality between the town and the mills and valued the material and social benefits the latter afforded to the community, the twentieth century brought with it growing labor dissatisfaction.

In 1912, as labor/management strife broke out elsewhere in New England, unionized Lancaster Mills employees—weavers and loom fixers—went on strike over wages. Even though non-unionized labor-

---

33  Ellen K. Stevens, "The First Half Century, 1850-1900," *Clinton Centennial Volume*, 6, 8; Thomas F. Gibbons, "Peace, Prosperity, and War, 1910-1920," *Clinton Centennial Volume*, 48, 50; Lewis S. Gordon, Jr., "The Old Order Changes, 1920-1930," *Clinton Centennial Volume*, 76-78, 86.

ers who performed other types of work still showed up, the striking employees were essential and their absence shut down production. A tentative rapprochement was reached, but tensions soon boiled over again, and the weavers went on strike a second time. Management refused to negotiate. Outside union organizers became involved, including William Haywood and Elizabeth Gurley Flynn of the Industrial Workers of the World. Protest, picketing, rioting, and violence ensued, and police assistance was brought in from Fitchburg, Framingham, Leominster, Milford, and Worcester. The situation eventually abated and employees returned to their jobs.[34] It was a sobering experience for the people of a town accustomed to equating local well-being and quality of life with the success of its mills.

In 1918, following the end of World War I, labor troubles resurfaced not only at the Lancaster Mills but also at the Clinton Wire Cloth Company and the smaller Roubaix Mill (a manufacturer of woolens and worsteds).[35] Such difficulties thus bookended the span of Jennie McLeod's diary. The ground on which Clinton's prosperity had been established was shifting as Jennie approached maturity.

The construction of the Wachusett Dam and Reservoir at the turn of the twentieth century also affected Clinton's economy and self-image. It engendered both pride and a dawning consciousness that local sovereignty did not always reign supreme—that the New England concept of local self-government could be overridden by agendas, politics, and decision-making at a higher level. Boston's need for more water and the state's identification of the south branch of the Nashua River as the best option to fulfill that need prevailed over self-determination at the municipal level. In the words of one town historian, the dam and reservoir

---

34   Gibbons, 54.
35   Ibid., 65.

were "in Clinton, but not of it."³⁶ State jurisdiction was hard to reconcile with the high value placed on local autonomy.

The Wachusett Dam and Reservoir project got underway with the approval of the Metropolitan Water Act in 1895. The dam was constructed between 1901 and 1905 and the reservoir filled in 1908, just six years before Jennie McLeod began her diary.³⁷

At a cost of fifteen million dollars, the project employed a huge workforce and required the power of hundreds of horses and a great deal of equipment.³⁸ Crude shanty towns sprang up near ongoing construction to shelter workers. The manpower consisted predominantly of Irish and Italians, some of whom remained in Clinton after completion of the undertaking. It also included transient Chinese and black workers.³⁹

Six and a half square miles in Clinton, Boylston, West Boylston, and Sterling were flooded for the reservoir. This entailed first removing soil and clearing away organic matter. Buildings had to come down and their owners and occupants relocated. Thousands of bodies had to be transported from the old St. John's Cemetery to another site. New railroad tracks had to be laid and existing ones moved. Tunnels, dikes, and a viaduct had to be engineered, and a new sewerage system for Clinton built.⁴⁰ The work was hard and often dangerous, and laborers protested conditions.⁴¹

The end result was a dam some two hundred and five feet in height and a reservoir with a capacity of nearly sixty-five billion gallons—the

---

36  Davis, 32.
37  Ibid., 31-32.
38  Ibid., 32.
39  Terrance Ingano, *Images of America: Clinton* (Dover, New Hampshire: Arcadia Publishing, 1996), 124-25.
40  Davis, 32.
41  Ingano, 124.

world's largest water supply reservoir at the time it was completed.[42] It was a man-made modern marvel, and the people of Clinton—however unsettled by their lack of control over its presence and operation—exercised bragging rights for it and made it a local destination for pleasure excursions. Jennie McLeod, for one, was fond of long walks to the dam. She wrote three times in her diary (on September 1, 1915, February 6, 1916, and June 2, 1916) of strolling there with friends.

In providing Boston and the metropolitan area with water, Clinton gained political capital within the Commonwealth of Massachusetts. Having accommodated the demands of the state, citizens of the town realized the value of involvement in decision-making at the State House in Boston. The voting district of which Clinton was part sent lawyer David Ignatius Walsh—a Democrat who had lived and attended public school in town—to the Massachusetts House of Representatives in 1900 and 1901, and a little later Republican Charles Mayberry, a Clinton native and resident.[43]

During the entire period Jennie McLeod kept her diary, Democratic president Woodrow Wilson was in the White House. For much of that time (January 8, 1914-January 6, 1916), David I. Walsh served as governor of Massachusetts, the first Catholic to hold that position. Traditionally Republican, Clinton was then gravitating toward a Democratic majority.[44] But discordant party loyalties in the vigorously political town did not diminish the jubilation and the boost to local self-esteem that Walsh's success roused.

Jennie's father George McLeod was a Road Commissioner in Clin-

---

42  Davis, 32; "1897—Wachusett Reservoir," http://www.mwra.com/04water/html/hist4.htm (accessed January 12, 2020).
43  Davis, 34.
44  Gibbons, 51, 56.

ton and a Republican.[45] Jennie revealed her solidarity with him on March 2, 1915, after he was defeated for reelection in a dramatic Democratic sweep: "Went down for 'Telegram' before class Clinton went dry and democratic—Not a single Republican elected. In ill humor all day." Politics was serious business in Clinton.[46] Still, when Governor Walsh spoke at a Democratic rally in Northampton (October 28, 1914), Jennie attended and shook hands with him. And on December 6, 1915 (nine months after Clinton Republicans were clobbered at the polls), she and her father went together to a Clinton Historical Society program at which Governor Walsh presented on "Humanitarianism in Govt."

Politics formed a major focus of public attention in Clinton, but a variety of other activities also brought local people together. Although Clinton's mill workers in 1915 did not have a great deal of leisure time, town residents, in general, relished their opportunities to enjoy themselves. They made the most of election-day celebrations; parades; local and national anniversaries and holidays (the Fourth of July was a big one); and church suppers, fairs, and entertainments. They took part in the events of social clubs like the Prescott and Lambsdec Clubs, of fraternal organizations (Elks, Hibernians, and Masons), and of women's clubs; debates; lectures, including those offered through the Weeks Institute and the Clinton Historical Society; and local Chautauqua series. They took pleasure in balls and dances; musical and theatrical programs; musters; sleigh rides, sledding, and ice skating in winter;

---

45   The elective office of Road Commissioner was compensated. The chairman and the clerk of the board were each paid $175 per year, other members $100 per year—"Elective Office," *Sixty-sixth Annual Report of the Town Officers of Clinton, Mass., for the Year Ending December 31, 1915* (Clinton: W.J. Coulter Press for The Town, 1916), 6.
46   Davis, 28; Gibbons, 53—"Bitter campaigns for election were waged and candidates were frequently targets for attack, not on their political records, but too often were subjected to personal vilification and abuse."

picnics and canoeing in warmer weather; sports and athletic competitions; roller-skating; movies in two High Street theaters (the Star and the Globe); and–of particular interest to young people—trolley rides to nearby amusement parks (Whalom Park in Lunenburg and Leominster Park).[47] And people paid calls on one another at home. Several German social clubs—Turnverein, Harugari, Schillerverein, Sons of Hermann, and the Colony Club—supported their own activities.[48]

Through 1915, the spectacular Clinton Fair (the Worcester East Fair) drew twenty-five thousand people annually from near and far. It featured lions and lion-tamers, dirigibles and hot air balloons, stunts of all kinds, horse racing, food and drink, and an assortment of vendors, as well as the types of exhibits and competitions traditionally associated with New England agricultural and livestock fairs.[49]

Clinton possessed a well-defined downtown surrounded by a densely inhabited residential village.[50] This configuration made it possible to walk or bicycle to work, town offices and shops, the library, and church. It made it convenient, too, for vendors of meat, fish, groceries, milk, and ice to deliver door-to-door to their regular customers.[51] People went downtown to buy dry goods and notions, hardware, clothing, shoes and boots, jewelry, tobacco, and flowers; to choose a piece of furniture for delivery; to visit a dentist, druggist, or barber; and to do their banking or consult a lawyer.[52] Merchants and service providers and their custom-

---

47   Davis, 30; Gibbons, 42; Ingano, 12.
48   John Dorenkamp, with addenda by Allan Mueller, *History of the "Germantown" Area in Clinton, Massachusetts (circa 1850-2000): A Collection of Photographs, Historical Research, and Recollections* (Clinton: The Germantown Historical Preservation Project, 2017), 11-44.
49   Ingano, 81-96.
50   Ibid., 7—"Clintonville's population was highly concentrated—90 percent of the population lived within ONE square mile!"
51   Davis, 23-24.
52   Ibid., 20.

ers and clients knew one another personally.[53] The bond of community was as important as the business transaction. Cliques formed around church membership, place of employment, and neighborhood of residence, but—despite its ethnic mélange and the rambunctiousness of its politics—Clinton was close-knit.

Transportation was evolving, allowing local residents to venture farther and faster. In the nineteenth century, railroad service had linked Clinton to Worcester, Boston, and Fitchburg.[54] The trolley had come to town in the 1890s, speeding travel from the neighborhood known as "The Acre" to the Lancaster line and to Leominster, Berlin, and Hudson.[55] Over the second decade of the twentieth century, the automobile edged out horse-powered conveyances for both personal and work-related purposes.[56] With the rise of the motorcar as a preferred means of transportation, road expansion and improvement became necessary. Public attention was devoted, in particular, to the elevation of railroad tracks above the level of street grade crossings, which posed hazards to public safety and to punctuality at busy intersections.[57]

Thanks to the Wachusett Dam and Reservoir project, Clinton residents in 1915 were assured of public water and an efficient sewerage system. The process of adopting twentieth-century amenities was ongoing. Running water, gas stoves, electricity, plumbed bathrooms, flush toilets, central heating, and telephones increasingly enhanced the quality of home life.[58]

Municipal services in Clinton satisfied a standard range of needs and wants, from the protection of public health and safety to the main-

---

53  Ibid., 23.
54  Stevens, 14.
55  Ibid.; Davis, 24-25.
56  Gibbons, 41.
57  Ibid., 42, 44.
58  Davis, 22-23; Gibbons, 42.

tenance of roads, sidewalks, bridges, street lights, and water and sewer pipes. The Town of Clinton handled sprinkling the streets to keep down the dust, moth control, tree care, and management of public parks and recreational facilities. Town services also included education of young citizens-in-the-making, operation of the town library, assessment and collection of taxes, oversight of public funds, and keeping the records and statistics required by the Commonwealth.[59] The municipal offices were located in the new town hall, dedicated in 1909 on the site of its predecessor, which had burned down in 1907.[60]

The town adopted some progressive reforms in municipal administration around the time Jennie was making entries in her diary. In 1914, a Finance Committee was appointed to make recommendations on appropriations presented at town meetings. An elected Planning Board also came into existence during this period. Additionally, implementation of the civil service system diminished the influence of politics and favoritism in local government.[61]

In 1915, public safety was ensured by a police force and fire department, both subject to civil service regulations.[62] That year, the police made a total of three hundred arrests—the most frequently occurring offenses were drunkenness, assault and battery, and vagrancy—and the Fire Department responded to one hundred and two calls.[63] At the time, people regarded fires as a form of public spectacle and showed up to see with their own eyes how bad they were. Jennie McLeod acknowledged

---

59  *Sixty-sixth Annual Report of the Town Officers of Clinton, Mass.*; *School Report, Clinton, Mass., for the Year Ending December 31, 1915* (Clinton: W.J. Coulter Press for The Town, 1916); *Forty-second Annual Report of the Directors of the Bigelow Free Public Library of the Town of Clinton, Mass. For the Year Ending December 31, 1915* (Clinton: W.J. Coulter Press for The Town, 1916).
60  Davis, 34, 36.
61  Gibbons, 52-54.
62  Ibid., 54.
63  *Sixty-sixth Annual Report of the Town Officers of Clinton, Mass.*, 32-33, 83.

this urge toward the sensational in a diary entry made at college on December 7, 1914, "Got back from fire at 2:30 A.M. Big fire—big crowd." She wrote in Clinton on January 18, 1917, "Expected Carl [whom she was tutoring] so couldn't follow impulse to go to High School fire which lasted but a short time."

Philanthropy contributed significantly to town life. The Clinton Hospital, the Holder Memorial building of the Clinton Historical Society, and Clinton's Home for the Aged on Central Park were all initiated by private benefactors for public benefit. The philanthropically-funded Bigelow Free Public Library—a Carnegie library—had its origins in the privately-held collection of the Bigelow Library Association, which had earlier incorporated the books held by the local Mechanics Association.[64]

Clinton had its own hospital and a training school for nurses from late in the nineteenth century.[65] The town maintained a small isolation hospital and also a Board of Health doctor and nurse to address matters relating to public health.[66] In 1915, tuberculosis represented a particularly concerning threat; forty-three cases of the illness and seventeen deaths from it occurred during the year.[67] Town Clerk James H. Carr reported a total of 362 births, 163 marriages, and 208 deaths for 1915; the number of deaths caused by tuberculosis thus represented a full 8% of the total.[68]

Clinton's school system in 1915 included grammar schools in twelve

---

64 Stevens, 10-12; Ingano, 26; Gibbons, 48.
65 Stevens, 11-12.
66 *Monthly Bulletin of the State Board of Health of Massachusetts*, Vol. 7, No. 2, New Series (February 1912), 67; *Sixty-sixth Annual Report of the Town Officers of Clinton, Mass.*, 103-104.
67 *Sixty-sixth Annual Report of the Town Officers of Clinton, Mass.*, 98.
68 "Report of Town Clerk," *School Report, Clinton, Mass., for the Year Ending December 31, 1915* (Clinton: W.J. Coulter Press for The Town, 1915), 75-76. (The town clerk's report for this year was published following and consecutively paged with the school report rather than in the general report of town officers, where it usually appeared.)

locations and a high school.[69] The philosophy of education that guided the operation of these schools reflected the social imperatives of the Progressive Era.

Superintendent of Schools Thomas F. Gibbons summarized the prevailing pragmatic approach in his report for the year: "The public school should aid the pupil in determining what position in life he is best fitted for; it should prepare him for that position; it should give him such general and cultural knowledge as will be necessary for him in his vocation whatever it may be; it should give him physical and moral training and some knowledge of the government of which he is to be a part, and his duties as a good citizen of the nation. Not solely nor primarily for the benefit of the pupil or his parents must the school strive to do all this, put [i.e. but] principally because it is the business of the State to render its future men and women economically as productive as possible, morally upright and intelligent participators in the government of the town, state and nation."[70]

Toward the achievement of these ends, the Clinton schools offered a slate of curricular options, including technical training. By state law, cities and towns were enabled "to establish and maintain as State-aided vocational schools, practical arts day and evening classes to be open to women over 16 years of age."[71] Clinton's Evening School gave local students the chance to acquire proficiency in mechanical drawing, commercial skills (including the Gregg system of shorthand for stenography), civil service qualifications, and citizenship, as well as a means for eighth and ninth graders who could not attend school during the day to pursue their studies.[72] As revealed in diary entries made during

---
69 *School Report, Clinton, Mass., for the Year Ending December 31, 1915,* 4-5.
70 Thomas F. Gibbons, "What Our Schools Ought to Do," *School Report, Clinton, Mass., for the Year Ending December 31, 1915,* 49.
71 *School Report, Clinton, Mass., for the Year Ending December 31, 1915,* 47.
72 Ibid., 54, 56.

the 1915-1916 school year, after graduating from Smith, Jennie McLeod availed herself of the opportunity to learn stenography at the high school.

Clinton was preoccupied not only by community concerns but also by matters of national consequence over the period Jennie kept her diary. The First World War—the "European War" until April 6, 1917, when it became America's war, too—and the women's suffrage movement demanded attention. War and suffrage belonged to the country as a whole, but the questions they raised and the challenges they posed played out everywhere. Neither reached resolution until after Jennie made her final diary entry—the war on November 11, 1918, suffrage with the ratification of the 19th Amendment to the United States Constitution on August 18, 1920. These issues formed the backdrop against which Jennie wrote. While their presence is subdued in the diary (it was, after all, meant to be a personal record), they affected Clinton in significant ways—certainly economically and socially, but also in forcing the realization that the town was part of a larger, more interdependent, more changeable world than previously understood.

## Jennie in Her Family

BORN IN CLINTON IN 1893, JENNIE MCLEOD WAS THE FIRST CHILD OF George and Jennie Durie McLeod, who had emigrated from Scotland in the 1880s, during a period of severe economic depression there.

George McLeod was born on February 11, 1863, to Findley and Georgina Mercer McLeod in the port city of Greenock, located in the west-central Lowlands of Inverclyde, in the county of Renfrewshire.[73] Greenock's nineteenth-century economy was based largely on shipping, shipbuilding and marine engineering, mercantile pursuits, sugar refining, and wool manufacturing.[74] As a young man there, George McLeod acquired skill as a plumber.[75] Seeking to capitalize on his proficiency in a more favorable economic climate, he came to America early in 1886 aboard the Cunard steamer S.S. *Catalonia*, arriving in Boston on March 15, and began his working life in America as a plumber in Boston.[76]

Jennie C. Durie was born in 1862 to Alexander and Jane Cramond (Crammond) Durie of Brechen, in the county of Angus.[77] An old market town, Brechen in the nineteenth century was home to paper and textile manufacturing, brewing, and distilling.[78] In 1887, Jennie Durie crossed the Atlantic on the Allan Line's S.S. *Austrian*. She reached Boston on May 19 of that year.[79]

---

73 "Death of Former Rep. George McLeod Occurred Last Night," *Clinton Daily Item*, February 8, 1936, 1. While George McLeod's obituary and other sources identify his mother as Georgina Mercer, the 1881 census of Scotland lists Findley McLeod's wife at that time as Christina—"George McLeod," *1881 Scotland Census*, Ancestry (electronic data base, accessible by subscription). The mother of George McLeod's younger sister Mary McLeod Johnston was Christina McCallum McLeod—"Mary McLeod Johnston," *Find A Grave*, https://www.findagrave.com/memorial/197975127/mary-johnston (accessed March 25, 2020). George McLeod's father apparently lost his first wife and married again.

74 "Greenock," *Wikipedia*, https://en.wikipedia.org/wiki/Greenock (accessed November 4, 2019).

75 "George McLeod," *1881 Scotland Census*.

76 "George McLeod," *Boston Passenger and Crew Lists, 1820-1943*, Ancestry; "Death of Former Rep. George McLeod."

77 "Jane C. Durie (Jane C. Cramond)," *1881 Scottish Census*. In the 1871 census of Scotland, she is listed as Jean C. Durie. The name of Jennie C. Durie McLeod's father is identified as Alexander on *Find A Grave*, at https://www.findagrave.com/memorial/199794035 (accessed November 4, 2019).

78 "Brechin (Angus)," BBC, *Scotland's Landscape*, https://www.bbc.co.uk/scotland/landscapes/brechin/ (accessed November 4, 2019).

79 "Durie," *Boston Passenger and Crew Lists, 1820-1943*, Ancestry; "The Allan Line," *Norway Heritage—Hands Across the Sea*, http://www.norwayheritage.com/p_shiplist.asp?co=allan (accessed October 16, 2019).

George McLeod and Jennie Durie were married in Boston on June 3, 1890.[80] They had relocated to Clinton by the beginning of 1893. The couple found in the town not only a welcoming community but also the economic opportunity that their native land did not provide at the time.[81]

By 1890, Clinton boasted a population of 10,424, including a significant number of residents of Scottish birth or descent.[82] Scottish immigration into Clinton in the nineteenth century was modest by comparison with the influx of Irish and Germans. There was no large-scale Scottish enclave here along the lines of the local Germantown community.[83] Nevertheless, from the period when Clintonville was still part of Lancaster, emigrants from Scotland had settled in the town and found employment, particularly in the mills.[84] A residential section known as the Scotch Block, or Scotch Row, was inhabited by Lancaster Mills employees of Scottish origin. Waldo Davis wrote of it, "And there was the old Scotch block on Cameron Street looking dourly down on the mills where its tenants earned their daily bread."[85] Thus, when George McLeod and his wife moved to Clinton, they readily found others who shared ties to their country of origin.

In Clinton, George McLeod expressed his continued interest in his Scottish heritage through membership in the St. Andrew's Mutual Benefit Society. This fraternal organization met the first and third Fridays of each month in the Odd Fellows' Hall on High Street, to perpetuate

---

80  "George McLeod," *Massachusetts Marriage Records, 1840-1915, Ancestry.*
81  "Migration and Empire: Emigration and Scottish History," Education Scotland, *NQ Scottish History,* http://www.sath.org.uk/edscot/www.educationscotland.gov.uk/higherscottishhistory/migrationandempire/migrationofscots/emigrationandsociety.html (accessed October 16, 2019).
82  Clinton's population in 1890: the federal census figure as published in the *Clinton Directory 1893-94* ... (Fitchburg: Price & Lee Co., copyright 1893), unpaged population lists bound in volume.
83  For an in-depth history of Germantown, see Dorenkamp and Mueller.
84  Ford, 256, 318-19, 326, 331.
85  Davis, 21.

Scottish culture, create social opportunities, and—like Clinton's lodge of the German Order of Harugari—to aid members in difficult circumstances.[86] In her diary, his daughter Jennie demonstrated her own consciousness of her Scottish ancestry. She occasionally used Scots words (for example, "micht" in place of the English "might"). She wrote of her family attending Clinton's Scotch Ball while she stayed home sick on January 21, 1916, and on February 9 of the same year of seeing a Mrs. Smart "about shortbread." A month after, on March 10, she and her mother assisted at a "Scotch supper" at the First Congregational Church (Jennie waited on tables; "Mother poured"). During the 1914-1915 academic year, she repeatedly referred (but not always favorably) to a course she was taking at Smith College on Scottish literature. Moreover, some years later, Jennie was her father's companion on a trip abroad, during which they visited Scotland together.[87]

The McLeods first appear in Clinton in the local directory for 1893, with a home address of 10 East Street.[88] George McLeod was initially identified not only as a plumber ("plumbing, steam and hot water heating, etc.") but also as a bottler. He was listed as the proprietor of McLeod Bottling Co. ("mfrs. soda water, ginger ale, etc.") at 10 East Street (his home address). The address of his employment as a plumber was given

---

86  "Death of Former Rep. George McLeod"; "St. Andrew's Society," *Wikipedia*, https://en.wikipedia.org/wiki/Saint_Andrew%27s_Society (accessed December 21, 2019); *Clinton and Lancaster Directory 1915* ... (Fitchburg: Price & Lee Co., copyright 1915), 229 (listing for St. Andrew's Mutual Benefit Society); *Celebration of the 137th Anniversary of the Birth of Robert Burns. Grand Concert and Ball of the St. Andrew's M.B. Society, Town Hall, Clinton* ... (printed program containing order of dances and menu; Clinton: Martin Printing Co. for The Society, 1896), "Social Organizations" pamphlet and ephemera box, Clinton Historical Society (Holder Memorial), Clinton, Massachusetts, documenting one major social offering of the local St. Andrew's Society; Dorenkamp and Mueller, 26, on the German Order of Harugari.
87  McLeod interview; "George McLeod" and "Jennie McLeod," *Massachusetts Passenger and Crew Lists, 1820-1963*, Ancestry.
88  *Clinton Directory 1893-94*, 77.

as 10 Mechanic Street. By 1896, his bottling concern had been dropped from the directory, his place of employment was given as 63 Church Street, and his home was still listed as 10 East Street.[89] The plumbing business of John B. Farnsworth, for whom McLeod then worked, was located at 63 Church Street.[90] McLeod subsequently worked for William H. Walker, to whom Farnsworth sold his business.[91] In 1905, George McLeod opened his own plumbing business on Church Street, in the former newspaper building.[92] He operated his plumbing shop at 162 Church Street until his death in 1936, and his family continued it for decades afterward.

Jennie Crammond McLeod was born on January 30, 1893, not long after her parents moved to Clinton. Having found a place where they felt their family might thrive, the McLeods had five more children over the next eleven years. Stanley Mercer was born on January 28, 1895, George, Jr. on January 7, 1897, Helen W. on March 28, 1900, Maybelle on April 15, 1902, and Norman on April 6, 1904.[93] The first five McLeod children all lived to adulthood. Norman arrived prematurely. He died and was buried the day he was born.[94] A decade after Norman's death, Jennie recalled her physical response to the event, writing in her diary on August 20, 1914, "Didn't get up until ten. Haven't been so lazy since the baby died." Hardly a sentimental remembrance, but one that nevertheless conveyed the emotional impact of the loss.

---

89    *Clinton Directory, 1896* ... (Fitchburg; New Haven: Price & Lee Co., copyright 1895), 75.
90    *Clinton Directory, 1896*, 36; "Death of Former Rep. George McLeod."
91    "Death of Former Rep. George McLeod"; *Clinton Directory 1897* ... (Fitchburg; New Haven: Price & Lee Co., copyright 1896), 109.
92    "Death of Former Rep. George McLeod"; *Clinton and Lancaster Directory 1905* (Fitchburg: Price & Lee Co., copyright 1905), 89.
93    Registered Births, Clinton, Massachusetts, Volumes 2, 1882-1898, and 3, 1899-1910 (manuscript records), Volume 2: 80 (Jennie), 100 (Stanley), and 121 (George); Volume 3: 16 (Helen) and 41 (Maybelle), Town Clerk's Office, Clinton, Massachusetts.
94    Registered Deaths, Clinton, Massachusetts, 1904-1928 (manuscript records), Volume 3: 3, Town Clerk's Office, Clinton, Massachusetts.

The McLeods' plumbing business was a successful, long-lived operation. During his management of it, George McLeod won some plum contracts. A notice in the September 1914 issue of *The Heating and Ventilating Magazine* announced, "George McLeod, Clinton, Mass., heating and ventilating Walnut Street School in Clinton, for $2,907. Other bids were: R. Maitland & Son, $3,232; O'Toole Bros., $3,875."[95] (Jennie thought this contract important enough to mention in her diary going with her father to Town Hall on June 27, 1914, in the effort to win it, a related visit by him to the School Committee on June 30, 1914, and, in her entry for July 9, its award to him.) And a 1918 issue of *Domestic Engineering* included the following notice: "George McLeod, of Clinton, has been awarded the contract to install plumbing in 14 two-apartment houses, being erected by the Lancaster Mills Co. for rental to its employees."[96]

The McLeod family moved frequently within Clinton prior to their purchase of 244 Water Street. They lived in a series of rental homes not far from the center of town between 1893 and 1916. George and his wife started out at 10 East Street when they first arrived and subsequently lived at 12 Orange Street, 32 Orange Street, 140 Cedar Street, 110 Orange Street, 96 Pearl Street, and 117 Pearl Street before finally moving into 244 Water Street.[97]

During the McLeods' earliest years in Clinton, George's younger

---

95  *The Heating and Ventilating Magazine*, Vol. 11, No. 9 (September 1914), 70.
96  *Domestic Engineering*, May 18, 1918, 265.
97  *Clinton Directory 1893-94*, 77; *Clinton Directory 1897*, 75; *Clinton Directory 1898* ... (Fitchburg; New Haven: Price & Lee Co., copyright 1898), 81; *Clinton Directory 1900* ... (Fitchburg; New Haven: Price & Lee Co., copyright 1900), 88; *Clinton and Lancaster Directory 1905*, 89; *Clinton and Lancaster Directory 1913* ... (Fitchburg: Price & Lee Co., copyright 1913), 104; *Clinton and Lancaster Directory 1915*, 102; *Clinton and Lancaster Directory 1917* ... (Fitchburg: Price & Lee Co., copyright 1917), 106.

"THIS IS THE LIFE"

244 Water Street, Clinton, June 2020

brother Findlay (Finlay) and sister Mary boarded in their household.[98] Findlay McLeod—identified as a bottler in an 1896 immigration record—was described in Clinton directories as an employee of George McLeod, presumably in his bottling business.[99] Miss Mary McLeod was initially characterized in Clinton directories as a dressmaker and then as an employee of the Lancaster Mills and the Bigelow Carpet Mill. She later married Joseph M. Johnston and lived with her husband and daughters in Sterling during the span of Jennie's diary.[100]

Jennie McLeod started keeping her diary while her family lived at 117 Pearl Street and continued it after they moved to 244 Water Street. She wrote on July 1, 1915, of hanging pictures at 117 Pearl, suggesting that they had not yet gotten fully settled. The following year, the McLeods moved *en famille* for the last time. On June 25, 1916, Jennie noted that she and her good friend Christine Beck had gone to "inspect the Water St house & barn," and soon afterward, on July 2, that she had toured the house in the company of her visiting "Aunt Mary" and "Uncle Andy" (the McCances, who were actually friends of the family rather than relatives).

---

98   Findlay is found in George McLeod's household in *Clinton Directory 1893-94*, 77, and *Clinton Directory 1894* ... (Fitchburg; New Haven: Price & Lee Co., copyright 1894), 73, Mary in *Clinton Directory 1894*, 73, *Clinton Directory, 1895* ... (Fitchburg; New Haven: Price & Lee Co., copyright 1894), 73, *Clinton Directory, 1896*, 75, and *Clinton Directory 1897*, 75; "George McLeod," *1881 Scotland Census*. This census lists the McLeod children as Charles, George, Finlay, John, Helen W., Mary, Isabella C., and Jane C. Allan, another of George's siblings, was apparently not part of the household in 1881 and was consequently not included in the census.

99   "Finlay McLeod," *Massachusetts Passenger and Crew Lists, 1820-1963*. The record is drawn from a "List or Manifest of Alien Immigrants for the Commissioner of Immigration" for April 8, 1896, which date indicates that Finlay made more than one trip from Scotland to Boston. He is identified as a bottler in the original document, although his occupation is not included in the summary transcribed record on Ancestry.

100  "Mary M. Johnston in the 1910 United States Federal Census," *HeritageQuest Online* (electronic data base); "Mary McLeod Johnston," *Find A Grave*.

"THIS IS THE LIFE"

The McLeods bought 244 Water Street in June of 1916.[101] Significantly, it is listed under Mrs. McLeod's name in the Clinton assessors' valuation book for 1917, beneath the entry for her husband, which includes as his assets only the stock in trade for his plumbing business and the value of his ratable personal estate.[102] This arrangement was presumably intended to protect the family investment in the house against potential business-related loss.

The purchase of the solidly middle-class Water Street house was an outcome of upward mobility, enlarging reputation, and a deepening connection to the community, all of which George McLeod enjoyed as he established his business and grew his family in Clinton. George was naturalized as a United States citizen on February 28, 1894.[103] He was elected one of Clinton's Road Commissioners in 1909, holding that position into 1915, and again, on reelection, from 1917 through 1919, serving as clerk and chair of the board.[104] (Jennie's diary includes multiple entries referring to her paid employment at the Road Commissioners' office in the Clinton Town Hall during her father's service in that capacity.) He was elected a Water Commissioner in 1926, serving as clerk throughout his term, which ended in 1929, and he was voted Town Moderator in 1928.[105] A Republican in a town trending toward Democratic dominance, he was elected a Representative in the Mas-

---

101  Assessors' abstract for 244 Water Street (manuscript card), Assessors' Office, Clinton, Massachusetts.
102  "McLeod, George" and "McLeod, Jennie C.," valuation list (manuscript commitment book), 1917, Assessors' Office, Clinton, Massachusetts.
103  "George McLeod," *U.S. Naturalization Record Indexes, 1791-1992, Ancestry.*
104  "Death of Former Rep. George McLeod"(the relevant years as published in the obituary confirmed against lists of town officers in Clinton's printed annual municipal reports for the period).
105  "Death of Former Rep. George McLeod"; "Town Officers," *Seventy-sixth Annual Report of the Town Officers of Clinton, Mass., for the Year Ending December 31, 1926* (Clinton: W.J. Coulter Press for The Town, 1927), 5 (confirmed in Clinton annual printed town reports through 1928).

sachusetts legislature in 1930 and reelected two years later.[106] He was clerk of the House Committee on State Administration and a member of the Committee on Public Health.

George McLeod belonged to the Prescott Club (a Clinton organization founded in 1886 for "the establishment and maintenance of a place for social meetings"), the Clinton Historical Society, and the Trinity Lodge, A.F. & A.M.[107] Jennie McLeod wrote in her diary on June 30, 1915 of his joining the Elks. He was active, too, in the Clinton Chamber of Commerce, serving on its membership committee.[108] He participated in the social and civic life of the community until his death on February 7, 1936. His obituary (published in the *Clinton Daily Item* the following day) stated that he was associated with the First Church of Christ Scientist. However, Jennie's diary makes clear that earlier in life he had belonged to the First Congregational Church, with which most of his family maintained ties. (The single exception was daughter Jennie, who became a member of the Episcopal Church of the Good Shepherd.[109])

It is more difficult to get a sense of Jennie Durie McLeod as a person than it is to form a picture of her husband. She lived an essentially domestic and private life in Clinton. As a young woman in Scotland, she had contributed to her family's income as a factory worker.[110] When she emigrated to America in 1887, she was twenty-five—an age by which many women of her time were already wives and mothers. Once the

---

106 "Death of Former Rep. George McLeod."
107 "Death of Former Rep. George McLeod"; Prescott Club, *By-Laws of the Prescott Club of Clinton, Mass., Incorporated April 2, 1886 ...* (Clinton: Press of Wm. J. Coulter for The Club, 1902), 3, "Social Organizations" pamphlet and ephemera box, Clinton Historical Society.
108 See, for example, the "Local Affairs" column in the *Clinton Daily Item* for October 11, 1915.
109 Church of the Good Shepherd, Parish Register, Volume B (manuscript volume), 22, 214, Church of the Good Shepherd Office, Clinton, Massachusetts.
110 "Jane C. Durie (Jane C. Cramond),"*1881 Scotland Census*.

McLeods arrived in Clinton, Jennie was preoccupied with bearing and raising children, and never ventured into the local workforce. When George McLeod died in 1936, Jennie was in her seventies. She subsequently remained at home at 244 Water Street with her three unmarried daughters, sheltered by the security her husband had created and by her eldest daughter's assumption of responsibility for the household. Like many women of her era, she left behind a limited documentary record and a largely invisible imprint on her community. Jennie Durie McLeod died in 1952 at about ninety years of age.[111]

In her diary, Jennie McLeod mentioned her father far more often than she did her mother. It is clear that the two were very close. She referred to George mainly as "Dad," but also more affectionately called him "Daddy" and "Papa," while Mrs. McLeod was with but one exception always "Mother" (the exception a single "ma"—lower-cased and in quotation marks—in the entry for February 19, 1916). Jennie spent a lot of what we would now call quality time in her father's company, frequently accompanying him to lectures, concerts, theatrical events, movies, vaudeville and minstrel shows, church, and baseball games. She looked things up for him at the library (she wrote on November 27, 1914, "Looked up St Andrew for Dad at the Libe"), worked in the Clinton Road Commissioners' office during his service as a commissioner, helped out at his plumbing store, and ran errands for him. She sent him frequent letters from Smith and, when home in Clinton, made special note of long conversations with him. He took her for rides in the family automobile (dubbed "the machine" or "the fliver"), and she dressed his hand after he and George, Jr. were in an accident that landed the vehicle in a brook late in August 1915.

---

[111] "Jennie C. Durie McLeod," *Find A Grave*, https://www.findagrave.com/memorial/199794035 (accessed January 2, 2020).

On May 9, 1914, in a psychologically telling passage in her diary, Jennie recalled a bad dream she'd had: "Horrible dream last night. 'funeraille de mon père' [my father's funeral]." Her relationship with George McLeod was so critical to her sense of well-being that she felt compelled to cloak the suggestion of his death in French.

Her relationship with her mother, on the other hand, revolved mainly around the management of home and family. Jennie wrote of shopping downtown with and for Mrs. McLeod and of taking care of some of the family sewing, cooking, and housekeeping. She sometimes assumed responsibility for her two younger sisters. She made social calls in Clinton with her mother, and ventured beyond Clinton with her on June 30, 1916, when the two made a trip to Camp Whitney in Framingham to visit Jennie's newly-enlisted brother Stanley. Occasionally, she accompanied her mother to the movies.

There is nothing in the diary hinting that the mother-daughter relationship was strained. Indeed, Jennie appears to have been comfortable in Mrs. McLeod's company. Moreover, she competently and willingly took care of the traditionally female tasks that devolved to her. Nevertheless, her diary strongly suggests that the place she held in her father's life was more gratifying than her part in her mother's narrower world.

Although he lacked the advantages of higher education and native birth, George McLeod made the most of his intelligence, judgment, capacity for hard work, sense of social responsibility, and Clinton's embrace of outsiders willing to adapt themselves to its values and possibilities. In the process, he transformed himself from labor for hire to successful business owner and respected public official. His prosperity and social standing benefited his entire family, his daughter Jennie in particular.

The five surviving McLeod children all attended the public schools of Clinton through high school. Jennie graduated with Clinton High

School Class of 1911, Stanley with the Class of 1913, George Class of 1914, Helen Class of 1918, and Maybelle Class of 1920.[112] Jennie alone among them went on to earn a college degree, an uncommon advantage for a girl of her time. In this she was fortunate.

As chronicled in her diary, Jennie McLeod and her father George shared a special affinity. Jennie was a smart, capable, strong girl, as well as the first-born child. One of her nephews—a son of her brother George—remembers her as the favored child of the family.[113] Her path through adulthood was formed by the space she occupied while growing up at home. Coupled with her intellect and temperament, her position in the family afforded certain prerogatives, among them her Smith education. Those prerogatives concomitantly imposed responsibilities that would be hers for the rest of her life.

Jennie and three of her four siblings made their lives in Clinton; only Stanley put down roots elsewhere. After his high school graduation in 1913, he worked in his father's plumbing business. On June 28, 1916, around the time his family moved into 244 Water Street, and before America entered the First World War, he enlisted.[114] During the war, he served in Company K, 101st Infantry Regiment in France and was wounded in action. Discharged at the end of April 1919, he married Clinton girl Pauline Vera Bartlett (Murray) in 1922.[115] The couple started their family in Clinton, then moved to Belmont, Massachusetts, where Stanley established himself as a plumber. Over time, they had five chil-

---

112 "Stanley M. McLeod, Sr." (obituary), *Clinton Daily Item*, October 6, 1955, 4; *Memorabilia, Class of 1914* (also 1918 and 1920), (Clinton: Clinton High School, 1914, 1918, and 1920), 25, 48, and 41, respectively.
113 McLeod interview.
114 "Stanley M. McLeod," *Clinton Military Case History* (Works Project Administration typescript compilation), Volume 2, 1937, Clinton Historical Society.
115 "Pauline Vera Bartlett," *Haskell Family History: the Haskell Family Tree genealogy database*, http://www.haskellfamilyhistory.com/haskell/4/82599.html (accessed January 11, 2020).

dren—William, Stanley, Jr., Kenyon, Russell, and Marjorie (Santello). Stanley McLeod was involved with the VFW in both Clinton and Belmont. A member of the Congregational church in Belmont, he died on October 5, 1955, at the age of sixty.

While his older brother built a life beyond Clinton, George McLeod, Jr. carried on the plumbing business his father had established.[116] At Clinton High School, where he was known as "Sprint," he was enrolled in the tech prep course.[117] He enlisted in the military on August 1, 1918, but did not fight in Europe; World War I ended a few months after his enlistment.[118] He was discharged on March 27, 1919. George married Marion Wahl, also of Clinton, and lived with his wife and children on East Street.[119] He and Marion had four sons—Malcolm, Donald, Robert, and Duncan. George was a Mason, a Shriner, a charter member of the James R. Kirby Post of the American Legion in Clinton, and a member of the town's First Congregational Church.[120] He retired from the McLeod plumbing business in 1967, at seventy, bringing the enterprise to its end. George, Jr. died in 1984, at eighty-seven.

Jennie McLeod's diary offers a glimpse of the camaraderie she shared with her brothers. She noted in her diary entry for March 3, 1914, that she had received a letter from Stanley, who enclosed $3.00 with which she might buy a fountain pen—a thoughtful gift, seemingly based on some understanding of things that mattered to his sister. On

---

116  "George McLeod" (obituary), *Clinton Daily Item*, May 2, 1984, 2.
117  *Memorabilia, 1914*, 25; McLeod interview.
118  McLeod interview; "George McLeod, Jr.," *Clinton Military Case History*, Volume 2.
119  "George McLeod" (obituary); George, Jr.'s involvement in the McLeod plumbing business and his residence at 35 East Street are documented in Clinton directories over a long span of years, including 1931, 1941, and 1956—*Clinton Lancaster Directory 1931* ... (New Haven: Price & Lee Co., copyright 1931), 123; *Clinton Lancaster Directory 1941* ... (New Haven: Price & Lee Co., copyright 1941), 170; *Clinton Lancaster Directory 1956* ... (New Haven: Price & Lee Co., copyright 1956), 188.
120  "George McLeod" (obituary).

July 14, 1914, she wrote, "Played cards with Sprint and Stan. Ate cherries and ice cream like mad."

But Jennie had a different type of relationship with her sisters. Seven years older than Helen and nine years older than Maybelle, she referred to them in her diary as "the kids." As she related on June 25, 1915, she took on the task of tutoring Maybelle: "Visited Maybelle's teachers to get instruction for tutoring her." She was, to some extent, a caretaker for her sisters while they were growing up, and her consequent sense of responsibility and authority persisted into maturity.

After the death of George McLeod, Sr. in 1936, the McLeod home at 244 Water Street became an entirely female environment. Jennie was the formally designated head of the household.[121] She held a visible place in the community, working in an occupation—insurance—that brought her into contact with many people. In some ways, she represented the family to the outside world as her father earlier had. Helen and Maybelle were cut from a different cloth. Both were more nurturing and home-oriented than Jennie. Family members recollect that they were kind and warm, while Jennie came across as sterner and more no-nonsense.[122] The four McLeod women were enmeshed in a dynamic that did not encourage any of the sisters to depart the family circle.

Helen—a pretty young woman in her high school yearbook photograph—was enrolled in the college course at Clinton High School, although she did not pursue higher education.[123] She did some substitute teaching in Clinton soon after graduation (it was possible at the time to do so without a college degree) and worked for many years as the secretary and bookkeeper for McLeod Plumbing & Heating, of

---

121 "Jennie C. McLeod," *1940 United States Federal Census, HeritageQuest Online.*
122 McLeod interview.
123 *Memorabilia, Class of 1918,* 48.

which she was part-owner with her brother George.[124] (An old safe still in the basement of 244 Water Street contains many volumes of McLeod plumbing business records in her manuscript hand.) Helen was a Girl Scout leader in town.[125] Although she never married, family and a long-time Water Street neighbor report that she had some love interests along the way.[126]

Maybelle—the baby of the family—also took the college course at Clinton High School. Her high school yearbook entry emphasizes her sense of humor as her most characteristic trait.[127] After high school, Maybelle did not work outside the home. Present-day Clintonians remember her fondly and recall that she and Helen used to sit on their front porch and chat as the local children passed by on their way to and from school.[128] Both Helen and Maybelle were members of the First Congregational Church of Clinton.[129]

Jennie C. McLeod died at the age of seventy-five on July 26, 1968, long before either of her sisters. After her death, Helen and Maybelle continued on into very old age in the Water Street house. Helen died on March 13, 1996, just before her ninety-sixth birthday. Maybelle McLeod died in March of 1999, at almost ninety-seven.

---

124  *Seventieth Annual Report of the School Department, Clinton, Mass., for the Year Ending December 31, 1919* (Clinton: W.J. Coulter Press for The Town, 1920), 64; "Helen W. McLeod" (obituary), *Clinton Daily Item*, March 13, 1996, 2; McLeod interview. The school report shows that Helen earned $78 for substitute teaching in 1919, her older sister Jennie $51.
125  Personal interview with Frances Mahan, December 19, 2019.
126  McLeod interview; Mahan interview.
127  *Memorabilia, Class of 1920*, 41.
128  Posts (in response to request for information by the author) by Elaine Marino, Ann Whalen, Cathy Porter Mahan, and others, "You know you're from Clinton, MA if…" (Facebook group), https://www.facebook.com/groups/276577909182016/ (September 14, 2019).
129  "Maybelle McLeod" (obituary), *Clinton Daily Item*, March 9, 1999, 4.

George and Jennie Durie McLeod and all of their children are buried in the family plot in Woodlawn Cemetery in Clinton.[130]

Clinton and the world at large changed enormously over the long span between George McLeod's arrival in Clinton in the early 1890s and the death of his youngest surviving child more than a century later. For people who still remember the McLeod sisters, they represent an earlier era. Yet, the path Jennie McLeod took through life often diverged from that which was generally anticipated for women at the time. Ultimately, she was a feminist by example, if not a self-conscious ground-breaker.

## The Education of Jennie McLeod

JENNIE MCLEOD GRADUATED FROM GRAMMAR SCHOOL AND ENTERED high school in 1907.[131] As she made her way through the Clinton school system, public secondary education across the country was undergoing a radical transformation.

Beginning in the late nineteenth century, educators turned away from the traditional academic, classically-oriented curriculum suited to the needs of an earlier time in favor of a differentiated approach geared to preparing students for evolving vocations and roles. Pragmatic considerations increasingly determined what was taught. Through the implementation of the differentiated curriculum, high school students were channeled into distinct programs of study, narrowing for some the

---

130 "George McLeod," *Find A Grave*, https://www.findagrave.com/memorial/199793897 (accessed November 4, 2019).
131 *School Report, Clinton, Mass., for the Year Ending January 31, 1908* (Clinton: W.J. Coulter Press for The Town, 1908), 30. The high school building was then located at the intersection of Chestnut and Union Streets, where the police station now stands.

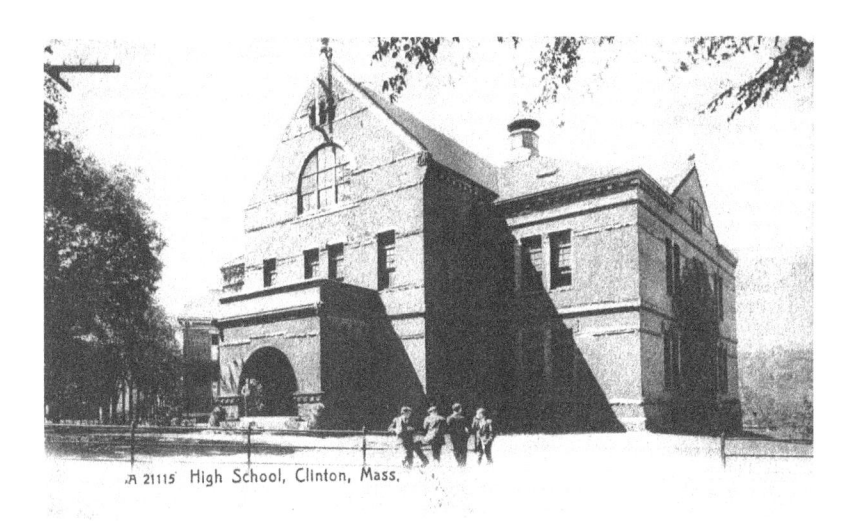

**Clinton High School, intersection of Chestnut and Union Streets**

opportunity for broad intellectual, cultural, and aesthetic development.[132]

The Progressive Era was a period of social reform. The improvements it introduced were motivated by the needs of society—its well-being, progress, and efficiency as a whole. The differentiated curriculum was aimed more at educating young people for future responsibilities at home and in the workplace than the achievement of individual fulfillment.

Women's lives improved significantly between 1870 and 1920 in terms of employment opportunities and conditions, suffrage, organizational involvement, the legalization of contraception, and in other ways. At the same time, the differentiated curriculum, with its focus on the

---

132  The summary in this and the following two paragraphs is based on Karen Graves, *Girls' Schooling During the Progressive Era: From Female Scholar to Domesticated Citizen* (New York; London: Garland Publishing, 1998).

ultimate usefulness of what was learned, discouraged the participation of high school girls in academic and scientific courses, as opposed to a business, teaching, or domestic program. Social pressure to conform to prevailing values thus impeded the aspirations of some who might have wanted to pursue a college education.

The differentiated curriculum had taken root in Clinton by the time Jennie McLeod entered high school. The students in the Class of 1911 (Jennie's class) each followed one of five courses: college preparatory; technical; normal (that is, teachers' training); commercial; or general.[133] Out of a total of forty-eight students, only eight—including Jennie— were in the college preparatory course. The technical course (seven students total) was all male in its composition, the normal course (two students) all female. The commercial course included the largest number of students (eighteen, sixteen of whom were girls). Thirteen students (four of them girls) were listed under the general course.

Clinton's annual school reports for the years Jennie attended the grammar and high schools reflect the ongoing national dialogue about the differentiated curriculum. A two-page exposition of the benefits of such a program appeared in the report for the year ending January 31, 1911.[134] The piece encapsulated key points of the philosophy behind differentiated education, specifically: "Because of difference in environment or life conditions, education ... has been differentiated and schools in each community are endeavoring to base their work to some extent upon the present and prospective environment of the pupils. Recognizing the difference in life aim or vocation, the schools are now being organized for the purpose of providing an education for each

---

[133] "Exercises of Graduation, Class of 1911," *School Report, Clinton, Mass., for the Year Ending January 31, 1912* (Clinton: W.J. Coulter Press for The Town, 1912), 45.

[134] "Differentiation in Education," *School Report, Clinton, Mass., for the Year Ending January 31, 1911* (Clinton: W.J. Coulter for The Town, 1911), 26-27.

child that will best fit him for his future position in life."¹³⁵ The once predominant academic curriculum was devalued: "It is recognized that by far the larger part of the children on completion of school studies will engage in some kind of vocational pursuit and but a small part will devote themselves to what may be called the cultural pursuits."¹³⁶

In opting for the college preparatory course at Clinton High School, Jennie McLeod represented a minority of young women in her class, the largest percentage of whom chose the commercial course, presumably with an eye toward clerical work or bookkeeping in the future. Why did she swim against the current? Family considerations and outside influences both factored into her choice.

Significantly, Jennie was not alone among her siblings in taking the college preparatory course. Her sisters Helen and Maybelle, neither of whom went to college, also followed the college prep track. The McLeod parents apparently thought a traditional academic education important for their daughters, while supporting a different approach for their sons.¹³⁷ They expected that Stanley and George would succeed to the family plumbing business and consequently did not press them to pursue academics. But they were more conservative as regards their daughters' schooling. Deeming an old-fashioned academic education best to prepare Jennie, Helen, and Maybelle for home and family life or teaching, they did not steer them down a vocational path.

Forces beyond family also affected Jennie's selection of the college preparatory course. Miss Ellen K. Stevens—a respected Clinton resident who had enjoyed a privileged education for a girl of her time (she was born in 1860)—took a special interest in encouraging young

---
135  Ibid., 26.
136  Ibid., 26-27.
137  George McLeod, Jr. was awarded a Mrs. Bayard Thayer Prize in manual training in the ninth grade for making a desk tray (*School Report, Clinton, Mass., for the Year Ending January 31, 1911*, 25) and took the technical course at Clinton High School.

women growing up in town during the early twentieth century. Miss Stevens's family had been able to provide private tutors for her. She had studied art and music in Boston and was known to residents of the town as an "[a]rtist, musician, poetess, linguist, student of nature and books ... one of Clinton's most highly esteemed citizens."[138]

Ellen Stevens was central to Jennie McLeod's religious and career choices in early adulthood. As Jennie's diary shows, she also made opportunities for local girls to get together, and was thus important in their social development. Miss Stevens was well poised to offer inspiration and possibly advice to academically promising girls at a crossroads in life. Because she embodied learning, culture, and investment in community, she may—either directly or indirectly—have advocated college preparation for those of scholarly inclination among her young protégées.

The predominant classically-focused nineteenth-century high school curriculum was in harmony with Emersonian notions of inherent human capability and the capacity of every person to evolve indefinitely toward the divine within. Jennie McLeod's familiarity with this humanistic line of thought is revealed by a quip in her diary about receiving a high grade on a written psychology test: "Haven't yet recovered from an A. 'We are infinitely perfectible'" (March 2, 1914). A tongue-in-cheek remark, for sure. Nevertheless, Jennie's educational decisions plainly reflected a comfortable acceptance of her own potential.

Whatever forces influenced Jennie's opting for an academic education, it is clear from her diary that she herself believed in the value of the path she had chosen, and that she found validation of her choice at Smith College. On February 24, 1915, she disclosed the debate subject

---

138 "Miss Ellen K. Stevens" (biographical note), *Clinton Centennial Volume*, 2.

she had been working on for Elocution 7, a course designed to cultivate skills in extempore speaking.[139] She wrote, "Resolved: That a general college education is preferable to a specialized training for a woman whether she is preparing for domestic or vocational activities."

Jennie graduated from Clinton High School with high honor in June 1911, her close friend Christine Louise Beck having taken highest honor.[140] In the fall of that year, Jennie entered Smith College. Founded in 1871 and opened in 1875, the academically rigorous, non-denominational liberal arts college for women is located in Northampton, a city with name recognition as the home not only of Smith College but also of Calvin Coolidge, president of the United States between 1923 and 1929. Some eighty miles from Clinton, Northampton was accessible by train via the Central Massachusetts Railroad.[141] The distinguished Smith faculty was committed to providing a strong education for young women, one equal to that available to members of the opposite sex.

Smith's student body in 1914-1915 (Jennie's senior year) consisted of 1,638 matriculants—580 freshmen, 355 sophomores, 365 juniors, 307 seniors, and 31 graduate students.[142] The college had high admissions standards. All students had to present prior coursework in English, mathematics, history, and Latin or Greek, plus some combination of elective subjects (among them French, German, chemistry, physics, botany, zoology, biology, astronomy, geology, and music).[143] Admission

---

[139] "Spoken English" (course listing), *Bulletin of Smith College ... 1914-1915*, 96.
[140] "Exercises of Graduation, Class of 1911," *School Report, Clinton, Mass., for the Year Ending January 31, 1912*, 45.
[141] See "Central Massachusetts Railroad," *Wikipedia*, https://en.wikipedia.org/wiki/Central_Massachusetts_Railroad (accessed December 21, 2019). The Clinton railroad station from which Jennie caught trains for Northampton was near the present Hamilton Square (Depot Square) and the brick buildings of the Clinton Wire Cloth Company.
[142] *Bulletin of Smith College ... 1914-1915*, 161.
[143] "Requirements for Admission," *Bulletin of Smith College ... 1913-1914*, 20-21.

College Hall, Smith College, Northampton, Mass.

**College Hall, Smith College, Northampton**

examinations were also required. Once admitted and enrolled, students followed a challenging curriculum that balanced the humanities, arts, and sciences, allowed for personal choice in the selection of electives, and required physical education.

Jennie's diary provides significant insight into the range and depth of her studies at Smith. She kept the diary through the second half of her junior year (1913-1914) and the whole of her senior year (1914-1915). Her academic life forms a major subject of entries written in that year-and-a-half period.

The classes that Jennie wrote about during the winter and spring of 1914 encompass a range of subjects: Chemistry 2 ("Qualitative and Quantitative Analysis. Laboratory practice, with lectures on the principles of chemical analysis");[144] Chemistry 4a (lectures on "the application

---

144 "Chemistry" (course listing), *Bulletin of Smith College ... 1913-1914*, 52.

of chemical facts and principles to common life");[145] Chemistry 10b ("Inorganic Chemistry," an advanced course);[146] English C ("Argumentative Paper, to be written after consultation with the instructor");[147] English 4:2 ("The Age of Dryden and Pope");[148] French 9 ("Romanticism. French literature in the first half of the nineteenth century");[149] Logic (Philosophy 1a, although Jennie did not refer to it by number; "The principles of correct reasoning, the methods of science, and an outline of the philosophical theory of thought");[150] and Psychology (she did not specify the course).[151]

During her senior year, her studies included Bacteriology (Chemistry 3a or Chemistry 3b, both of them titled "Chemistry of Microorganisms");[152] Elocution 7, or Spoken English 7 ("Extempore Speaking");[153] Education 2a ("Principles and Problems of Contemporary Education");[154] English 8 ("The Elizabethan Age and its Influence, exclusive of the drama");[155] English 12 ("Modern Drama");[156] English 25 ("Scot-

---

145 Ibid., 53.
146 Ibid.
147 "English Language and Literature" (course listing), *Bulletin of Smith College ... 1913-1914*, 61.
148 Ibid., 59.
149 "French Language and Literature" (course listing), *Bulletin of Smith College ... 1913-1914*, 64. The syllabus included "Chateaubriand, Lamartine, Hugo, Vigny, Musset, Dumas, Th. Gautier, G. Sand, Stendhal, Mérimée, Balzac."
150 "Philosophy" (course listing), *Bulletin of Smith College ... 1913-1914*, 88.
151 Like Logic, Psychology fell under the heading "Philosophy" in the Smith catalog, *Bulletin of Smith College ... 1913-1914*, 88-90.
152 "Chemistry" (course listing), *Bulletin of Smith College ... 1914-1915*, 52-53.
153 "Spoken English" (course listing), *Bulletin of Smith College ... 1914-1915*, 96-97.
154 "Education" (course listing), *Bulletin of Smith College ...1914-1915*, 56. The course is described as follows: "Lectures, discussions, readings, use of educational reports and other documents; school visiting."
155 "English Language and Literature" (course listing), *Bulletin of Smith College ... 1914-1915*, 59.
156 Ibid.

tish Vernacular Literature");[157] English D ("Themes in connection with the class work of the student");[158] French 7 ("Advanced Prose. Advanced grammar and composition");[159] and French 12:3 ("The Short Story (Nouvelle) in the nineteenth century").[160]

Jennie was serious about her studies in Clinton and at Smith. That said, it is clear that while at college, she was no slave to the academic grind. She did her work, got good grades in some courses, and found that success in others came only with greater effort. She did, in fact, struggle in some of her classes, and had to work to overcome one long-standing academic condition. During the spring semester of her junior year, she referred in her diary to a condition imposed in English B (a course required for sophomores), which, as described in the Smith College catalog, focused on "[t]hemes affording practice in collation and arrangement of material."[161] Between June and September of 1914, Jennie worked on a paper on domestic water to satisfy the condition. She rejoiced on September 17, 1914, "Miss Tetlow phoned Paper satisfactory Dieu soit loué [God be praised]. I am free from a condition for the first time since I entered." Strong student though she was at Clinton High School, she nevertheless had to apply herself to get through Smith.

Jennie McLeod embraced her educational opportunities, but she also displayed a certain indifference to academic achievement as an objective in and of itself. She razzed her friend Hutch—Mildred

---

157   Ibid., 61. The course covered early Scottish poets from Barbour to Lindsay, the prose of Bellenden, Pitscottie, Knox, and Melville, and Scottish ballads and songs (Robert Burns and Sir Walter Scott).
158   Ibid.
159   "French Language and Literature" (course listing), *Bulletin of Smith College ... 1914-1915*, 63. "Recommended especially for those who expect to teach French."
160   Ibid., 65. "Xavier de Maistre, Chateaubriand, Nodier, de Vigny, de Musset, Balzac, Mérimée, Flaubert, Gautier, Laboulaye, Daudet, Maupassant, France, Coppée, Villiers de l'Isle Adam, de Régnier and others."
161   *Bulletin of Smith College ... 1913-1914*, 58.

Hutchinson—over her election to Phi Beta Kappa in March 1915.[162] She wrote on May 9 of that year, "Hutch came over and I insulted her Φ.B.K."

Her diary shows that Jennie took a lot of English and chemistry during her junior and senior years. Her membership in Colloquium further demonstrated a particular interest in chemistry. (Colloquium was a departmental chemistry club "where informal discussion about the subject could be conducted between students and faculty similar to seminars in the German universities."[163]) Had Jennie entered Smith a few years after she did, she might have chosen one of those subjects as her formal major. But although juniors and seniors had to pursue courses in a "main study" while Jennie was at Smith, the Academic Council there did not adopt a curriculum requiring students formally to declare a major until the year that she graduated.[164]

After graduation from Smith, as Jennie grappled with finding immediate employment and some line of work that might hold her interest over the long haul, she acknowledged the usefulness of certain practical skills that were not part of the college preparatory course at Clinton High School. As recorded in multiple diary entries, during the 1915-1916 school year, Jennie and her friend Christine Beck (who had graduated from Wellesley) took Stenography III at Clinton High on an

---

162  Hutch's identity is established in Smith College, *1915 Class Book*, "Phi Beta Kappa, Zeta Chapter," 83.
163  Biographical/historical note, "John Tappan Stoddard Papers" (finding aid), *Smith College Libraries*, https://findingaids.smith.edu/repositories/4/resources/247 (accessed November 13, 2019). Departmental clubs at Smith were "organized under the joint management of teachers and students," with membership "by election, to which students of approved standing" were eligible—"Departmental Clubs," *Bulletin of Smith College ... 1914-1915*, 117.
164  Marion LeRoy Burton, "The New Curriculum," *Smith Alumnae Quarterly*, Vol. 7, No. 1 (November 1915), 1-8.

extension basis.[165] Jennie and Christine both had opted to cultivate the broad intellectual awareness, drive to learn, and self-confidence imparted by a well-rounded education before attending to more hands-on skills.

Writing on the day she graduated from Smith (June 15, 1915), Jennie cast a stone at the idea that receipt of a bachelor's degree represented the pinnacle of education: "Commencement Day. Got our little Dips and think we're educated." Within a few months, she, Christine, and a small group of their friends in Clinton staked a claim to self-culture and continuing education through the formation of a Spanish study group. Jennie observed on September 24, 1915, "[W]ent to Christine's for first Spanish conference with her & Helen Plummer." Participants met at one another's homes with considerable perseverance—Jennie mentions such gatherings well into 1917. Ellen Stevens sometimes participated. On January 3, 1917, Jennie wrote, "Spanish club met with me. All present except Marg. Usual jovial time. Miss Stevens the teacher the questions most difficult." And a week later, on January 10, she noted, "Weekly Spanish at Miss Stevens. Full attendance."

Jennie's post-college diary entries show her maintaining an intellectual life on her own through reading. Between her graduation from Smith and her final diary entry, she made note of the books, plays, poetry, and periodicals she read. Her encompassing literary embrace included plays by George Bernard Shaw; French nouvelles by Guy de Maupassant; Delos F. Wilcox's *The American City: A Problem in Democracy*; Arnold Bennett's *How to Live on 24 Hours a Day*; *The Teaching of Civics* by Mabel Hill; *Dracula*; and the *Smith Alumnae Quarterly* (which she borrowed from high school and college classmate Carolyn Woodruff

---

165 Christine's graduation is documented in *Legenda*, 1915 (yearbook) (Wellesley: The College, 1915), 89.

Sprague).[166] She read *Alice in Wonderland;* plays by Ibsen and Strindberg; an unspecified title by H.G. Wells which she pronounced "weird" (October 29, 1915); the best-selling 1913 novel *The Inside of the Cup* by popular American author Winston Churchill (not to be confused with the British statesman); and Jeffery Farnol's 1915 novel *Beltane the Smith.* She devoted attention to poetry by Paul Shivell; *Sentimental Tommy* by Scottish novelist and dramatist J.M. Barrie; Jacques-Henri Bernardin de Saint-Pierre's *Paul et Virginie* (first published in 1788); Francis Hopkinson Smith's novel *Felix O'Day* (1915); and something she referred to on February 16, 1916 as "lives of illustrious women"—possibly Mary Elizabeth Hewitt's *Lives of Illustrious Women of All Ages.* She tackled the poetry of Rupert Brook, Robert Frost, and Lincoln Colcord for a Lenten study group organized by Ellen Stevens; *Just David* (a 1916 children's novel by Eleanor H. Porter); *The Contagion of Character: Studies in Culture and Success,* by Newell Dwight Hillis (published 1911); C. Hanford Henderson's *What Is It to Be Educated?* (1914); and Gautier's *Jettatura* (which she read to Miss Stevens "while she carved" on January 17, 1917). Her reading also included Margaret Slattery's *The Girl and Her Religion* (this at a time when Jennie was moving toward a denominational change); Jane Addams's *The Spirit of Youth and the City Streets;* and the free-verse poetry of Edgar Lee Masters in *Spoon River Anthology.*

This literary grab bag paints a picture of Jennie McLeod holding on to the high culture she had imbibed at Smith even as she moved away from her four years there, simultaneously balancing respect for the academic canon with attention to more popular and more avant-garde authors, books, and ideas, while also maintaining awareness of social issues.

---

166   Carolyn (sometimes spelled Caroline) Sprague's graduation with honor from Clinton High School is documented in *School Report, Clinton, Mass., for the Year Ending January 31, 1912,* 45, and her graduation from Smith in the college's *1915 Class Book,* 54.

## "THIS IS THE LIFE"

If attending Smith College was pivotal in Jennie's life of the mind, it was also important to her social development, which was a part of her education. College friendships were fostered by shared housing, class attendance, and membership in departmental and other clubs. For students who hailed from relatively close by, friends from home could visit the campus to make social calls. Jennie wrote a number of times in her diary about escorting outside visitors to her classes. Camaraderie and hospitality were characteristics of the climate at Smith.

Senior Euphemia Lofton (later Mrs. Harold A. Haynes) was a resident of 17 Belmont Avenue when Jennie lived there as a junior.[167] Jennie's diary contains more than thirty references to Euph, as she was familiarly known, during the spring semester of 1914. The two spent a good deal of time together. Participating in a Smith College centennial oral history project in 1972, Euphemia Lofton Haynes recalled Smith as a highly sociable place: "[E]verything had the social flair. You would think of the choir as singing on occasions, nothing else, but they had a concert and then they'd meet regularly ... I think the thing that Smith people would remember is that kind of life ... has the social flair. Everything was done on a social basis."[168]

The residence system at the College encouraged the formation of friendships. It was described in the school's 1914-1915 *Bulletin:* "Smith College has eighteen halls of residence, housing almost eight hundred students. It is the aim of the College to make these houses home-like and pleasant, as well as to create in them conditions favorable for study."[169] Most of the houses had their own kitchens, dining rooms, and communal living rooms. A full-time Head of House managed op-

---

167 *Bulletin of Smith College ... 1913-1914*, 149.
168 Euphemia Lofton Haynes, oral history interview with Mary Jo Deering, October 26, 1972 (typed transcription February 7, 1973), 19, Smith Centennial Study, Smith College Archives, Northampton, Massachusetts.
169 *Bulletin of Smith College ... 1914-1915*, 107.

erations in each and looked after the students, with a faculty member also in residence. The congenial atmosphere so carefully maintained in Smith's houses facilitated camaraderie.

As noted, Jennie McLeod lived at 17 Belmont Avenue during her junior year and in Gillett as a senior. The former was basically a boarding situation used by Smith students at a time of scarce college housing. The latter opened in 1911, the year Jennie arrived at Smith.[170]

During Jennie's junior year (1913-1914), two other Clinton girls resided at 17 Belmont—freshman Anna Teresa Comaskey and junior Marguerite Frances Philbin, both of whom, her diary shows, formed part of her social circle at home as well as in Northampton.[171] Carolyn Sprague, who had graduated from Clinton High School in 1911 with Jennie, lived at 109 Elm Street during the 1913-1914 school year.[172] The double bonds of hometown and college strengthened the social connection and support system between these girls.

In her diary, Jennie McLeod used both first and last names in writing about some of her Smith College comrades. But more often, she mentioned friends simply by first name or by nickname—Euph, Lolo, Babes, Hutch, Carp, and Neugy. (She herself was dubbed Joney, and referred to herself in the third person by that sobriquet a couple of times.[173]) Because of the familiar way she referred to friends, it is sometimes difficult to pin down their identities with certainty—some guesswork is involved in connecting the dots.

---

170  Eleanor Terry Lincoln and John Abel Pinto, *This, the House We Live In: The Smith College Campus from 1871 to 1982* (Northampton, Massachusetts: The College, 1983), 92.
171  *Bulletin of Smith College ... 1913-1914*, 119 (Anna Comaskey), 142 (Marguerite Philbin).
172  Ibid., 144.
173  Her nickname is given under the entry "Jennie C. McLeod," *Smith College, Class of 1915: 25th Reunion Report* ([Chestnut Hill, Massachusetts: Elizabeth Dewey Perry], 1940), 77.

"THIS IS THE LIFE"

College friends who appear frequently in diary entries for the 1913-1914 academic year and who may be identified with reasonable confidence include Lois Brantly (another 17 Belmont housemate), Catherine Carpenter, Arlene Deware, Ada Hill, Helen Irving, and Florence Quilty (all residents of other houses).[174] Of these, Lois was a member of the Class of 1917, Arlene of the Class of 1916, and the rest of the Class of 1915. Lois and Ada came from out of state, Catherine, Arlene, Helen, and Florence from Massachusetts.

In moving from a small residential situation to a larger one in her senior year, Jennie gained an expanded pool of potential friends. More college comrades thread through diary entries for 1914-1915 than for the previous year. (To be sure, the fact that she kept the diary for only half of her junior year but for her entire senior year affects the numbers to some extent.)

Housemates at Gillett who surface in 1914-1915 entries include Anna Potter, Anna Sparks, Elizabeth (Betty) Reed, Amy Walker, Margaret (Peg) Jones, Dorothy Sykes, Margaret Dunne, Etta Boynton, and Rebecca Painter.[175] This group embraced four seniors, three juniors, and two freshmen; three—Betty, Peg, and Dorothy—were Massachusetts girls. Girls from other houses were again important in her circle of friends and acquaintances—Lois Evans, Louise Wood, Helen Hannahs, Anna McQuoid, Elsie Heinrich, Mary Martin, Martha Wells, Marion Poole, Agnes Jones, Alice Richardson, Florence Hanford, and Hyla Watters.[176] Including Anna McQuoid, a freshman from Clinton, five of

---

174   *Bulletin of Smith College ... 1913-1914*, 118 (Brantly), 131 (Deware), 141 (Hill and Irving), and 143 (Quilty).
175   *Bulletin of Smith College ... 1914-1915*, 125 (Dunne), 133 (Sparks), 148 (Jones), 150 (Reed), 151 (Sykes), 153 (Boynton), 157 (Painter and Potter), and 159 (Walker).
176   Ibid., 126 (Evans), 127 (Heinrich), 129 (Martin and McQuoid), 141 (Richardson), 143 (Wells), 147 (Hannahs), 148 (Jones), 155 (Hanford), 157 (Poole), 159 (Watters and Wood).

these girls came from Massachusetts, seven from other states. They ran the gamut in terms of class membership—four seniors, two juniors, two sophomores, and four freshmen.

The role of club involvement in Smith College social life is reflected in references in Jennie's diary to members of Colloquium, the departmental chemistry club she was invited to join in the fall of 1914. She wrote on October 17, 1914, "Amy Walker pinned me into Colloquium." She had been to an open meeting of the club the previous May 7, and attended her first meeting for members on November 12. In addition to Amy Walker, Colloquium members who show up in the diary include Irene Boardman, Elizabeth Carpenter, and Mildred Hutchinson.[177]

Among all of Jennie's college friendships, that with 17 Belmont housemate Euphemia Lofton is perhaps the most interesting. The two shared a companionable relationship during the 1913-1914 academic year.

Euph and another friend met Jennie at the train station in Northampton when she returned from Clinton at the end of Christmas vacation. Jennie read O. Henry all of one January evening with Euph and Lois. With Lois and May, she "decorated" Euph's room while the latter was at a meeting, and a week later took part in a surprise party there. The pair studied, attended concerts and lectures, and walked downtown together. On February 8, 1914, Jennie went with a group to the Catholic Church expressly to hear Euph—a Catholic—sing "Ave Maria." (Euph was in the choir and glee club at Smith and also studied organ.[178]) On February 19, Jennie was one of several girls who accompanied Euph to a wake. On June 9, Euph promised Jennie her senior pin, and hosted a "swell spread." On June 16, Jennie attended Euph's commencement

---

177 "Colloquium," 1915 *Class Book*, 90.
178 Haynes, oral history interview, 19.

("So glad I stayed"), and the following day shared a taxi to the train station with her. Euph disappeared from Jennie's diary after that.

There is nothing extraordinary about such interactions. However, what Jennie neglected to say about Euph is noteworthy. Nowhere in the diary does she give away the fact that Euphemia Lofton was black. Her seemingly uncomplicated acceptance of Euph and her disinclination to focus on race speaks volumes about Smith's socially progressive atmosphere, which was a conspicuous part of the college environment. Unlikely to have had much chance to associate with black children while growing up in Clinton, Jennie seems to have absorbed the lessons Smith aimed to impart.

Black applicants began attending Smith around the turn of the twentieth century, opening up the student body to intelligent, motivated students who were not so different in their attainments and aspirations from their white counterparts.[179] The exposure to young women of color and Smith's institutional commitment to upholding inclusiveness and respect for all in the college community created an awareness—indeed, for some, a revelation—of the capabilities of girls like Euphemia Lofton.

Born and raised in Washington, D.C., Euph went on to make a difference in the world she occupied. She married soon after graduating from Smith. She received a master's degree in mathematics from the University of Chicago in 1930, and in 1943, a Ph.D. from the Catholic University of America, the first black woman in this country to earn a doctorate in the subject.

Euphemia Lofton Haynes spent her adult life teaching black students and working to improve the quality of public education available to them in the District of Columbia school system. She served for ten years

---

[179] Leidholdt, 31-33.

on the District's Board of Education, pushing for desegregation and against a tracking system that worked to the disadvantage of minority students. In addition, she devoted energy to multiple local and national committees and organizations that advanced social welfare, particularly across race, class, and gender lines. A devout Catholic, she belonged to several denominational associations, as well, and to the Washington Chapter of the National Conference of Christians and Jews.[180]

In her 1972 Smith oral history interview, Mrs. Haynes commented on not having encountered discrimination at Smith.[181] It was for her, as for Jennie, a place where she could be judged on her own merits and efforts. The college climate allowed Jennie to regard Euph as simply one of her circle of chums.

During the time Jennie was a student at Smith, the college's progressivism expressed itself in relation to other areas, as well, among them the support of settlement houses, advocacy of social work, opposition to employer exploitation of working women and children, and women's suffrage.[182] The Smith student thus gained encouragement to take a stand on important social issues as part of the college experience.

Assuming her diary provides an honest record of what went on in Jennie's world during her time at Smith College, romance was conspicuously absent from her life. Male names turn up from time to time, as do the beaux of some of her friends, but she revealed nobody with whom she shared a strong personal connection. Expressing neither

---

180 Haynes, oral history interview; supplementary materials filed in the Smith College Archives with the oral history transcript (curriculum vitae; Euphemia Lofton Haynes, "The Identity Crisis" (typescript address given by E.L.H. at Smith Class of 1914 Class Reunion, May 30, 1969); Nancy Weiss, "Leader for the Public Schools, *Smith Alumnae Quarterly,* November 1967, 12-14); "Euphemia Lofton Haynes Biography," Biography.com, https//www.biography.com/scientist/euphemia-lofton-haynes (accessed August 30, 2019).
181 Haynes, oral history interview, 17-18.
182 Leidholdt, 33-35.

hopes nor complaints in this regard, she appears to have accepted her single status early on. Whether or not she was troubled by it, following graduation, her lack of romantic prospects meant that marriage was not on the horizon. Bachelor's degree in hand, Jennie McLeod had to consider other options for a meaningful and sustainable life going forward.

## The Bigger Picture—World War

THE FIRST WORLD WAR AND WOMEN'S SUFFRAGE HOVER BEHIND THE more quotidian themes of Jennie McLeod's diary.

The assassination of Archduke Franz Ferdinand of Austria in Sarajevo on June 28, 1914, precipitated World War I, but Jennie did not note the event. In short order, one European nation after another became involved, but she did not call attention to any war-related event until May 8, 1915, when she squeezed the brief line "Lusitania sunk" above the space formatted for her entry. She read the newspapers and must have been aware of what was going on in Europe, but held back in reacting to it.

Presidential directive no doubt contributed to Jennie's indisposition to highlight headlines about the war in her diary entries for 1914 and 1915. In August 1914, Woodrow Wilson declared that the United States would remain neutral in thought and feeling as well as in official action.[183]

Cloaking American impartiality with a mantle of righteousness, President Wilson designated October 4, 1914, Peace Sunday, "a day of prayer for the restoration of peace."[184] Jennie noted the occasion in her diary. Back home at the First Congregational Church in Clinton, the Reverend Jordan delivered a sermon based on Isaiah 9:6, "Of the

---

[183] David M. Kennedy, *Over Here: The First World War and American Society* (New York: Oxford University Press, copyright 2004), 46.
[184] "Peace Sunday Sermon," *Clinton Daily Item*, October 9, 1914, 5.

increase of his government and peace there shall be no end."[185] Upholding Wilson's commitment to non-intervention, ministers across the nation preached similar sermons.

The administration hoped that the stance of neutrality would inhibit support for potential American involvement in the war. But the attempt to engineer public opinion was a losing proposition almost from the outset: "The pleas had been in vain, for Americans began to divide about the war and its implications for their country as soon as they received the first news of the European armies clashing in Belgium and East Prussia in the summer of 1914."[186]

Wilson was narrowly reelected in November 1916 on the platform of keeping America out of the war. Vocal pro-war interests motivated by a variety of agendas had, from the outbreak of hostilities, made non-intervention increasingly difficult to sustain. The United States held the line until early in February 1917, when Germany escalated its threats to American ships. America declared war on Germany on April 6, 1917, requiring an about-face on the subject of neutrality. What Jennie might have written on the day America entered the war remains a matter of speculation. By then, she was no longer keeping her diary.

Having made non-involvement the cornerstone of his reelection, the president knew his reversal was politically problematic. To ensure support for the war initiative, he needed to keep dissension between anti- and pro-war factions under control. He attempted to frame America's entry into the war as a means of achieving peace. But ideological debate was not so easily tamped down. Consequently, the administration looked aside as conservative forces pursued citizen support of America's involvement by vigorous methods.

---

185   Ibid.
186   Kennedy, 46.

Although the progressive preference was to obtain public buy-in for the war through education about citizenship, organizations like the National Security League, the National Board for Historical Service, the Committee on Public Information, and the American Protective League tended toward the suppression of dialogue and the enforcement of unquestioned loyalty. Conservative elements derailed measured attempts to influence opinion through education and objective journalism. They worked to introduce patriotic propaganda into school curricula and released reactionary news stories and publicity for broad consumption. Those inclined toward nationalism, censorship, emotionalism, and anti-immigrant sentiment were emboldened. In this volatile climate, liberals, socialists, labor advocates, and the foreign-born became targets of suspicion and vigilantism.[187]

Jennie McLeod was raised in a town full of the well-assimilated descendants of German immigrants, whose number included neighbors and friends in Germantown, which was situated just beyond 244 Water Street. The parents of her close friend Christine Beck were both of German background.[188] In addition, Jennie was educated at Smith College, a progressive bastion. For these reasons, she was unlikely to have been swayed by the reactionary hysteria that afflicted the nation in the months leading up to and following America's involvement in the war. Interestingly, her diary entry for February 14, 1916, suggests some ambivalence about the public display of militarism. She wrote of her discomfort in handling a firearm as part of a preparedness exercise in Clinton: "Went with Helen and Ruth to drill and had a miserable time carrying a gun."

A piece in the *Clinton Daily Item* for October 25, 1915, makes clear

---

[187] Kennedy, 45-92.
[188] 1910 federal census information for Louis and Josephine Beck, as published in *HeritageQuest Online*.

that early in the war, those of German birth or descent in Massachusetts spoke out freely against the president and his policies. At a meeting in Worcester of the Massachusetts branch of the National German Alliance, neutrality was denounced as a "shameful farce" in light of the "attitude of President Wilson toward the exportation of munitions," and a resolution was passed opposing Wilson's reelection.[189] The state's German-Americans seemed not to fear reprisal at that moment.

In his essay for Clinton's centennial history, Thomas Gibbons described the local displays of patriotism that took place following America's entry into the First World War, including observances by the German community: "A most significant incident took place on April 8 when the members of the Turn Verein, the leading German organization of the town, assembled on their grounds and raised the flag of the United States while their choral group sang 'The Star-Spangled Banner.' There followed a concert in their hall and an address by President Ludwig Baer pledging loyalty without reservation by all residents of German birth and descent. The position of these good people had long been a most difficult one. While the United States remained officially neutral, they had been, quite properly and naturally, sympathetic to the German cause in a war against other European nations. Now that the United States and Germany were at war, they promptly displayed their loyalty to the land of their adoption, and from that day forth no one had cause to doubt their allegiance and patriotic service in every war effort."[190]

Although Gibbons put a positive spin on this spontaneous pledge of loyalty, it surely revealed some underlying apprehension among Clinton's German-Americans. Entry into the war put them in a vulnerable

---

189 "Germans Will Not Vote for Wilson: Resolution to That Effect Passed at Worcester Meeting," *Clinton Daily Item*, October 25, 1915, 6.
190 Gibbons, 58.

position as potential objects of mistrust. Clinton was historically a welcoming community, but changing circumstances exposed fault lines.

America's participation in World War I prompted many cities and towns to forbid the teaching of German: "District after district did its patriotic bit for the war effort by banning the teaching of the German language. Many states did likewise ... The anti-German animus soon extended to teachers. An Iowa politician charged that 'ninety percent of all the men and women who teach the German language are traitors.' Loyalty oaths were increasingly demanded of school personnel."[191] Clinton's apparent avoidance of such excesses did not mean that the people of the town were oblivious to the danger posed by conspicuous interest in German heritage and culture. Still, on October 7, 1915 (a year and a half before America entered the war), Jennie McLeod wrote in her diary, "Tutored Florence S in German." We cannot know if Jennie might have hesitated to do the same in 1917, but in 1915 she had no misgivings.

Certainly, Clinton valued the war contributions of its German population. In writing the history of Company K, 101st Infantry in World War I, James T. Duane memorialized an incident in which one Clinton soldier's ability to speak German directly advanced American objectives. George Schobert of Branch Street in Germantown was positioned close to the enemy. When the commands to prepare for attack were given, Schobert "issued several commands in German which counteracted the German officer's commands, and thus confused the groups about to attack in his location. The Germans starting to disperse afforded a lovely opportunity for our boys to open fire and caused a great number of casualties."[192]

Whatever suppressed tensions rose to the surface during the Great

---

191  Kennedy, 54.
192  James T. Duane, *Dear Old "K"* (Boston: Thomas Todd Co., 1922), 134, 180.

War, the people of the town nevertheless banded together to provide humanitarian aid to Europeans affected by warfare and, eventually, to support American soldiers fighting abroad. They dutifully went to see patriotic war movies promoted by the government.[193] (Jennie wrote on August 21, 1915, "To Star at night with Mildred to see War pictures.") They sent much-appreciated letters, newspapers, and care packages to local men fighting in Europe.[194] They organized drives for the sale of war bonds and put their money into this form of "patriotic contribution toward winning the war."[195] And in response to shortages caused by the shipment of food supplies to Europe for American servicemen, they planted war gardens.[196]

In the autumn of 1915, Clintonians took advantage of the opportunity to educate themselves about the war through a free public lecture series on the conflict.[197] (The Weeks Institute lecture series were funded through the bequest of George W. Weeks to provide high quality, nonpartisan, nonsectarian programs for community benefit.[198]) In her diary, Jennie noted attending all of the Monday evening lectures in the series: on September 27, John Cowper Powys on Russia (which she described as the "[c]rowning feature of life since June 15," the date of her college commencement)—an event attended by 750 people, "the largest number ever present at a Weeks' course lecture"[199]; on October 4, J.C. Powys on England; on October 11, Charles Herbert Levermore on "The

---

193 Kennedy, 62.
194 Duane, 17, 20, 21, 25.
195 Gibbons, 60.
196 Ibid.
197 Ibid., 56.
198 *The Weeks Institute, Clinton, Massachusetts. Season of 1907 and 1908* ([Clinton: The Institute, 1907]) (printed schedule of programs), 4, "Social Organizations" pamphlet and ephemera box, Clinton Historical Society.
199 "Russia's Reasons: Prof. J.C. Powys Tells Large Audience Why That Country is in the War," *Clinton Daily Item*, September 28, 1915, 1.

European Conflict";[200] on October 18, Edmund von Mach on Austria and Germany (following which "the local German societies tendered a most enthusiastic reception to Prof. von Mach at Turner hall, where he gave a short address in German");[201] on October 25, Louis K. Wilkenson on France and Italy; on November 8, Edwin A. Grosvenor on Turkey and the Balkan states (a lecture she did not like); and on November 22, Brooks Adams on "War as the Ultimate Form of Economic Competition" (which also displeased her).[202]

Similarly, Smith College took measures to raise campus consciousness of issues related to the war. Jennie noted on March 8, 1915, "Went to Mr. Fays lecture on probable results of the war." Historian Sidney Bradshaw Fay, who taught at Smith, went on to write an influential study titled *The Origins of the World War* (1928).

Red Cross work was a focus of community energy both at Smith and in Clinton. During the autumn of 1914, just months after the outbreak of war, a Red Cross committee for war relief work was organized at Smith. Through contributions, supplies were purchased to make mufflers, towels, bandages, and pillowcases. Parties were organized to accomplish the work, and the completed items were collected and packed. The effort produced 357 mufflers, 307 bundles of absorbent pads, 2,006 bandages, 1,668 towels, 210 pillowcases, and 50 "miscellaneous articles." Sheets and blankets were purchased with contributions. The mission having been completed, leftover materials, knitting needles, and crochet hooks were sent to the women of Belgium. A total of $1,323.37 was raised for materials and for distribu-

---

200   Jennie's report of Charles Herbert Levermore's lecture ("Lecture in Grammar Hall") appeared in the *Clinton Daily Item* on October 13.
201   *Clinton Daily Item*, October 19, 1915, 3.
202   The title of Adams's lecture is printed on the front page of the *Clinton Daily Item* for November 9, 1915, at the end of the report on Edward Grosvenor's lecture the previous evening.

tion, including $183.93 designated for food for countries involved in the war.[203]

Jennie's diary shows that she took part in this collective endeavor. She wrote on October 22, 1914, "Miss McElwain read to us for one hour while we did Red Cross work. Fascinating." On November 7, she commented that "everybody" was knitting gray mufflers for the Red Cross.

Between 1917 and 1920, the Smith College Relief Unit substantially aided a cluster of villages in France, providing medical care, transportation, and farming assistance, addressing matters of public health, distributing food and supplies, and organizing educational and social services for children.[204] As a Smith alumna, Jennie must have felt some pride in the undertaking.

By the beginning of 1917, Clinton fully accepted the reality of the European War as an American concern which would impact all citizens, not just those in the military. In the early part of the year, the local branch of the Special Aid Society for American Preparedness initiated a multi-session program series to study elementary hygiene and home care of the sick, supervised by the Red Cross. As her diary documents, Jennie took part in this program. In April 1917, six Red Cross members—Ellen K. Stevens among them—met at the Star Theater in Clinton to plan the formation of a local chapter, which also included the towns of Lancaster, Harvard, Bolton, Berlin, and Boylston. The chapter threw itself into sewing, knitting, preparing bandages and dressings, and collecting money for the Red Cross War Fund.[205] Jennie may well have volunteered her time to the local Red Cross effort, but she was no longer making diary entries when the chapter was formed. Other local

---
203   *1915 Class Book*, 166-67.
204   Lettie Gavin, *American Women in World War I: They Also Served* (Niwot, Colorado: University Press of Colorado, copyright 1997), 157, 162, 169-70, 176, 204.
205   Gibbons, 59-60.

organizations also contributed to relief. Many women with husbands, sons, or brothers in the service took part in such work.

On June 27, 1916, as Germany wooed Mexico and attempted to inflame border hostilities between Mexico and America to keep America out of Europe, Stanley informed his family of his intention to enlist. He enlisted the next day, and was sent to Camp Whitney in Framingham, Massachusetts, located roughly 30 miles south of Clinton.[206] Jennie wrote in her June 30 diary entry of visiting him there with her mother. On January 20 and 21, 1917, she noted buying material and sewing items for a "Co. K. Bazaar." Such devotions made the families of Clinton's soldiers feel useful, but they did little to alleviate the anguish caused by the absence of loved ones. In September 1917, Stanley McLeod sailed to France as part of Company K, 101st Infantry, which included many soldiers from Clinton.[207]

America's involvement in the Great War diminished Jennie McLeod's interest in her line-a-day. Except for one isolated entry on April 18, 1918, she left off keeping it just as the country was about to enter the war. Her personal record must have seemed inconsequential, the small events it captured dwarfed by the headlines in the news. Moreover, anxiety over the possibility that one or both of her brothers might be wounded or killed in the line of duty probably factored into her laying her pen down.

---

[206] A June 24 article in the *Clinton Daily Item* ("Mustering Begins Today") announced that the mustering of 6,500 Massachusetts militia men into service at Camp Whitney in Framingham had begun. The action was described as "the first step toward the Mexican border so far as Washington orders were concerned."

[207] "Stanley M. McLeod," *Clinton Military Case History*, Volume 2; Duane, 186; Gibbons, 62.

## Reform Unfolding—The Suffrage Movement

JENNIE NEVER EXPLICITLY DECLARED HERSELF A SUFFRAGIST IN HER diary. Nevertheless, she demonstrated a more apparent attention to the suffrage movement than to the First World War. She displayed a pragmatic engagement with voting rights for women that eventually revealed itself in practical, hands-on action if not in public protest or dramatic rhetoric.

It might seem self-evident that a Smith girl reaching womanhood at a time of feverish political activism toward equal suffrage would, of course, be a suffragist. But the choice was not black-and-white for those trying to fathom the issue, not even for a smart young woman attending a progressive female college.

With great organization and persistence, early twentieth-century suffrage advocates pushed to gain the vote for women. Their crusade suffered many political setbacks at the state and national levels along the way to the passage and ratification of the 19th Amendment. A significant number of women did not believe that electoral politics was the most appropriate or effective channel of influence for members of their sex. This group was headed by some capable women leaders who allied themselves with a range of powerful interests in the effort to defeat suffrage—brewing and liquor interests, manufacturing, corporate, and business interests, political machines, Southerners determined to block black voting rights, and New England social conservatives among them.[208]

In 1879, reflecting acceptance of education as a traditional "woman's sphere" activity, Massachusetts passed a law allowing women to

---

208 Eleanor Flexner and Ellen Fitzpatrick, *Century of Struggle: The Woman's Rights Movement in the United States,* enlarged edition (Cambridge: The Belknap Press of Harvard University Press, copyright 1996), 255-317.

vote for local school committee members. But this did not go nearly far enough for those who wanted political equality. As the suffragists soldiered on, opponents of suffrage mobilized, too, posing significant challenges to suffrage efforts in the state. Rooted in earlier state anti-suffrage organizations, the Massachusetts Association Opposed to the Further Extension of Suffrage to Women was founded in 1895.[209] Other states subsequently formed similar organizations, but the Massachusetts association remained the most vigorous and vocal.[210]

Both suffragists and anti-suffragists were outspoken in promoting their respective causes. Each point of view was represented by articulate and convincing speakers who lectured whenever and wherever the opportunity arose. Her diary shows that Jennie attended programs on both sides of the suffrage argument and that she listened closely to the merits of each. On August 1, 1914, for example, she attended a pair of presentations on suffrage, part of a Clinton Chautauqua series. She wrote in response, "Mrs. Oliphant against woman suffrage was splendid. Frank Stevens in favor at night not so good." As she deepened her understanding of suffrage, Jennie demonstrated an objective appreciation of a reasoned, well-presented argument, whether or not she agreed with its content.

On February 10, 1915, during the second semester of her senior year, she heard an extemporaneous speech by a fellow student in elocution class: "Irene Boardman made star speech on suffrage." (Emma Irene Boardman—the first student at the college to finish the four-year degree program in three years—went on to a distinguished career as a physician.[211]) A month later, on March 12, she took in a speech by poet,

---

209  Ibid., 287-88.
210  Ibid., 288.
211  "Dr. E. Irene Boardman never stopped Serving the Public," *Connecticut History*.org, https://connecticuthistory.org/dr-e-irene-boardman-never-stopped-serving-the-public/ (accessed February 2, 2020).

playwright, and suffragist Marion Craig Wentworth. Two and a half months after that, on the evening of May 25, she attended a "brilliant convincing talk on equal suffrage" by Dr. Anna Howard Shaw, a leader of the suffrage movement in the United States and also a physician and an ordained Methodist minister. In Clinton on June 7, 1915, she heard "O. Stone Mrs George & Miss Dorman on anti suffrage"—a program organized by the Clinton branch of the Women's Anti-Suffrage Association of Massachusetts.[212] And October 14, after she had graduated from college, she heard suffragist and workers' rights advocate Helen M. Todd speak in favor of suffrage, summing up the occasion with a single word, "Great."

By the end of her senior year at Smith, Jennie knew her own mind regarding suffrage. In April, May, and June 1915, she joined college friends in the effort to canvass voters in Northampton in advance of a vote on a proposed amendment to the Massachusetts constitution to grant women the franchise.

Jennie wrote in her diary on April 28, 1915, that she had attended a suffrage canvassers meeting "at local headquarters." She noted dictating ward lists on May 13, 14, 17, 18, 19, and 20 (on May 20, referring to the task as her "reg occupation"). Although she declared "Finished Suffrage canvas" on May 21, on June 12—three days before commencement—she was still plodding away on the lists. This was not scintillating work, but it reflected a willingness to tackle the issue with boots on the ground.

The proposed Massachusetts amendment came to a vote on November 2, 1915, five months after Jennie graduated from college. The

---

212 "Campaign Opens Tonight: Mrs. George and Miss Dorman to Address Anti-Suffragists Meeting in Music Hall," *Clinton Daily Item*, June 7, 1915, 1.

anti-suffragists had thrown their energies into its defeat.[213] Although suffragists had been optimistic about its chances to pass, it failed by an almost two-to-one margin.[214] Jennie learned the results of the election as they were coming in at the newspaper office, noting in her diary, "Watched election return at Item Off. Suff. Lost."

A summary of the Worcester County votes in the *Clinton Daily Item* for November 3, 1915, showed that 504 Clinton voters had been in favor of the amendment, 1,504 against it—a higher margin than the state average.[215] Perhaps the town's manufacturers, economically motivated to maintain the social status quo, hampered suffrage support. Perhaps also the strong male dominance of some of the immigrant cultures represented in the town's population contributed to the result. But the amendment was also trounced in the primarily agricultural and more ethnically homogeneous towns surrounding Clinton. Lancaster had voted 68 in favor to 232 opposed—the margin even wider there than in Clinton. Bolton had voted 48 pro, 85 con; Boylston 29 to 93; Harvard 42 to 149; and Sterling 58 to 155.

The failure of Massachusetts voters to give women the vote in 1915 did not suppress Jennie McLeod's interest in the political process. On February 26, 1916, she and Christine Beck became registered local voters. On March 6, 1916, she observed, "Cast my first vote all alone." A momentous occasion, even if only in a municipal election.

As women proved their loyalty to the country through relief work and other types of service in World War I, suffragists continued to do battle. The significant contributions that women made to the war ef-

---

213  See Women's Anti-Suffrage Association of Massachusetts, *Anti-Suffrage Essays by Massachusetts Women* ([Boston: J. Haier], 1916).
214  "Massachusetts Woman Suffrage Victory Parade: Instructions for Marchers," *Massachusetts Historical Society Collections online*, https://www.masshist.org/database/1892 (accessed February 2, 2020).
215  "In District Contests," *Clinton Daily Item*, November 3, 1915, 1.

fort and persistent political pressure by suffrage advocates eventually pushed President Wilson to express support for the cause.[216] This by itself was not enough to give women the vote, but it was a factor in moving the struggle toward a successful conclusion.

The 19th Amendment to the Constitution was passed by the United States House of Representatives in May 1919 and by the Senate in June. It was ratified (again after a good deal of contention) on August 18, 1920. Had Jennie McLeod still been keeping her diary, she would almost certainly have made note of these milestones. Be that as it may, by the time she settled in earnest into the occupation that afforded her an independent life as a working woman, she was a politically empowered citizen, as well.

## Jennie's Life, Going Forward

AFTER GRADUATING FROM SMITH COLLEGE IN JUNE 1915, JENNIE resumed life at home in Clinton. Her immediate challenge was to find employment. Although she had acquired valuable work experience along the way, it took her some time to gain a professional foothold.

While still a Smith student, she had taken advantage of several opportunities to earn money, presumably contributing to the significant cost of her education. The fees for attending Smith during the 1913-1914 academic year were: $150 for tuition; $300 for room and board in college houses; a $10 fee for elementary courses in astronomy, chemistry, physics, zoology, and botany; a $5 fee for required physical education; and additional fees for particular offerings in physical education, art, and music. It all came to a minimum total of approximately

---

216   Flexner and Fitzpatrick, 271-72, 300-08.

$450.[217] At a time when the average income for an American man was about $687 per year, a Smith education represented a serious financial commitment.[218] Jennie's college fees were likely covered by some combination of her own and parental funds. However generous her family may have been in that regard, Jennie herself displayed a sense of personal responsibility in the financial management of her education. She wrote matter-of-factly in November 1914 and March 1915 of paying the bills for her tuition, room, and board.

Jennie earned occasional income by reporting on local events for the *Clinton Daily Item,* both before and after graduating from Smith. On January 5, 1914, over Christmas break, she noted in her diary that she and her father had attended a lecture on Keats in the Clinton Town Hall by Professor John Cowper Powys of Cambridge University in England. (She liked the lecture.) The next day, working from her notes of the event, she submitted an account to the *Item* for publication. The report appeared in the paper that evening.[219] On January 7, she wrote, "Rec'd $1.00 from Item for report on Keats." On October 11, 1915, four months after graduating from college, she wrote, "Prof Levermore's lecture on The European Conflict. Took notes to report." The next day, she pulled together a piece for the paper from her notes. On October 13, the article appeared in the *Item* and Jennie received seventy-five cents for her work.[220]

Although it engaged Jennie with town life and honed the listening and writing skills developed in the college classroom, writing for the paper brought in little more than pin money.

---

217 *Bulletin of Smith College ... 1913-1914,* 104.
218 Geoff Williams, "A Glimpse at Your Expenses 100 Years Ago," *U.S. News & World Report,* https://money.usnews.com/money/personal-finance/articles/2015/01/02/a-glimpse-at-your-expenses-100-years-ago (accessed December 2, 2019).
219 "Prof. Powys' Lecture," *Clinton Daily Item,* January 6, 1914, 1, 3.
220 "Lecture in Grammar Hall," *Clinton Daily Item,* October 13, 1915, 5.

Jennie's work in the Town Hall office of the Clinton Road Commissioners during her father's service on the board was more remunerative. Her diary entries for the entire summer of 1914 and for Christmas break that year contain multiple references to the hours she spent working for the commission. In a period when the approach to what might now be considered nepotism was relatively laissez faire, George McLeod's office-holding likely favored his daughter's Town Hall employment.

As the annual Clinton town report for 1913 shows, Jennie's municipal employment preceded her first diary entry. The financial itemization in the Road Commissioners' report for that year includes a line for "McLeod, Jennie C., office work—$20.00."[221] Because the expenses for office labor for 1914 are presented less explicitly, the 1914 report is not helpful in identifying how much she made the next year. However, several of her diary entries document payments made to her during the summer of 1914. She received $16.75 on July 15, $10.00 on July 29, $12.25 on August 12, and $6.38—"[l]ast pay from Rd Dept for the season"—on September 9. Regardless of whether she actually earned more from the Town of Clinton in 1914 than is noted in her diary, the total of those four payments by themselves ($45.38) was significant.

The work of bookkeeping for Clinton's Road Commissioners required attention to detail, accuracy, and a sense of responsibility. The duties of the commission as spelled out in town bylaws demanded as much: "The Road Commissioners shall keep an accurate account of all money expended and all work done upon all public ways and sewers of the Town, and a detailed record of the number of teams and men employed, the extent and nature of the work done and the amount

---

221 "Report of Road Commissioners: Financial Report," *Sixty-fourth Annual Report of the Town Officers of Clinton, Mass. For the Year Ending January 31, 1914* (Clinton: W.J. Coulter Press for The Town, 1914), 39.

expended on each street, way or sewer."[222] Since there is no hint of workplace dissatisfaction in her diary, Jennie appears to have fulfilled her municipal office duties satisfactorily. Her part-time job in the Clinton Town Hall was valuable experience in that it built up her skill set and simultaneously helped secure her college education.

During her college years and after, Jennie also pitched in at George McLeod's plumbing store on Church Street. Entries in her diary refer to her keeping the store open, working at bookkeeping and accounting, taking care of odd jobs as they arose (for example, washing the windows and tidying the shelves on November 5, 1915), and spending time with her father. Her younger sister Helen, who would later become the secretary and bookkeeper for the family business, was already a regular presence there. Jennie wrote of filling in for Helen when the latter was otherwise occupied. While her diary offers no insight into whether Jennie was paid for her hours in the plumbing store, or whether her involvement was a means of offsetting parental contributions toward college, or whether stepping up to the job was simply expected of the McLeod girls as a family duty, this practical experience reinforced Jennie's developing understanding of what it meant to work.

Seeking a job fresh out of college, Jennie looked first to the most traditional of female occupations—teaching. On August 10, 1915, while vacationing in Boston with the McCances (family friends), she visited the Fisk Teachers' Agency on Park Street. On August 19, she applied for a vacancy in the public high school of the neighboring town of Sterling, writing the following day to two of her Smith professors for recommendations. The job did not materialize. However, a few weeks later, on September 9, she noted her "début as a school marm"—substitute

---

222 "Duties of the Road Commissioners," *By-Laws of the Town of Clinton, Massachusetts, 1914* (Clinton: W.J. Coulter Press for The Town, 1914), 21.

teaching four Latin classes for Clinton High School teacher Guy Jordan. That fall, she also wrote about tutoring someone named Cameron (probably Cameron Duncan) in algebra and French and "Florence S." (likely Florence Shutts) in German.

On February 26, 1916, Jennie answered a letter from the Fisk Teachers' Agency regarding "reg. position as governess," which suggests that the job search had not been overwhelmingly successful. Nineteenth-century horror stories of ill-treated governesses underscore the fact that service in that capacity was not always a means to quality of life.

That spring, she landed several temporary teaching jobs. On April 10, she began substituting at Peters High School in nearby Southborough, teaching Latin and English, a situation lasting through April 28. On her last day in that post, she called on the high school superintendent in Marlborough on her way home. The following Monday, May 1, she began substituting in French at Marlborough High School, and the next day was offered "English in M.H.S. for rest of year as soon as released from French assignment." Her diary entries for the remainder of the year show her engaged in the responsibilities of that position. Early in 1917, she tutored one "Carl" in Latin and algebra. As late as 1920, her name appears in listings of substitute and night school teachers in Clinton.[223]

Although Jennie made a valiant effort to establish a career as a teacher, the initiative did not yield permanent results. In fact, it appears to have been a false start, entered into in good faith, and probably with the encouragement of others, but not especially suited to her nature. Indeed, she revealed some ambivalence toward her students in commenting with irony on June 18, 1916, "Made out average for year and

---

223  *Seventy-first Annual Report of the School Department, Clinton, Mass., for the Year Ending December 31, 1920* (Clinton: W.J. Coulter Press for The Town, 1921), 68, 69.

Ellen K. Stevens, from Clinton
High School *Memorabilia*
(yearbook), 1922

examinations for Marlboro cherubs." Fortunately, she had the opportunity to explore another occupation better suited to who she was. Less than a year and a half out of college, Jennie secured a clerical position in a respectable profession then opening up to her sex: insurance. Having likely influenced Jennie's decision to go to college, Ellen K. Stevens was also pivotal in her vocational path.

Educator, temperance reformer, and suffrage advocate Frances Elizabeth Willard wrote about women in insurance in 1897: "The soliciting of insurance and the management of insurance business, as a legitimate and practical work for women, has recently come to attract widespread attention. At first this work was almost wholly restricted to life insurance, but following the successful work done in that direction, the women agents are extending their lines to embrace fire risks also. Nearly all the prominent life insurance companies now have a woman's department, efficiently directed by a woman manager. Such positions as these, demanding unusual executive ability, and commanding more than generous salaries, must of course be comparatively few in number: but the field now opening to women for soliciting life insurance and placing fire risks and for managing local agencies, is almost unlimited."[224]

Willard observed that insurance operations were eager to hire intelligent women. She also pointed to specific female exemplars in the field, Ellen Stevens of Clinton among them: "When Mr. C.G. Stevens, of Clinton, Mass., retired from business at an advanced age, his daughter Miss E.K. Stevens took charge of the several agencies which he had managed."[225] At a point in Jennie McLeod's life when it was unclear how she would make a living, Ellen Stevens provided a possibility.

In 1920, a prominent insurance weekly ran a notice of the sale by Mrs. Elizabeth M. Pope of her interest in the Clinton insurance agency of S.R. Merrick & Co. to C.G. Stevens & Son. The piece went on to outline the history of the Stevens business: "The purchasing agency, C. Stevens & Son, was founded by the late Charles Stevens over fifty years ago, the first insurance agency in Clinton. Edward G. Stevens became a member of the firm in 1872, when the present agency name was adopted. Ellen K. Stevens became sole owner of the business in 1896, and for the last nineteen years has occupied the office from which the agency is now removing [205 Church Street] to the larger quarters of the Merrick Agency [104 High Street].[226] Miss Jennie McLeod is now

---

224  Frances Elizabeth Willard, *Occupations for Women: A Book of Practical Suggestions for the Material Advancement, the Mental and Physical Development, and the Moral and Spiritual Uplift of Women* (Cooper Union, New York: The Success Co., 1897), 165.
225  Ibid., 167.
226  Documenting the location of the Stevens agency: *Clinton and Lancaster Directory 1915*, 139; *Clinton and Lancaster Directory 1922* ... (Fitchburg: Price & Lee Co., copyright 1922), 140. The 1922 listing for the business reads "Stevens CG & Son (Ellen K. Stevens & Jennie C. McLeod) fire life accident and automobile insurance agents and brokers 104 High."

a member of the firm and will be business manager for this year."²²⁷

Jennie's promotion followed an apprenticeship chronicled in her diary. On November 17, 1915, some five months after graduating from Smith, she wrote, "Kept Miss Stevens office open from 2-5:30." Not long after that, on January 3, 1916, she mentioned that Miss Stevens was ill and that she "kept office for her with doubtful success." She reported two weeks later, on January 17, "My last day at the insurance business after a pleasant two weeks."

Jennie noted working at the Stevens insurance office a number of days in February and early March 1916. In the second half of February, she also kept office for Miss E.F. Merrick at the S.R. Merrick insurance business, which was later absorbed into the Stevens company.²²⁸ And on January 8, 1917, she wrote, "Spent A.M. soliciting accident insurance."

A notice of Jennie McLeod's increasing responsibility in C.G. Stevens appeared in the November 1920 issue of the *Smith Alumnae Quarterly*: "Jennie McLeod was admitted, September 1, as a junior member of an insurance firm in Clinton, Mass. While her business partner is taking a year's leave of absence in order to teach in the high school, Jennie is in charge of the office."²²⁹

Twenty-five years out of college, Jennie summarized her career in insurance for the Smith Class of 1915 reunion book: "Since the fall of 1916 my interests have centered around insurance. Entering the office of C.G. Stevens & Son as a clerk, I remained in that position for four

---

227   *The Standard*, Vol. 87 (December 4, 1920), 687.
228   The identity of the "Miss Merrick" in Jennie's diary and her association with the S.R. Merrick Company is confirmed in *Clinton and Lancaster Directory 1916* ... (Fitchburg: Price & Lee Co., copyright 1916), 261.
229   *Smith Alumnae Quarterly*, Vol. 12, No. 1 (November 1920), 79. "Miss Ellen K. Stevens was appointed to succeed Miss Fury as teacher of history and civics"—*Seventy-first Annual Report of the School Department*, 35.

years, becoming junior member of the firm in September 1920. Upon the retirement of my partner, May 1, 1939, I became sole owner of the business now conducted in my own name. The work of running a general insurance agency in a small town ... involves inspection of risks, underwriting, counselling, clerical details, accounting and loss adjustment."[230] Through a network of local women in which Ellen Stevens was central, Jennie McLeod found lifelong work. Insurance gave her a visible place in the community and allowed her to exercise her abilities. She operated her business from her office on the second floor of the building at the corner of High and Church Streets, very near the McLeod plumbing business, until 1965, retiring three years before she died.[231]

In the period immediately following her graduation from Smith, Jennie grappled not only with finding employment but also with her denominational commitment. Although raised in the First Congregational Church of Clinton, she was increasingly drawn to the Episcopal Church of the Good Shepherd.

While in college, she attended chapel—which was mandatory at Smith—and vespers. Smith spelled out its approach to cultivating the religious capacities of its students in its annual *Bulletin*: "The College is Christian, seeking to realize the ideals of character inspired by the Christian religion. It is, however, entirely unsectarian in its management and instruction. As there is no college church, the students are expected to attend the churches in the city. They are expected also to be present at the daily religious exercises of the College. A voluntary vesper service is held on Sunday afternoons in the John M. Greene Hall. The religious life of the College is further expressed in the Smith Col-

---

230 *Smith College, Class of 1915: 25th Reunion Report*, 78.
231 "Private Services for Miss McLeod Are Held Today," *Clinton Daily Item*, July 29, 1968, 1.

lege Association for Christian Work, membership in which is open to students and faculty, whatever their religious affiliations."[232]

Not surprisingly, chapel and vespers feature prominently in Jennie's diary entries at Smith. She wrote, too, of attending services in several Northampton churches.

Her diary offers evidence that Jennie paid close attention to discussions of religion and had definite opinions about some aspects of belief. On January 26, 1914, she wrote that her friends Euph and Florence had talked about religion. On September 25 of that year, she reported having discussed atheism with Bertha, and on October 21, that Ada and Bertha had had a "long rel. argument." On January 23, 1915, she referred to a conversation among Bertha, Eleanor, and Mira on "Catholic Belief."

The October 21 exchange came the day after Jennie reported in her diary, "Went to Catholic mission with house crowd." The visit prompted her to comment about the Catholic focus on the afterlife, "Life is only a preparation for death!!" Her double exclamation point suggests some skepticism.

Jennie wrote that she had attended "[c]hapel with the Jewish contingent" on March 21, 1914. Whatever subtle rebellion against parochialism may have been implicit in the act had its limits, however. Three weeks later, on April 13, she backtracked, writing, "Told Florence I wasn't a Jew." While it is difficult to say with certainty what those two statements mean, the first implies some impulse to push beyond the religious comfort zone, or at least to be seen doing so.

Church life was important in Clinton, and it runs through Jennie's diary as a recurrent theme. When she was at home, Jennie regularly attended Congregational services and Sunday school, recreational events organized by her own and other local churches, and church-sponsored cultural offerings and programs on social issues.

---

232   *Bulletin of Smith College ... 1914-1915*, 15.

She made special note on May 2, 1915, of going to church with her father "to hear Dr J: on Minimum Wage." "Dr J" was the Reverend William W. Jordan, D.D., pastor of the First Congregational Church. Well-respected in Clinton both as a clergyman and as a community leader, he had become the minister of the church around the time Jennie was born and remained in the position until 1921, having presided for twenty-eight years.[233] As members of Dr. Jordan's congregation, the McLeods enjoyed occasional pastoral visits to their home. Jennie noted his calling on January 1, 1914.

Jennie moved away from the First Congregational Church when she returned to Clinton after graduating from Smith. Finding her own way as an adult in the community in which she had been raised encouraged a desire to shape her religious identity as well as an independent working life. Social considerations played a role in her ultimate denominational change. For starters, her high school and college classmate Carolyn Sprague was the daughter of Clinton's Episcopal minister. Moreover, two other important people in her life directly influenced her conscious decision to become a member of Clinton's Episcopal Church of the Good Shepherd late in 1918.

Jennie's high school classmate Christine Louise Beck was a member of Good Shepherd.[234] During and after college, Jennie and Christine sometimes attended Sunday school and church events together in Clinton. As good friends who spent a lot of time in each other's company, they probably talked about religion. Their shared trust in speaking of this personal matter apparently extended to Christine's mother. In February 1917, Mrs. Beck lent Jennie *The Girl and Her Religion,* a 1913 book by Margaret Slattery. The loan attests to Jennie's consideration during

---
233  Gordon, 79-80.
234  She was baptized there on April 22, 1905 and confirmed on November 20, 1910 (Church of the Good Shepherd, Parish Register, Volume B, 8, 207).

this period of the role of religion in her life. On February 25, 1917, Jennie wrote in her diary, "Went to church with Mrs Beck much to Dr Jordan's chagrin." She was beginning to assert autonomy in relation to her religious choices.

Mentor and role model Ellen Stevens was also a force in this process. Miss Stevens was a charter member of the Church of the Good Shepherd and is credited with having suggested that name for the church.[235] She was organist, choir member, and Sunday school teacher there as well as a leader of the Girls' Friendly Society, a church organization for young women, which Jennie mentioned in her diary.[236]

On Sunday, January 30, 1916 (her twenty-third birthday), Jennie recorded that she had attended a Sunday school class taught by Miss Stevens. On April 26, 1916, she noted that she and Christine had attended a Bible class party at Miss Stevens's home. On January 8, 1917, she wrote, "Discussed religion with Miss Stevens with much satisfaction." Less than two years later, she became an Episcopalian.

On December 29, 1918, Jennie McLeod was baptized by the Reverend Robert R. Carmichael in the Church of the Good Shepherd.[237] Ellen K. Stevens was her sponsor. She was confirmed in the church on February 16, 1919, by Bishop Thomas Frederick Davies of the Episcopal Diocese of Western Massachusetts.[238] What Jennie might have written about these transformative events would have been illuminating, but by this point she was no longer keeping her diary.

While her siblings remained Congregationalists, Jennie was a member of Good Shepherd until her death. Like Ellen Stevens, she was

---

235 Church of the Good Shepherd, Parish Register, Volume B, 465.
236 "Miss Ellen K. Stevens"; Ellen K. Stevens, "The Associate's Responsibility Toward the Religious Life of Her Girls," *Girls' Friendly Society in America Associates' Record*, Vol. 23, No. 1 (January 1915), 9-11.
237 Church of the Good Shepherd, Parish Register, Volume B, 22.
238 Ibid., 214.

active in the Girls' Friendly Society, the records of which refer to her serving refreshments at meetings, holding card parties at her home on Water Street, and talking to the group about a recent trip.[239]

Between 1915 and 1920, as she was resolving important issues relating to work and religion, Jennie enjoyed the fellowship afforded by town life and by membership in local and area organizations. As in college, her friendships and associations appear to have been primarily with members of her own sex. To all appearances, no young man inspired love. She remained a member of her parents' household, listed in town directories for the period as boarding at 244 Water Street.[240] Her sisters Helen and Maybelle stayed on, too, but her brothers Stanley and George left to start their own families.

In addition to her involvement in the Girls' Friendly Society of the Church of the Good Shepherd, Jennie was active in the Clinton Chamber of Commerce and the Clinton Historical Society. She applied her executive abilities to community benefit, serving as chair of both the local Junior Red Cross and the Clinton Council of the Girl Scouts. She was also treasurer of The Wanocksett Girl Scout Camp, Inc. She belonged to the Clinton Women's Club (she was a member of the Student Loan Committee) and to the Fitchburg Smith College Club (serving on its Scholarship Fund Committee).[241] She wrote in her diary on October 23, 1915 of joining the Worcester Smith College Club. In 1940, she served on the 25th Reunion Committee and the Class Book Committee for the Class of 1915 at Smith, and she purchased advertis-

---

239 Church of the Good Shepherd, Girls' Friendly Society, Secretary's Book, 1919-1931 (manuscript record volume), 61, 142, 143, 170, 180, Church of the Good Shepherd Office.
240 *Clinton and Lancaster Directory 1917*, 107; *Clinton and Lancaster Directory 1918* ... (Fitchburg: Price & Lee Co., copyright 1918), 107; *Clinton and Lancaster Directory 1920* ... (Fitchburg: Price & Lee Co., copyright 1920), 103.
241 *Smith College, Class of 1915: 25th Reunion Report*, 78.

ing space for her insurance business at the end of the reunion book.[242]

Women's clubs in the early twentieth century provided a mechanism for self-culture and a means of contributing to community and society at a time when women had limited agency beyond the home.[243] Such organizations attracted working women and homemakers alike. Established in 1896, the Clinton Women's Club shared the mission of American women's clubs in general in championing both self-improvement and civic responsibility, as indicated by the range of committees listed in the club yearbook for 1899-1900—Social Service, Philanthropy, Art, Literature, Current Topics, Hospitality, Educational, and Music.[244]

Jennie McLeod's adult life encompassed work, family and home, church, friendship, and community. It included a few personal indulgences, too, foremost among them the theater and travel. She stressed how important these were to her in writing for her twenty-fifth college reunion book, "As a recreation, the theater holds first place for me, with motoring a close second."[245]

Jennie had enjoyed a rich menu of possibilities to satisfy her taste for theater as a student in Northampton—so much so that during a lull in theater attendance in March 1914, she complained in her diary, "Haven't been to theatre in 2 wk."

She studied modern drama during her senior year at Smith, but her love of the theater went beyond the academic. With equanimity, she attended and applied her critical judgment to all types of college

---

242 Ibid., 6, 134, 182.
243 Anne Firor Scott, *Natural Allies: Women's Associations in American History* (Urbana and Chicago: University of Illinois Press, 1991), 111-74.
244 Clinton Women's Club, *Yearbook of the Clinton Women's Club, Clinton, Massachusetts, 1899-1900* ... (Clinton: W.J. Coulter for The Club, 1900), 7-8, "Social Organizations" pamphlet and ephemera box, Clinton Historical Society.
245 *Smith College, Class of 1915: 25th Reunion Report*, 78.

productions. On June 11, 1914, she pronounced the senior class performance of *The Tempest* superior to the previous year's offering, and, on October 31 of the same year, deemed the Halloween vaudeville show given by Gillett sophomores "swell." She favored neither high nor popular culture exclusively.

With more than a passing interest in the theater, Jennie welcomed the easy access Smith provided to what journalist Warren Barton Blake described in 1914 as "America's Only Municipal Theatre."[246] Blake reported that Northampton had had a municipal theater from 1892 and its own company of players from 1912. By the time Jennie began to keep her diary, the Northampton Players were co-managed by Bertram Harrison and actress Jessie Bonstelle, who shaped a vigorous and profitable slate of productions. Smith College students comprised a significant component of the audience for this local asset.

In 1914, Jennie was a regular at Northampton Players performances—for example, *Peaceful Valley*, a play in three acts by Edward E. Kidder; *The Amazons*, a farcical romance by Edward Wing Pinero; *A Gentleman from Mississippi*, a comedy by Harrison Rhodes and Thomas A. Wise; *The Lion and the Mouse* (which she judged "Best yet"); *The Travelling Salesman*; *The Dawn of a To-morrow* (based on a novel by Frances Hodgson Burnett); and *The Girl with the Green Eyes* (which Jennie found "Awfully good"). Her companions on these outings varied, but her attraction to the art form was constant.

In May 1915, near the close of her senior year in college, Jennie McLeod reveled in one of the thrills in her life as a theater aficionado. The great English actor Johnston Forbes-Robertson—"considered the finest Hamlet of the Victorian era and one of the finest actors of his time"—

---

246 Warren Barton Blake, "America's Only Municipal Theatre," *The Theatre Magazine*, Vol. 20, No. 164 (October 1914), 166-70, 188.

stopped in Northampton as part of his first farewell tour of the United States.[247] Jennie wrote on May 20, "Stood in line for tickets for Forbes Robertson in Hamlet—#486—excellent seats." On May 24, she enthused, "An eventful day in my life. Saw Forbes Robertson in 'Passing of 3rd Floor Back' in P.M. and in 'Hamlet' in the evening. His last appearance in Hamlet. Never have seen such acting & interpretation." The following day, Forbes-Robertson spoke in chapel "about his art and made a plea for attention to spoken Eng." Jennie must have cherished the memory of this rare access to thespian eminence.

Live theatricals also formed a regular part of life in Clinton. Before the rise of the countless distractions that now bombard us, people eager for entertainment turned out in force for amateur plays, musicals, tableaux, and pageants within walking distance of home. Like town celebrations, concerts, and lectures, such events boosted local spirit and cohesion. Entries throughout Jennie McLeod's diary show her enjoying all kinds of theatrical amusements through Clinton's schools, churches, Chautauqua, and organizations. In this regard, Clinton resembled countless American towns at the time.

Jennie noted attending a Unity Dramatic Club production with her father on March 27, 1914. Ellen Stevens wrote about this club for Clinton's centennial history: "The Franklin Unity, named for Franklin Forbes [agent of the Lancaster Mills, local benefactor, and active member of the Unitarian church], later becoming the Unity Dramatic Club, has brought together young people of Unitarian and other denominations in the interest of clean amusement."[248]

Community taste in theater was wide-ranging, embracing low culture as well as a higher aesthetic. Those who valued Shakespeare did

---

247 "Johnston Forbes-Robertson," *Wikipedia*, https://en.wikipedia.org/wiki/Johnston_Forbes-Robertson (accessed December 30, 2019).
248 Quotation: Stevens, 8; supplied information regarding Forbes: Ford, 306-22.

not turn up their noses at humbler forms of stagecraft. Jennie and her father took in a "Somerset minstrel show"—a then-acceptable and popular genre—on Thanksgiving (November 26) in 1914.[249] With seeming enthusiasm, she declared it the "[c]oursest ever!!"

But in the early twentieth century, live performance in Clinton was surpassed as a crowd-puller by the cinema, references to which fill Jennie's diary. From the 1890s, silent film made theatrical entertainment available to anyone who could pay the entrance fee. It created a shared popular culture and reinforced common tastes and values across the country. Jennie's love affair with the movies (silent through the late 1920s, talkies after that) was satisfied by the offerings of two local theaters in the center of Clinton, the Globe at 111 High Street and the Star at 136 High Street.[250] She attended movies whenever she had the chance, with family members and friends. She also went to the movies in Northampton and while she was away from home on summer vacations.

Jennie's diary opens a window on some of the movies she saw and sometimes what she thought of them: *Lucille Love, Girl of Mystery* (a serial action film directed by Francis Ford, starring Grace Cunard and Francis Ford; not favored—"Lucille Love bores me to death and distraction"); *Your Girl and Mine* (which Jennie characterized as "'Suffragette' movy");[251] D.W. Griffith's controversial blockbuster *Birth of a Nation* (viewed while on vacation; pronounced a "Marvellous picture"); *A Girl of Yesterday* (a comedy starring Mary Pickford, viewed with a party of Clin-

---

249 A printed program for a November 27, 1919 minstrel show by the Somerset Club survives in the "Clinton Drama Shows" box, Clinton Historical Society.
250 "Silent film," *Wikipedia,* https://en.wikipedia.org/wiki/Silent_film (accessed December 20, 2019); "Sound film," *Wikipedia,* https://en.wikipedia.org/wiki/Sound_film (accessed December 20, 2019); *Clinton and Lancaster Directory 1915,* 217.
251 *Your Girl and Mine* is described in a Globe Theater advertisement in the *Clinton Daily Item* for April 6, 1915 (the day Jennie saw it) as "a dramatic photoplay in 7 acts, produced under the auspices of the National Women's Suffrage Association."

ton friends); *Under Cover;* and *Salvation Joan* (which she found "Very good").

Jennie's experience as a theater-goer constitutes a significant theme of her diary. She also wrote throughout the little volume about getting out and about in the world around her, within Clinton and beyond, revealing the great and enduring pleasure that travel in its various forms provided.

She made frequent outings on foot in and around Clinton. She walked up Water Street to Harris Hill; to the Wachusett Dam; to Sterling to attend the Cattle Show there; to an observation tower on the Felton property in Bolton with Miss Nellie Kent (a teacher at Clinton High School);[252] and back home from the Unitarian church in Lancaster.

Jennie also took full advantage of the street railway and train systems that connected Clinton to the world outside town bounds. She wrote in her diary of excursions to Worcester—a city then accessible from Clinton by street railway and train as well as automobile—to shop and sometimes to have lunch.[253] (Twice she mentioned having lunch at the Esca, a cafeteria restaurant on Main Street in Worcester. [254]) She often traveled by train within Massachusetts. Near the end of her junior year at Smith, she took the train to Springfield for lunch at the Worthy

---

252 Documenting Nellie Kent as a Clinton High School teacher: *Sixty-seventh Annual Report of the School Department, Clinton, Mass., for the Year Ending December 31, 1916* (Clinton: W.J. Coulter Press for The Town, 1917), 70.
253 "Boston and Worcester Street Railway," *Wikipedia,* https://en.wikipedia.org/wiki/Boston_and_Worcester_Street_Railway (accessed December 16, 2019); "Fitchburg and Worcester Railroad," *Wikipedia,* https://en.wikipedia.org/wiki/Fitchburg_and_Worcester_Railroad (accessed December 16, 2019).
254 *The Worcester House Directory and Family Address Book* ... (Worcester: Drew Allis Company, 1916), 582.

Hotel, shopping, a baseball game, and an overnight stay.[255] She routinely journeyed back and forth between Clinton and Northampton by railroad. Back home the autumn after graduating from Smith, she met Christine Beck at the Clinton train station for a visit to Wellesley College, afterward continuing by train to South Station in Boston. Mass transportation made it possible for Jennie to enlarge her experience of the world before she had a vehicle of her own.

The automobile was fast becoming a means of transportation for the average American during Jennie McLeod's young womanhood. Henry Ford's Model T opened up new horizons for many, the McLeod family included. Jennie embraced the sense of freedom that joyriding afforded. Her delight in Ford's invention and her affinity for popular culture were simultaneously reflected in her diary entry for June 20, 1915, in which she alluded to the song "And the Little Ford Rambled Right Along," recorded in 1915 by singer Billy Murray.[256]

Jennie's diary shows that her father had a car by the summer of 1915. The McLeods' "fliver" provided opportunity for family time. On June 9 of that year, Jennie wrote that she had gone "to Sterling with Dad in the machine." She noted an automobile trip "with family to Hudson Bolton Lanc." on June 20 and a drive to Leominster on July 4. On July 11, the destination was historic Concord: "In the afternoon went autoing. Milkshakes at Italian store in Hudson. Went to Concord. Saw historic pts. Home via Littleton, Harvard & Lanc." On July 13, there was

---

255 Springfield had been accessible by rail from Northampton from the 1840s—"Union Station (Northampton, Massachusetts)," *Wikipedia*, https://en.wikipedia.org/wiki/Union_Station_(Northampton,_Massachusetts) (accessed December 17, 2019); "Worthy Hotel," *Wikipedia*, https://en.wikipedia.org/wiki/Worthy_Hotel (accessed December 17, 2019).

256 "Model T Music and Lyrics" (webpage), https://www.fordmodelt.net/music.htm#The_Little_Ford_Rambled_Right_Along (accessed December 17, 2019); "Billy Murray (singer)," *Wikipedia*, https://en.wikipedia.org/wiki/Billy_Murray_(singer) (accessed December 17, 2019).

a short auto trip "out Shirley Road" and on July 17 an outing to North Lancaster "to cool off." "Autoing" followed evening church services on Sunday, July 18.

George McLeod's car accident on August 28 did not deter him from replacing the broken windshield and getting behind the wheel again. A newspaper notice of the mishap two days after it happened concluded, "Mr. McLeod was driving the car today."[257] Later, on May 17, 1916, he attended a school event at Marlborough High School, where Jennie was then substituting, and the two returned home in the car at midnight. And on June 26, 1916, he drove with Jennie to Worcester.

Other people in Jennie's life also had cars. In Clinton on April 5, 1914, she went "automobiling" with her friend Mildred Hamilton. (It snowed, but "we took our chances"). At college a month later, she rode "to Easthampton with Anna & Lois" and on May 15 took a drive "to Amherst with Mrs Carpenter Lois and Cath." On July 15, 1914, during summer break from college, she wrote, "Cath Carp Mrs C and 2 friends came in new machine." On September 13, Mildred drove her to Concord.

During the summers of 1914 and 1915, Jennie wrote in her diary of vacationing away from Clinton, with friends. These junkets—which involved train, street railway, and automobile—took her to some well-known Massachusetts sites and attractions: Pepperell Springs; Paragon Park at Nantasket Beach; Franklin Park in Boston; Revere Beach; the town of Salem, which had been devastated by fire on June 25, 1914; the Shawmut Theatre on Blue Hill Avenue in Roxbury; Chinatown in Boston (for supper); and the Dudley Street Baptist Church in Roxbury "to hear Dr. Rees, the Evangelist." She was moved to observe a personal

---

257 "Auto Goes Into Brook. George McLeod Cuts His Hand in Accident at West Berlin Saturday," *Clinton Daily Item*, August 30, 1915, 1.

milestone on August 15, 1914, "Crowd went to Manchester, N.H[.] in the machine. First time I was ever out of the state."

Such travels were not especially long-distance, but they reinforced Jennie's growing sense of independence. Her own ability to drive eventually became a means of exercising personal freedom while remaining firmly bound to Clinton by family, work, and community involvements. By the time she submitted notes for her twenty-fifth college reunion book, "motoring" was a part of who she was and how she reconciled her desire for self-determination with the boundaries of her life.

On September 11, 1915, less than three months after graduating from Smith, Jennie penned a diary entry, the beginning of which was nothing if not a study in contrasts: "Darned stockings & smocked all day. Hutch sailed for Spain on Cetric." Agreeable though Jennie was to doing her share of "woman's work," her college friend's adventure abroad must have given her pause for thought. In fact, once Jennie was well-established on a career path, she looked to faraway places to satisfy her wanderlust.

In 1924, at the age of thirty-one, Jennie traveled to Bermuda. She returned to the United States on the ocean liner S.S. *Orduña* via the Port of New York, docking on April 21.[258] The records of the December 2, 1924 meeting of the Girls' Friendly Society reflect the local celebrity that this trip conferred on her: "Miss Jennie McLeod gave a very interesting talk on her trip to Bermuda."[259] As her diary reveals, Jennie was a shutterbug. Her talk was probably complemented by some of her own photographs.

Jennie is remembered by a nephew as a "world traveler" for a trip she made at the age of thirty-six with her father in 1929—on the brink

---

258 "Jennie McLeod," *Massachusetts Passenger and Crew Lists, 1820-1963*.
259 Church of the Good Shepherd, Girls' Friendly Society, Secretary's Book, 1919-1931, 61.

of the stock market crash at the outset of the Great Depression.[260] George McLeod chose his oldest daughter from among the members of his family to accompany him on this major expedition, which took them to Britain—in particular, to Scotland, his native country—and to the Continent, as well. His doing so reflected the sympathetic connection the two shared. They traveled with Andrew McCance, a friend of McLeod's and a seller of secondhand and rare books who had a store on Ashburton Place in Boston, and McCance's daughter Catherine, who appears in Jennie's diary as a visitor to Smith in February 1914.[261] The four made the return trip from Boulogne-sur-Mer in France, arriving in Boston on August 18, 1929. This expedition conferred upon Jennie a then-uncommon exposure to the world.

Jennie engaged in more domestic recreations, as well. She wrote in her diary of learning to tat late in 1915. She reported for her twenty-fifth college reunion book, "Knitting bedspreads and spiral socks is my hobby. It has long been my ambition to own a small loom and to do hand weaving."[262] Poker, pool, and bowling show up in her diary as occasional pastimes. And she enjoyed the company of friends.

After the death of George McLeod in 1936, the McLeod women carried on with Jennie at their head. For years, they occupied the apartment on the upper two floors of 244 Water Street and rented the smaller first-floor apartment to tenants.[263] Jennie had the best bedroom

---

260 McLeod interview; "George McLeod" and "Jennie McLeod," *Massachusetts Passenger and Crew Lists, 1820-1963*.
261 "Andrew McCance" and "Catherine McCance," *Massachusetts Passenger and Crew Lists, 1820-1963*; "McCance, Andrew," Donald C. Dickinson, *Dictionary of American Antiquarian Bookdealers* (Westport, Connecticut: Greenwood Press, 1998), 139.
262 *Smith College, Class of 1915: 25th Reunion Report*, 78.
263 McLeod interview. Robert McLeod remembers a family by the name of Morton, in particular. Clinton directories for the early 1940s show that insurance solicitor Hawley E. Morton and his wife Iris then lived in the downstairs apartment—*Clinton Lancaster Directory 1941* ... (New Haven: Price & Lee Co., copyright 1941), 178; *Clinton Lancaster Directory 1943* ... (New Haven: Price & Lee Co., copyright 1943), 173.

in the house—the large third-floor room facing Water Street. Following her death in July 1968, her sisters Helen and Maybelle preserved it untouched, just as Jennie had left it.[264] They ultimately moved into the downstairs apartment, which was easier for two aging, increasingly fragile women to navigate.[265]

When Jennie died, her passing was marked by an honor not accorded to many Clintonians. Although obituaries and death notices are traditionally published within the pages of the *Clinton Daily Item*, her combined burial announcement and obituary appeared on the front page of the July 29, 1968 issue.[266] Her father's obituary had also made the front page in 1936, but no other member of her immediate family received the same distinction.

Jennie McLeod was born in the Victorian Era and died while Americans were fighting and dying in Vietnam. She weathered the impact of two world wars, the trauma of the influenza pandemic of 1918, the privations of the Great Depression, the chill of the Cold War, and the upheaval of hard-won social change. Writing in 1940, Jennie's Smith classmate Esther Root Adams pinpointed the radical world transformation witnessed by those born in the 1890s and raised prior to World War I: "[W]e were sufficiently grown up before the World War to have accepted the world of peace and security as our world, and therefore old enough to appreciate, after the war, the contrast between the settled standards, which we had been led to expect and the turning kaleidoscope into which we were propelled."[267]

In some respects a nonconformist, Jennie nevertheless followed a mediate path between social and cultural norms and the challenges

---

264 McLeod interview.
265 Mahan interview.
266 "Private Services for Miss McLeod Are Held Today."
267 *Smith College, Class of 1915: 25th Reunion Report*, 164.

and opportunities created by the life that was hers to negotiate. It was not an extraordinary life by any definition, but she exercised the scope it allowed for the expression of her strength, intelligence, character, and adaptability. She remained true to herself while coming to terms with change, fulfilling her responsibilities, and commanding community respect.

A few Clinton people today remember Jennie. It surprises some to learn that the diary of a woman they recall might be considered historical. Jennie's little line-a-day volume is a reminder that history is in the making all the time, and that it enfolds us all.

# THE DIARY

"THIS IS THE LIFE"

## Note on Transcription and Annotation

TO PRESERVE THE SENSE AND FLOW OF JENNIE MCLEOD'S DIARY IN transcription, I have "undone" the five-year format (entries for a given day of the year over five years following one another on a single page) and have run entries day-by-day, in normal chronological order. The headers for each date are presented in bold, in a standardized format that does not always reflect Jennie's varying abbreviations for days of the week.

By and large, Jennie's spellings, misspellings, punctuation, and lack thereof are retained in the transcription, although errant or odd punctuation has occasionally been normalized or omitted. Sometimes a correct spelling or usage is supplied in square brackets following Jennie's idiosyncratic one.

With a few exceptions, an explanatory annotation for a person, place, event, or thing appears just once, in connection with its first appearance. This means that the reader who cares about the information in the notes will want to pay attention to them as they occur, through a close and consecutive reading.

Since many entries can be understood without knowing the details of people and events mentioned within, not every name or incident in the diary is represented in a note. In some cases, unexplained names and events show up only once or twice in the diary. Sometimes, the difficulty of tracking down information makes the pursuit a process of diminishing returns. Knowing the minutiae of every baseball game Jennie mentions would not, after all, significantly enhance the reader's appreciation of her life.

I have intentionally avoided re-explaining in the notes to the diary those topics presented in depth in the introduction. For example, the specifics of Jennie's coursework at Smith College are fully covered in "The Education of Jennie McLeod" and consequently not repeated in the diary annotations.

While the footnotes in the introduction to the diary cite relevant documentation systematically, the primary purpose of the notes to the transcription is to provide context for understanding Jennie's words. Consequently, I have not routinely included source information in the notes to the diary transcription (although I did make some effort to cite significant documentation not used in footnotes to the introduction—especially articles and notices found in the *Clinton Daily Item*).

Like any product of research, *"This Is the Life"* undoubtedly contains errors and omissions—all of them mine. I welcome any information that will set the record straight.

— L.P.W.

## — 1914 —

*January 1 1914 Th.* New Year's party at Mildred's Alpha Club and friends.[268] Delightful reunion. Dr Jordan called in the afternoon.[269] Hope to keep this 5 yr without fail.

*January 2 1914 Fri.* Sewed all morning. Down town in the afternoon. Waldo Davis here in the evening on Pickwick trial[270] Coasting with Eliz Hayter in evening[271]

---

268 Mildred R. Hamilton graduated from Clinton High School in 1911 (Jennie McLeod's class). Daughter of William and Rebecca Hamilton, Mildred lived on Forest Street. She took the commercial course at the high school and was described in town directories as a stenographer. The Alpha Club was a local girls' social club. A notice of the January 1 party Jennie mentions appeared in the *Clinton Daily Item* for January 3, 1914: "The Alpha cub [club] had a reunion at the home of Miss Mildred Hamilton on Forest street, on Thursday evening, most of the members and a few invited guests being present. The evening was pleasantly spent socially interspersed with music and games. The guests were Misses Frances Thissell, Carolyn Sprague, Esther B. Towne, Gladys M. Howe, Edith Strout, Merl Beaven, Jennie McLeod, Margaret McGinn, Catherine Gibbons, Margaret Shaw, Marion Whitham, Elizabeth Hayter, Myrtle Peters, Ruth, Dorothy, and Mildred Hamilton." This circle of young women included some of Jennie's close Clinton friends.
269 The Reverend Doctor William W. Jordan was pastor of the First Congregational Church in Clinton.
270 Lawyer Waldo T. Davis lived at 98 West Street. Jennie refers to the "Pickwick trial" in the following diary entry (January 3) as the "Brotherhood mock trial." Waldo Davis and George McLeod were both active members of the Congregational Brotherhood, a church organization. An announcement ("Church Meetings") in the September 20, 1915 issue of the *Clinton Daily Item* provided information about an upcoming Congregational Brotherhood meeting, concluding, "A lively time is expected, with Waldo T. Davis and George McLeod opening the discussion." George McLeod served as a president and director of the Brotherhood, his son Stanley as secretary ("Brotherhoods in Session," *Clinton Daily Item*, September 22, 1915). Mock trials—simulated trials—were popular as a form of entertainment. They also encouraged the development of effective public speaking skills, logic, and quick thinking.
271 Elizabeth M. Hayter—daughter of Elias and Lizzie Hayter—lived at 23 Henry Street, which parallels Pearl Street, where the McLeods lived in 1914. She was about Jennie's age.

*January 3 1914 Sat.* Spent whole day in Rd Comm Office typewriting for Brotherhood mock trial except trip to Belle Vue Mills with Merl.[272] Chafing dish supper at Esther Towne's[273] basket ball game in evening

*January 4 1914 Sun.* Visited Mrs Donald's Sunday school class with C. Bowers[274] Mother Marg and I at Anna's for afternoon and evening[275] Delightful time

*January 5 1914 Mon.* Sewed and shopped morning and afternoon. Powy's lecture on "Keats or the Cult of the Beautiful" with Dad at 8:00[276] Rare treat  Went to party at Caroline Bowers after lecture.

*January 6 1914 Tues.* Spent morning at store on account books[277] Keats lecture to Item from notes  Sewed in P.M.  Store and m p's in the evening.

---

272 Incorporated in 1902, the Belle Vue Mills (manufacturers of worsted goods) were located at 172 Sterling Street. Merl Beaven was one of the young women present at the Alpha Club reunion on January 1.
273 A daughter of William and Ellen Towne, Esther Towne was a member of Clinton High School Class of 1912. She lived at 74 Haskell Avenue. Her father had a meat market on Water Street.
274 Mrs. Donald: Elizabeth Donald (born in Scotland), widow of John; the Donald family lived at 42 Henry Street. Caroline Adams Bowers, a student at Wellesley College, lived at 287 Chestnut Street. Her mother was widow Caroline Bowers. Jennie sometimes refers to Caroline by her initials (C.A.B.).
275 Marg and Anna: Marguerite Frances Philbin and Anna Teresa Comaskey (last name spelled variously), who were not only Jennie's friends in Clinton but her housemates at Smith during the 1913-1914 academic year. Marguerite—like Jennie, a Smith junior—lived at 179 John Street in Clinton. Her parents (John and Margaret) both came from Ireland. Her father superintended Clinton's Water Department. Freshman Anna Teresa Comaskey was also a daughter of parents from Ireland, James and Bridget. She lived at 22 Burdett Street.
276 The lecture was held in the Town Hall. As the following two diary entries show, Jennie wrote it up for the *Clinton Daily Item* and was paid $1.00 for the effort.
277 The plumbing store of Jennie McLeod's father George McLeod, on Church Street.

*January 7 1914 Wed.* Rec'd $1.00 from Item for report on Keats Back to Hamp on the 6:45[278] In on time. Euph and Minnie met us.[279] All back before ten. In bed by 11:00 Saw 1st pre-payment electric in Hamp.[280]

*January 8 1914 Th.* Registered in S.10 Down town with Cath in a.m.[281] Afternoon in Chem Lab. Loafed around all the evening. Pres Burton spoke after chapel[282] 40¢ of every American dollar wasted on ac of lack of efficiency—Exams—

*January 9 1914 Fri.* Cut chapel and slept until 11:00 Then unpacked and settled. Spoiled experiment in Lab and burned my thumb most off. No Chem 4a Lect.

---

278  Hamp: short for Northampton.
279  "Euph": senior Euphemia Lofton, a black student from Washington, D.C.—one of Jennie's housemates. "Minnie": Minnie is identifiable through Jennie's multiple diary mentions of her. The entries for August 12 and 13, 1914 refer to a visit by Minnie (no last name given) to Anna (Comaskey). The Minnie in these entries is identified as Minnie Long of Brattleboro, Vermont in a notice in the "Local Affairs" section of the *Clinton Daily Item* for August 13, 1914. However, it is evident from what Jennie writes in diary entries for 1914 and 1915 that Minnie lived in Northampton. Northampton directories for 1915 and 1916 do, in fact, list Minnie Long's residence as 35 Graves Avenue and describe her as a telephone operator at Smith College. The 1917 Northampton directory indicates that she had removed to Brattleboro. In the 1910 federal census, the Long household on Hudson Street in Brattleboro included father Thomas, mother Katherine C., and daughters Minnie A. (then 18), Ellen I. (17), Kathleen (12), and Alice S. (11). Jennie's diary entry for May 20, 1914 notes a visit to Smith by three of Minnie's sisters (no names given). The *Brattleboro Vermont Directory 1917* (Greenfield, Massachusetts: H.A. Manning Company, copyright 1917) gives Minnie's next oldest sister's name as Irene E. rather than Ellen I. Long, supporting the possibility that she was the Irene Long mentioned in Jennie's diary entries for March 25 and November 8, 1914.
280  Pre-payment electric: an electric streetcar for which the fare was paid in advance.
281  Junior Catherine May Carpenter, who lived at 13 Belmont.
282  Marion LeRoy Burton (1874-1925) was Smith's second president, serving in that capacity from 1910 to 1917. He was subsequently president of the University of Minnesota and the University of Michigan.

*January 10 1914 Sat.* Woke up by fire bell at Dippy Hill[283] Barn on fire. Went with Lou and Anna  Downtown with Lois in P.M.[284] Bought Keats poems. Read O'Henry with Lo. & Euph all eve. "Feed."

*January 11 1914 Sun.* Got up for breakfast  Read Keats all morning. Studied Logic in the afternoon. Vespers with Lolo and Cath  Booker T. Washington.[285] J.M. Greene over crowded[286]

*January 12 1914 Mon.* Attended all regular classes  Got course cards for 2nd semester and went down on Paradise to look at the ice.[287] C. Sprague called in the evening[288]

*January 13 1914 Tues.* Chapel with C.W.S. Got back Logic written. Last hope shattered  Studied all afternoon and most of the evening.

---

283  Dippy Hill: a hill next to the Smith campus, on which was located the Massachusetts Asylum for the Insane. Also known as Hospital Hill.
284  Lois Brantly (Lolo): another of Jennie's housemates during her junior year.
285  Born a slave, Booker T. Washington (1856-1915)—black educator, author, reformer, and orator—was the first president of the Tuskegee Normal and Industrial Institute in Alabama.
286  Smith opened John M. Greene Hall—an auditorium building—in 1910.
287  Paradise Pond on the Smith campus, originally created by damming the Mill River.
288  Like Jennie McLeod, Smith student Carolyn Woodruff Sprague, daughter of David and Anna Sprague, graduated with the Class of 1911 at Clinton High School. Her family lived at 353 Church Street. Her father was rector at Clinton's Episcopal Church of the Good Shepherd. Jennie sometimes referred to Carolyn (occasionally spelled Caroline) by her initials, C.W.S.

*January 14 1914 **Wed.*** Northampton players—matinee Peaceful Valley—Lois and M. Deware[289] "We" liked it. Others!! Fritz Kreisler violinist.[290] S.C. [Smith College] concert course in evening

*January 15 1914 **Th.*** Slept late and finally succeeded in "working" wt cc O for Chem 2[291] Lab and lecture in P.M. Lois, May and I decorated Euph's room while she was at meeting[292] H.P.

*January 16 1914 **Fri.*** Took myself by the hand and went to chapel with a girl C. Judd who missed her date[293] Wrote Chem 4 paper Domestic Water Handed course card in with note on ac of Chem 4a class at 5. Lecture on Culte de Jeanne d'Arc by André Bellessort[294]

*January 17 1914 **Sat.*** Euph and Anna visit Rahar's Inn!!![295] Spent 2 hr. extra in Lab. And then apparatus broke. Errands before lunch Downtown with Lolo and Catherine. Wrote letters and cards rest of afternoon and all evening

---

289 The Northampton Players were a local theatrical company formed in 1912. *Peaceful Valley* was a play by Edward E. Kidder. M. Deware: freshman Marguerite Deware, sister of sophomore Arlene Theresa Deware; both lived at 6 Bedford Terrace in 1913-1914. Jennie used the nickname "Mugger" for one of the Dewares, most likely Marguerite.
290 Friedrich Kreisler (1875-1962) was a virtuoso violinist.
291 The abbreviation "wt cc O": weight of a cubic centimeter of oxygen.
292 "May": possibly May Heines, who appears in Jennie's diary entries for June 12, 1914 and September 30, 1914.
293 Senior Clarise Sophia Judd.
294 André Bellesort (1866-1942): a French poet and essayist.
295 Rahar's Inn: a hotel and restaurant at 7 South Street in Northampton.

*January 18 1914 Sun.* "Go to church" Sun. in Hamp. Went to Edwards with Lois.[296] Prof Pierce and Prof Gardner at "17" to dinner.[297] Pleasant time. Vespers with Cath & Lolo. Studied all evening Rev. Maner of N.H. vespers

*January 19 1914 Mon.* Mid-years "start" Chapel with Anna & Lois. Studied Logic all day long. Company to dinner. Took 10-25¢ pledge to N. Players. "The Amazons"[298] Lolo Anna & Minnie

*January 20 1914 Tues.* Studied Logic all morning and greater part of afternoon. Budged pungs with Lolo Anna and Cath.[299] Studied Logic all evening. Bed 10 P.M. sharp[300]

*January 21 1914 Wed.* Logic exam. G.H. 9-11[301] Never did so miserably in anything. Thoroughly disgusted with myself. Punged with Lolo and Cath. Dippy to Dickinson Hospital[302]

*January 22 1914 Th.* Studied French all A.M. Studied English at Libe all evening "Surprise" party in Euph's room, i.e. surprise to her

---

296 Edwards Church of Northampton (established in 1833 by members of the First Church) was located at the corner of State and Main Streets.
297 Arthur Henry Pierce was Professor of Psychology. "Prof Gardner" was Harry Norman Gardiner, Professor of Philosophy. "17" was short for 17 Belmont Avenue (Jennie's residence in 1913-1914).
298 The play *The Amazons: A Farcical Romance* was written by Arthur Wing Pinero.
299 Pung: a type of horse-drawn sleigh.
300 Smith maintained a policy of lights-out at 10:00 p.m.
301 G.H.: (John. M.) Greene Hall.
302 Dippy: the Class of 1915 twenty-fifth reunion book (1940) identifies "Dippy" as the nickname of Dorothea T. Allen, who was a senior in 1914-1915. Northampton's Cooley Dickinson Hospital was founded in 1885 through the bequest of Caleb Cooley Dickinson.

*January 23 1914 Fri.* Studied French from 9 A.M. till 12 P.M. Light cut shared by house and noise put an end to the gaiety.[303] Mrs. H in "delightful" humour [304]

*January 24 1914 Sat.* French 9 exam 9-11 "It micht be unwise."[305] Studied Eng 11-1. Libe at 2. Stood it until 3. Slept rest of P.M. Libe 7-9:45 Eng 4:2

*January 25 1914 Sun.* Spent the best part of the day cramming Eng 4:2. Stayed in all day. Light cutted with Euphy and light lunched at 11:30

*January 26 1914 Mon.* Spent morning at Libe on Eng 4:2. Spent afternoon and evening studying for Chem 2. Took a light cut. Euph and Florence rel. [religion] discussion[306]

*January 27 1914 Tues.* Chem 2 exam 9-11 Perfectly fiendish. Eng 4:2 exam 11-1 Good exam. No surprises. Shopped with Lolo Read for pure pleasure with Lolo all evening

---

[303] "Light cut": an approved release from Smith's strict policy of lights out at 10:00. This policy caused much student grumbling and interfered with attendance by college girls at off-campus evening events like Northampton Players productions.
[304] Mrs. H. was widow Helen Hoagland, who ran 17 Belmont Avenue.
[305] Micht: Scots for might.
[306] "Florence": likely Florence Lillian Hanford (Class of 1915), who lived at 29 Belmont in 1913-1914 and at 41 Elm Street in 1914-1915, and who shows up elsewhere in Jennie's diary (see, for example, the entry for January 16, 1915).

*January 28 1914 Wed.* Holiday between semesters  Ideal weather. "The Little Minister" matinee at Academy with Lolo and Anna.[307]  Borrowed Mrs Parker to chaperone at Plaza at night.[308]  Cath and Lolo

*January 29 1914 Th.* Wrote Chem 4a paper on "Solutions" and handed it in. Did exp on analysis of air by Fe for 5th time and apparatus collapsed  Miss Mason then worked it for me with mg.[309]  Chem 10b at 5. Cut dinner  was desperately homesick all evening

*January 30 1914 Fri.* No Chem 10b lecture  My twenty-first birthday and without question the unhappiest day of my life. Letter from home after 19 days. Little spread cheered a trifle

*January 31 1914 Sat.* Trip to C.H. to put in exercise cards at 7:00[310]  Alas Too Late  Rained all day. $H_2O$ 8" deep on walks. Lolo and I ploughed through to the station and back. Soaked to the skin. Forgot to hand in exercise card. Lolo and I made comballs that didn't ball[311]

---

307  *The Little Minister* was a production based on a book by J.M. Barrie. It was made into a silent film in 1921. Opened in 1891, the Academy of Music Theatre at 274 Main Street in Northampton was deeded to the City of Northampton in 1892, making it the first municipally owned theater in the United States.
308  Mrs. Parker: Clara M.W. Parker, Head of House at Hatfield House. The Plaza Theater at 79 Pleasant Street in Northampton opened as a movie house in 1912.
309  Fe: in chemistry, the symbol for iron. Mg: magnesium.
310  C.H.: College Hall. Smith juniors and seniors maintained and passed in exercise cards to document their physical activities.
311  Comball: a Scots verb (meaning to meet together for amusement, or to plot) and related noun (a company of plotters or cabal). Jennie is engaged in some wordplay here.

*February 1 1914 Sun.* Beautiful day. Walked with Cath in the A.M. Wrote letters and read all P.M. Arlene, Helen, Marg. & Sally Dow to tea[312] Music all evening. Lolo left for Yale Prom.

*February 2 1914 Mon.* Handed in exercise card at 9:00 at gym office Got Logic exams back. The inevitable confirmed! Alas!! E [the "E" in a box] Grade in exam 58% Juniors invited to observatory to see moon. Went.

*February 3 1914 Tues.* Attended all classes. Flunked in first Psych recitation. Studied all P.M. and evening except 2 short rehearsals for Frolic.[313] My part: Sandwich boy in station

*February 4 1914 Wed.* Classes as usual. Prepared but didn't have to recite. Studied in Psych Lab all P.M. while Euph experimented. Lolo got back Studied and read all evening. Last bell rang 9:49

*February 5 1914 Th.* Studied all morning. Prof Stoddard cut Chem 2 Lect.[314] Classes adjourned at 12:30 Lab 2-5 10b Lect at 5 on Manufacture of Paper Jr. Frolic rehearsal in Wallace cellar.[315] Before committee at 8:50[316]

---

312  Arlene Deware, Helen Irving, Marguerite Philbin, and Sally Eaton Dow. (Sally lived in Albright House and was a year behind Jennie at Smith.)
313  Frolic—a Smith ritual—was a dance with entertainment. Older students invited and escorted freshmen to the event.
314  John Tappan Stoddard was Professor of Chemistry.
315  Wallace House: a Smith residence.
316  "Before committee": there is not enough context here to know what Jennie means. The committee may have been related to the academic condition for English B that she satisfied by writing a paper during the summer of 1914, between her junior and senior years.

*February 6 1914 Fri.* Studied all A.M. Down town 12-1 with Lolo. Frolic rehearsal after lunch. Then Lab 2-5 & lecture 5-6. Got formula for ink Feed in Anna's room. Anna's treat 1917 Sing at 7:00 House meeting 7:15. Euph mad!!! Florence and Mrs H present

*February 7 1914 Sat.* Lab 9-10:30 Downtown with Cath to get clothes for Frolic. Downtown in P.M. Matinee "The Gentleman from Mississippi" with Lolo and Anna.[317] Great. Lolo and I sent Euph violets as peace offering Her majesty placated. Dinner and dress rehearsal at Wallace. Frolic in Gym. Best time ever. Trip to Niagara— Pass word Sllaf Aragain.[318] Bully time

*February 8 1914 Sun.* Whole whole [sic] went to Catholic Church at 10:30 to hear Euph sing Ave Maria. Miss Hunt here to dinner.[319] Cath and I took 12 Frolic snapshots. "Silence reigned supreme" at tea. Studied all eve

*February 9 1914 Mon.* Classes as usual. Downtown with Cath after lunch to return articles rented for Frolic. Studied rest of P.M. "John" is born 1915 class meeting and sing at 7:00. Libe after.

---

317   The popular 1908 play *The Gentleman from Mississippi* was written by Harrison Rhodes and Thomas A. Wise.
318   References to the Junior Frolic production, titled "A Trip to Niagara Falls, " and to the password which admitted juniors into the gym for the event. The password "Sllaf Aragain" was "Niagara Falls" spelled backwards.
319   Agnes Hunt was Associate Professor of History.

Main Street, Northampton, ca. 1905-1910

*February 10 1914 Tues.* Up at 6 A.M. to study  Classes all morning  Miss Jordan incensed over S.C.A.C.W. invitations to Congregationalists.[320]  Studied first of afternoon—then downtown with house.  Met Mrs McSherry.[321]  Studied all evening.

*February 11 1914 Wed.* Chapel with Mrs Elms and Lolo  Classes all morning.  Recited in Psych!!  Yea vraiment![322]  Lyric with Cath and Lolo  Wrote letters all evening

---

320  Mary Augusta Jordan, who was displeased with the Smith College Association for Christian Work, was Professor of English Language and Literature.
321  Clinton High School Principal Francis McSherry resigned from his position in 1912 to become Superintendent of Schools in Holyoke, which is a little more than eleven miles from Northampton. His wife was Alice A. McSherry.
322  Vraiment: truly (French).

*February 12 1914 Th.* No Chem 2 Lecture temp 7.2° C Mrs Philbin came at 12:00.[323] Lab. all P.M. Euph sang "Marguerite" to Jim at his request before the whole house.[324] "Nuff said" Euph heartbroken over letter from home

*February 13 1914 Fri.* Mrs Philbin spent the morning in my room with me. I sewed and studied  Lab. 3-5. Lecture 5-6. Went to theatre in evening with Lolo and Anna. "The Lion and the Mouse"[325] Best yet

*February 14 1914 Sat.* Blizzard. 18" snow. Drifts 4-6 ft. Lab. 9-11. Studied rest of P.M. Downtown ploughing thru' drifts with Lois on errands. Lab. 3:20-4:40 Studied all evening on Chem problem in Euph's room

*February 15 1914 Sun.* Lolo and I up for breakfast. Mirabile dictu!![326] Mrs. Philbin left for home at 9:15  No guests for dinner or tea. Mugger Deware and Helen Irving give vaudeville stunt as robber and chorus girl[327]

*February 16 1914 Mon.* Cold and more snow. Psych written sprung. Also French—the most unkindest cut of all. Studied all afternoon  N.Y. Philharmonic Soc. Concert Course J.M. Greene Hall

---

323  Margaret Philbin of Clinton, mother of Jennie's classmate Marguerite Philbin.
324  "Marguerite": song by C.A. White. Jim: Jim Martin (Jennie refers to Jim's father as "Mr. Martin" in her diary entry for February 20).
325  The play *The Lion and the Mouse* was written by Charles Klein. It was made into a silent film released in January 1914.
326  *Mirabile dictu*: Latin, meaning amazing (or strange) to say.
327  Helen Anna Irving of Framingham, Massachusetts, Class of 1915.

*February 17 1914 Tues.* Classes in the morning. Miss Cutler lectured in Psych.[328] Prof Pierce ill. Maddening trip downtown for paper clips, ruler, etcetera for Psych. Performed inane cutaneous sensation exp. all evening

*February 18 1914 Wed.* Classes unusually dull and interminable. Miss Clark lectured on eye in Psych.[329] Fooled around and experimented some in P.M. Euph tired out  Jim's father died. Lolo and I changed napkin rings at the table  Response "All eight out without my permission!!"

*February 19 1914 Th.* Straightened up my room and got laundry ready to send. First Chem 2 Lect in 5 weeks. Lab and lecture from 2-6  Studied all evening. Girl tooks [Girls took] Euph to the wake

*February 20 1914 Fri.* Mr Martin's funeral. Euphemia sang "Face to Face."[330] Catherine McCance came 5:25[331]  1915 Sing and watched Jr. gym. Beckmann's[332]  Death of Prof A.H. Pierce 6:55 P.M. of dble pneumonia

---

328  Anna Alice Cutler was Professor of Philosophy.
329  In 1914, there were two Miss Clarks on the Smith faculty—Laura Sophronia Clark (Instructor in Chemistry) and Ruth Swan Clark (Assistant in Philosophy). The Miss Clark in this entry was likely Ruth.
330  The Hymn "Face to Face with Christ, My Savior," by Carrie Ellis Breck.
331  About five years younger than Jennie, Catherine McCance was the daughter of Boston book dealer Andrew McCance and his wife Mary, who were both born in Ireland. Andrew McCance and George McLeod were friends, and their families visited one another.
332  Beckmann's: a confectionary and ice cream place at 249 Main Street in Northampton.

*February 21 1914 Sat.* Chapel—awfully sad. Pres. Burton spoke of Prof Pierce. Almost all classes dismissed. Special services at Plymouth Inn—Burial in Westboro Mass.[333] Mrs Stebbins and theatre party[334] "Anna" The Travelling Salesman[335] Lolo C.M.C. C.M.McC. F.L.H. HN[336]

*February 22 1914 Sun.* Bitter cold. Catherine McCance & Cath C went out sightseeing while I studied in A.M. Trip to Art Gallery Thrilled? Vespers—very few present Big crowd here to tea Bernice Blackmer here[337] High School destroyed by fire.[338] Leading lady here in the evening

*February 23 1914 Mon.* Florence birthday—Breakfast party Exercises in J.M. Greene. Pres Taft speaker[339] Faculty robed for first time. Rally given up by vote of students. Great game in P.M. Seniors beat Jrs 20-15 Went to Springfield with Cath McC. Studied until 11:45

---

333  The Plymouth Inn: a hotel and boarding house at 31 West Street. Professor Pierce had lived there. Westborough: a town in Worcester County.
334  Mary D. Stebbins, mother of Smith student Eunice Burr Stebbins (Class of 1916), lived at 267 Crescent Street.
335  *The Travelling Salesman*: a four-act play by James Forbes.
336  Catherine May Carpenter, Catherine McCance, Florence Hanford, and others.
337  Visitor Bernice Blackmer graduated from Worcester Classical High School in 1911.
338  Northampton High School was severely damaged by fire late in the afternoon on February 22, 1914.
339  Republican William Howard Taft (1857-1930), President of the United States from 1909 to 1913.

*February 24 1914 Tues.* Classes again. Bernice went to Eng 4:2 with me. Miss Cutler spoke to Psych class and Miss Clark went on with class. Spent afternoon on Psych experiments. Studied all evening with Millie. Cath went to Mary Angland.[340] Funny enough

*February 25 1914 Wed.* Classes in the morning. Recited in Psych and French. Did Psych experiments all afternoon and evening  Ash Wed and its consequences—as regards meals

*February 26 1914 Th.* Finished up Ch I of Psych exp. Chem classes 12-6. Nothing unusual. Went to house president's meeting for Catherine in the evening. Talked with Lois.

*February 27 1914 Fri.* Psych experiments and Eng 4:2 all morning. Lab all afternoon and absolutely nothing accomplished. Inspiration to blow up a safe. Went to bed at 7:30 and read  Got report card

*February 28 1914 Sat.* Chapel with Lolo. Lab 9-1. Got something done at last. Downtown after lunch  Went to bed and red [read]. Miss Welch called[341]  Theatre with Vina  The Dawn of a To-Morrow  Jessie Bonstelle[342]

---

340 "Mary Angland": clearly a performance or performer, although the reading of the title or name is uncertain. It is perhaps a variation on the title *Merrie England*, an English comic opera in two acts that opened in 1902 and subsequently became a popular production choice for amateur theatrical groups.

341 Miss Welch: possibly junior Mary Louise Welch from Holyoke, Massachusetts, a Wallace House resident in 1913-1914 (although Jennie does not usually use the term of respect "Miss" for other students).

342 Vina: Vina Mary Allan (Class of 1916). *The Dawn of a To-Morrow*: a play based on a novel by Frances Hodgson Burnett, performed by the Northampton Players. Jessie Bonstelle (1871-1932) was an actress, theater director, and a manager of the Northampton Players.

*March 1 1914 Sun.* Water inches deep on all walks  Dismal day. Studied and loafed all day. Went to vespers with Florence. Memorial service for Prof Pierce—Prof Gardiner of S.C.

*March 2 1914 Mon.* Dr Haines took charge of Psych class for rest of the year.[343] Got back Psych written. Haven't yet recovered from an A. "We are infinitely perfectible." Studied afternoon and evening. Dead tired

*March 3 1914 Tues.* Brisk letter from Stanley, with cash enclosed ($3.00) for fountain pen.[344] Studied for Psych written. Mr and Mrs Sherman of Amherst and Miss Forbes, Mt Holyoke to dinner

*March 4 1914 Wed.* Written in Psych. Called on in French. It's getting to be a Wed habit with "Port"[345] Freshman—Soph basketball game with Anna. Soph won 23-13. Ah what a fall was there my countrymen  Florence fell!!! S.C. Symphony Orchestra concert 8. Euph & Flor

*March 5 1914 Th.* Nothing terribly exciting or irregular. Called around with Chem Hall as usual from 12-6. Lois and I called on Cath. Hid in closet and scared her to pieces. Bed at 9.

*March 6 1914 Fri.* Chapel with Vina and Lolo. Studied and sewed in the morning. Lab all P.M. Theatre with M. Deware. Awfully good. "The Girl with the Green Eyes."[346]

---

343  "Dr Haines": Thomas Harvey Haines (1871-1951), who taught psychology at Ohio State University.
344  Stanley: Jennie's younger brother Stanley Mercer McLeod (born in 1895).
345  Port: nickname for Alice Portère-Baur, Instructor in French.
346  *The Girl with the Green Eyes*: a play in four acts by American dramatist Clyde Fitch (1865-1909).

*March 7 1914 Sat.* Lab all morning and from 2-3:30 Loafed rest of afternoon Lois friend, Helen Longmaid came. Spent the night with Helen and Arlene at 6 Bedford.

*March 8 1914 Sun.* Breakfast in Arlene's room. Home at 11. Studied until dinner. Music until 3. Studied. Vespers. Eight guests to tea. Much music. Studied and wrote letters latter part of evening

*March 9 1914 Mon.* Helen Longmaid went to Eng 4:2 with me. Classes as usual. Called on Mrs Sprague at "109" in the afternoon.[347] Properly squelched for sending Anna's napkin ring around table. Studied French with Mildred in evening[348]

*March 10 1914 Tues.* Regular classes. Spent afternoon and evening on Psych. Whole house excited over "What is it?"—Ugly face—landscape, baby—Dog curled up on a rug[349]

*March 11 1914 Wed.* Classes. Men much in evidence. Little reverie while counting the seconds rudely interrupted by Mme "Porte" Batted around the laundry with the kids.[350] Telegram excitement

---

347 Anna Sprague of Clinton was visiting her daughter Carolyn, who lived at 109 Elm.
348 Mildred Hutchinson, Class of 1915, lived at Wallace House. In 1914-1915, she and Jennie were both members of Colloquium, a departmental chemistry club. Jennie often referred to Mildred by the nickname "Hutch."
349 What is it?: a children's guessing game.
350 "Batted": Jennie uses "bat" in her diary both as a verb and a noun. The verb means to discuss informally (something along the lines of "chewing the fat"), the noun an (extended) informal discussion. As a verb, "to bat" can also mean to wander about. In some diary entries, Jennie seems to intend both meanings simultaneously.

*March 12 1914 Th.* Spent the best part of the day studying Chem of one variety or another. P.M.—Read 3 hr from S.C. Chem Lab. Helen Longmaid chaperoned Lolo Marg and me to Plaza at night

*March 13 1914 Fri.* Chapel with Minnie. Worked 2 hr at Libe on Eng. C. Chemistry all P.M. Psych experiments on attention worked with Florence all evening. Another Fri the 13th

*March 14 1914 Sat.* As usual. Spent the entire morning in the Chem. Lab. Also one hour in the P.M. Tired to death when I got back. House sent Mrs H violets for birthday

*March 15 1914 Sun.* Helped Mary make the salad for surprise birthday dinner for Mrs H and Minnie.[351] Most gorgeous spring day. About ten guests at our regular little fireside tea.

*March 16 1914 Mon.* Classes. Thoroughly peeved at Porte—she called on me and didn't give me a chance to recite. Spent the rest of the day studying Psych for the next week

*March 17 1914 Tues.* Classes—Strange isn't it? Got over my peeve with Porte. Wellesley Coll. Hall burned to ground so probably won't visit Christine on tue 26th[352] Wrote up Psych experiments. "Petite extension du jour."[353]

---

351   Mary: possibly Mary Rose, a domestic in Helen Hoagland's 17 Belmont Avenue boarding house.
352   From the opening of Wellesley College, the massive College Hall building encompassed under one roof all aspects of college life. It contained classrooms, offices, laboratories, library, and housing for the college community. It was destroyed by fire in just four hours. Jennie's good friend and Clinton High School classmate Christine Louise Beck was a Wellesley student at the time.
353   "Petite extension du jour": small one day's extension.

Christine L. Beck, from
1915 Wellesley College
*Legenda* (yearbook)

*March 18 1914 Wed.* All classes interesting. Drew #10 for campus assignment. M. Deware to dinner  Miss Ellis on Min's trail & Grace on Euph's[354]  Never told so many lies successfully in my life

*March 19 1914 Th.* Finished up Scottish Lyrics for 4:2  Haven't taken so much genuine pleasure in a subject for some time. Lab. all afternoon.  Libe in the evening to read for Wed's Psych written

*March 20 1914 Fri.* Went over to Lab and left things ok for vacation. Spent the day at the Libe on Psych and Eng. C. "Jim" sent us all chickens  Dedicated mine to Jim and "Wee-Jokey-birdie"[355]

---

354  Grace Hovey of Cambridge, Massachusetts (Class of 1916) was a resident of Gillett.
355  "Wee-Jokey-birdie": "Wee chookie birdie," a Scottish children's song.

*March 21 1914 Sat.* Chapel with the Jewish contingent  Phi Beta Kappa announcements. Stuck to resolution not to go near Lab. Libe all A.M. Not much in afternoon or evening but rest

*March 22 1914 Sun.* Decided to devote the day to Eng C. Didn't have any distraction but it seemed an interminable task. Mrs H grouchy. Miss Childs worse.[356] Haven't been to theatre in 2 wk

*March 23 1914 Mon.* Regular routine of classes. Recited in Psych. Downtown on short business trip. Studied Psych for to-morrow's written  Too dull and stupid for any exertion. Skunks

*March 24 1914 Tues.* Recited on Burns in Eng 4:2  Psych written. Miss Childs called but I didn't see her. Spent P.M. and eve on Eng C. Took bath at 11:00  Nobody heard me. Packed for home

*March 25 1914 Wed.* Finished Eng C at 11:30. Irene Long went to Eng 4:2.[357] Miss Jordan called roll!! Home on 12:30 Boston special. Hated to leave Lolo. Movies with mother. Dad in Boston

*March 26 1914 Th.* Didn't go to Wellesley to visit Christine on acct of College Hall fire  Slept late and loafed around all A.M. Called on Esther at store in P.M. Went down town with Elizabeth. Met Merl and walked to Harris Hill  Gorgeous bat together

---

356  Jennie L. Childs, a teacher, boarded at 17 Belmont at the time.
357  Irene Long: probably one of the younger sisters of Minnie Long (see Jennie's diary entry for January 7, 1914, and the accompanying note). There is another, contextually tenuous possibility in Irene Long, the sixteen-year-old daughter of laundryman John C. Long and his wife Minnie M. Long of Laurel Street in Clinton.

*March 27 1914 Fri.* Sewed for Maybelle.[358] Went to food sale in Baptist church—benefit district nurse. Gift of ten dollar bill—John "The Runaways." Unity Dram. Club.[359] Went with Dad

*March 28 1914 Sat.* Wet and muddy. Crossman's truck stuck on Pearl St and thereby hangs a tale.[360] Down to Mildred's to tea. Went to Globe with Mildred and Elizabeth.[361] Visited Burke's and Gordon's

*March 29 1914 Sun.* Slept late. Mildred came up and we went over to Carolyn's to tea. Nice time. Everybody home. Church in evening with Mildred and Elizabeth. 78 present

*March 30 1914 Mon.* Rained all day. Downtown in the morning. Store in the afternoon. Called on Louise Sprague and Mrs Shutts.[362] Wrote letters. Spread with Dad

---

[358] Maybelle: Jennie's youngest sister (born in 1902). Jennie sometimes refers to her as "Baby."
[359] *Teddy; or, The Runaways,* a comedy in three acts by Walter Ben Hare. The Unity Dramatic Club was a Clinton amateur theatrical organization.
[360] Located at 662 Main Street, G.F. Crossman was a Clinton moving company. Crossman's relied on horse and wagon to move pianos and furniture locally and for all kinds of jobbing. The company also advertised long distance moving by "auto truck." The McLeod family lived on Pearl Street when Jennie wrote this diary entry.
[361] The Globe at 111 High Street was one of Clinton's two movie theaters in 1914.
[362] Louise Kathrine Sprague of Worcester, daughter of Gorham and Almeda (Bell) Sprague. Louise was described in a notice in the *Clinton Daily Item* for June 23, 1914 as being "of Worcester, formerly of Clinton." Widow Nellie Shutts of 73 Prospect Street was the mother of Florence M. Shutts, Jennie's Clinton High School classmate, who attended the New England Conservatory of Music in Boston.

*March 31 1914 Tues.* Pleasant once more. Sewed most of day. Awful cold in my head so didn't go to Wellesley whist party. Store with Dad and then "movies." Ice-cream—Mrs Duncan's treat[363]

*April 1 1914 Wed.* Slept late. Sewed for mother Went down and did some office work in afternoon. Again in evening with Dad Merl down in P.M. Took Maybelle to dentist

*April 2 1914 Th.* Spent most of the day at the store. Marshmallows— oui, encore[364] Sprint says 5 & 10 are wise.[365] Vaudeville and pictures at Star.[366] Went with Dad. Fair.

*April 3 1914 Fri.* Went down to store for a while. Christine came in. We called on Miss Parsons.[367] Worcester. Lunched with Mildred. Got suit. Home with Mitchell's. Met Florence Smith's father.[368] Look her up

*April 4 1914 Sat.* Went to the dentist with Maybelle. Got hat. Mildred's to birthday dinner. Met Mr. Mill. Like him ever so much. He's a mason. Spent the night at Mildred's

---

363 Mrs. Duncan: there was more than one Mrs. Duncan in Clinton. One possibility was Jessie Duncan, wife of Clinton's Unitarian pastor James Duncan. The James Duncans (both born in Scotland) lived at 168 Walnut Street. Another was Marion Duncan, wife of lawyer William S. Duncan. Marion was born in Scotland, William in England of Scottish parents. They lived at 45 Boynton Street.
364 "[O]ui, encore": yes, again (French).
365 Sprint: nickname for George McLeod, Jr., the younger of Jennie's two brothers (born in 1897).
366 Star: Clinton theater at 136 High Street.
367 Miss Parsons: Clinton public school teacher May Parsons, who roomed at 203 High Street.
368 Likely Florence Smith from East Orange, New Jersey, a member of Jennie's class at Smith.

*April 5 1914 Sun.* Church in the morning with Dorothy Hamilton.[369] Stayed to Sunday School  Automobiling with Mildred. Blizzard but we took our chances. Called at Mildred's in evening

*April 6 1914 Mon.* Went down to store. McKnight in hospital—appendicitis.[370] Nearly went crazy trying to work problems. Cut out dress for Helen.[371] Too tired to go to bed.

*April 7 1914 Tues.* Stayed home all day  Snow. Sewed most of the day. Made candy and read in the evening.

*April 8 1914 Wed.* Telephoned, sewed, ironed, shopped and everything else as usual before going back with the whole crowd on the 6:45. Terrible rain when we landed 9:40

*April 9 1914 Th.* Chapel with Anna. Pres Burton lead [led] but did not give his usual talk after  Worked Chem problems until 12. Lectures & Lab (2-5)  Unpacked and studied for Sat exam

*April 10 1914 Fri.* Studied Logic all the live long day. French lecture on L'explication française by Prof Morize of John [Johns] Hopkins[372]  Studied Logic all evening

---

369  Dorothy Hamilton was a younger sister of Jennie's friend Mildred Hamilton.
370  George McKnight (age twenty-three in 1914) was a Clinton plumber whose parents had emigrated from Scotland.
371  Helen: Helen W. McLeod (born in 1900), one of Jennie's two younger sisters.
372  André Morize (1883-1957): Associate Professor of French Literature at Johns Hopkins from 1913 to 1914, later Professor of French Literature and Culture at Harvard.

*April 11 1914 Sat.* Anna and I both got up at 5:30. Studied Logic all morning. Exam at 2 in C.8 About 20 took it. Went walking with Florence after exam. Wrote letters all eve

*April 12 1914 Easter Sun.* Lolo Cath and I went to Edward's church. Dr Keeler back for the day[373] Pres Seelye assisted.[374] Style of 5th Ave! Hugh Black at vespers: "The open door"[375] Girls here to tea. Went to call on A. Hill with Arlene[376]

*April 13 1914 Mon.* Classes. Recited in French. Beware of Mondays hereafter. Studied in every room of the house in turn. Told Florence I wasn't a Jew. Lolo engaged to "Ted." Euph got back.

*April 14 1914 Tues.* Cut Eng 4:2 on account of cold and sore throat. Other classes O.K. Anna and I both passed our Sat makeups. Paid bills down town. Bought & played with comeback balls[377]

*April 15 1914 Wed.* Classes. Recited in Psych and flunked in French. Penalty: write résumé of story for next Mon. Chem. Lib. all P.M. Studied and read in the evening

---

373   The Reverend W.P. Keeler was pastor of the First Church in Northampton.
374   Laurenus Clark Seelye (1837-1924): Smith's first president (in office from 1875 to 1910).
375   Hugh Black (1868-1953) was a Scottish-American theologian and author. He was Professor of Practical Theology at the Union Theological Seminary in New York. His book *The Open Door* was published in 1914.
376   A. Hill: Ada Hill, a member of Smith's Class of 1915.
377   Comeback ball: a recreational and exercise ball secured to an elastic string and wrist fastener.

*April 16 1914 Th.* Rec'd campus assignment–rm 14 Gillett.[378] Studied all A.M. for Chem written Worst thing ever. Everybody hysterical Lab 3-5. Mr Adamson spoke in 10b.[379] Interesting

*April 17 1914 Fri.* Read Musset's plays in French all morning. Lab 2-5—Note extra hour. Lecture at 5. Senior sing with Lois. Went over to see Rm 14. Studied rest of evening.

*April 18 1914 Sat.* Spent half of morning at Chem Libe. Wrote paper on paper-making. Hall locked so couldn't hand it in. Handed in acceptance of assignment Theatre once more. "The House Next Door"[380] Arlene, A. Hills etc

*April 19 1914 Sun.* Slept late. Bert Leahys friend here to dinner. Impending war with Mexico frightened Euph. into missing desert [dessert].[381] Wrote French paper. Hot!!

---

378 Jennie's residence during the 1914-1915 academic year, Gillett House had opened in 1911.
379 Mr. Adamson: George P. Adamson, founder and president of Baker and Adamson Chemical Company (Easton, Pennsylvania) and a member of the American Chemical Society, the Society of Industrial Chemistry, the Chemists' Club of New York City, and the Electro-Chemical Society.
380 Possibly the 1912 comedy in three acts *The House Next Door* by J. Hartley Manners, adapted from *Die von Hochsattel* by Lee Walther Stein and Ludwig Heller.
381 Jennie refers in this diary entry and in those for April 20 and 21 to the tense situation that followed the Tampico Affair of April 9, 1914. Nine American sailors were arrested in Tampico in the state of Tamaulipas in Mexico, during a period of unstable relations between the United States and Mexico associated with the ongoing Mexican Revolution. The occupation of the port of Veracruz began on April 21 in response to intelligence of an impending delivery of arms there. The occupation continued for seven months.

*April 20 1914 Mon.* Chapel. Classes. Much joking about the war. Studied most of the afternoon and evening. Three days late in making this up and my memory is hazy.

*April 21 1914 Tues.* News of Battle of Vera Cruz in Mexican war. Classes. Afternoon party or feed in Lolo's room. Sport imitating the hens. All the neighbors joined in. Studied in eve.

*April 22 1914 Wed.* Chapel again and classes. F. Quilty fell out of her seat. Porte mad at disrespect of back row. High pitch all the hour. Walked with Anna and Min. German and dance on the ave Tel call from Miss Woodward[382] Lab 2:30-5:00 with Ev. Warren[383]

*April 23 1914 Th.* Beautiful day. River is high. Chemistry 12-5. No 10b lecture. Read round-robin letter from a Texas "nut." Wrote letters and read in the evening.

*April 24 1914 Fri.* Restless all day and hysterical. Didn't go to Lab. Went out with Marg. All the house went to Senior sing.

*April 25 1914 Sat.* Spent the morning on exp. Psych. Dull afternoon. Guest from Spfld. Finger bowls!! Yea verily. Lecture Mysticism & Logic Bertrand Russell: Trinity Coll Cambridge[384]

---

382 Katherine Shepherd Woodward was an instructor in English.
383 Evelyn Warren of Northampton was a junior in 1913-1914.
384 Bertrand Russell (1872-1970), British philosopher, mathematician, logician, historian, writer, social critic, and activist. He won the Nobel Prize in Literature in 1942.

*April 26 1914 Sun.* Wet and disagreeable. Lolo in bed all day. Louise Elms to dinner. Called on N. Kastl—Failed to see KZ Wells[385] Disappointed Vespers—fireside tea. Read all evening

*April 27 1914 Mon.* Classes. Did a back chapter in Psych exp. Nothing particularly interesting all day Studied in the evening.

*April 28 1914 Tues.* Chapel with Marg. Classes. Plaza with Lolo and Cath. Got in free—"too late to buy tickets" Senior sing. Read Cowper all evening.

*April 29 1914 Wed.* Took Mildred Hutchinsons sister Gertrude to chapel & 4:2. Recited in French. Loafed most of afternoon. Tired Rifled the pantry in evening. Spread Cath here to dinner

*April 30 1914 Th.* Went down town to send laundry & letters. Lecture at 12. Lab. 2-5 Started Chem of cooking in 10b. Studied in the evening. It's always safe to. Mouse last night

*May 1 1914 Fri.* May-day but alas—no excitement. Did Normal Illusions & thank fortune Miss Welch here to lunch. Lab. 2:30-5:00. Senior Sing. Loafed rest of the night

*May 2 1914 Sat.* Stood in line at Academy 1 ½ hour for 3 50¢ tickets for Disraeli—Got them[386] Lab. 10:15-12:15. Car-ride to Easthampton with Anna & Lois.[387] Libe for a dozen books in evening

---

385  Norma Bogard Kastl: a senior who lived in Chapin House.
386  *Disraeli* was a play by British writer Louis N. Parker, commissioned by actor George Arliss and first staged in 1911. It was later made into silent and sound films.
387  Easthampton, Massachusetts is bordered by Northampton.

*May 3 1914 Sun.* Delightful day. Read on upper porch all morning. Lower porch in afternoon. Cath Arlene & Ada here. President Burton at vespers "In nothing be anxious." C. & A. to tea Studied in eve

*May 4 1914 Mon.* Took Miss Smith (Mrs H's cousin) to chapel. Classes. Studied in the afternoon. Went to lecture on Byron in Spain 1809 with Marg & Euph. Mr Churchman of Clark U.[388]

*May 5 1914 Tues.* Classes! Written in Psych. Open question if "it micht be worse." Studied in the P.M. Disraeli—George Arliss Wonderful! Best ever! Went with Cath & Lolo

*May 6 1914 Wed.* Classes! Prof Haines recommended reading the text!! Went to walk with Ada Hill Had a circus reading "Pigs is Pigs."[389] Mrs. Carpenter came.[390] Chaperoned crowd to Plaza—Pretty fair

*May 7 1914 Th.* Family feud at its height There are keys—and keys. Lab. 3-5:30 No 10b. Went to open meeting of Colloquium Lecture on Coffee by Harris head of Agri. Dept[391]

*May 8 1914 Fri.* Peace reigns supreme once more. Florence The common spy Lab. 3-5. Went to bed after dinner. My spine cracks in sympathy with Anna's toe

---

388 Philip Hudson Churchman, Professor of Romance Languages at Clark.
389 "Pigs is Pigs": a popular short story by American author Ellis Parker Butler (1869-1937).
390 Mother of Jennie's classmate Catherine Carpenter.
391 William B. Harris was the expert on coffee at the United States Department of Agriculture in 1914.

*May 9 1914 Sat.* Went over to Lab for an hour & a half. Horrible dream last night. "funeraille de mon père"[392] "Invited to go batting but turned out to be the 5th wheel of the coach" Felt wretched over it.

*May 10 1914 Sun.* "A Perfect Day" Mother's Day Went to church with Cath & her mother. Pres Burton on criticism. Dinner at Lawrence with Vince B. Fuller G. Moore etc. to tea.[393] Pres. Burton's brother lead [led] vespers Marg. Wiesman called in eve.[394]

*May 11 1914 Mon.* Took Marg Wiesman to Eng 4:2 Other classes as usual. Didn't open a book all day. Penalty of getting up early. Mrs. C. and clairvoyant called on Mrs Harris

*May 12 1914 Tues.* Continued wetness. Looks bad for garden party. Went to Lyric with Anna and Lolo.[395] Spent the evening at the Libe with Lolo.

*May 13 1914 Wed.* Classes. Written sprung in French. Afternoon in Browsing room. Too wet for Garden Party. Tea dances a true blessing Helped Florence dress. She looked lovely. Bed 9:30

*May 14 1914 Th.* Delightful for batting. Went to all classes. Not a single regret that I am not fussing. Batted with Hutch all evening Easthampton. Most lost car buying pop-corn.

---

392  "'[F]uneraille de mon père'": my father's funeral (French).
393  Lawrence House was a cooperative venture in which residents managed household work beyond cooking.
394  Margaret Wiesman: a visitor from Clinton, daughter of dry goods and fancy goods merchant Anton W. Wiesman and his wife Elizabeth. The Wiesmans lived at 310 Church Street. Margaret was accepted at Bryn Mawr College in 1917.
395  The Lyric Theater at 24 Pleasant Street in Northampton was a movie house. It closed in 1917.

***May 15 1914 Fri.*** Cleaned up room. Sent laundry. Studied. Handed in course card at 12 to Mr. Abbott.[396] Early. Chem Lab 3-5. Car ride to Amherst with Mrs Carpenter Lois and Cath. Lots of fun

***May 16 1914 Sat.*** Left for Springfield at 11:02. Helped an old German lady who couldn't speak English find her relatives. Mr Hamilton and I met Mildred at 12.30.[397] Lunch at The Worthy[398] Went shopping and then to the ballgame Springfield 3 Hartford 2 (in the 9th inning) Front Room with private bath (à la Mrs H) at Nelson Haynes up in campeneilled Tower.[399] Poli's.[400] Thoroughly good time

***May 17 1914 Sun.*** Great rush to catch 9:05. Walked off Sun. with hotel key. Train leaves at 9:30 Sunday. Telephoned Isabel and went to college church service with her. Inspected the campus Isabel took us to dinner at Croysdale Inn.[401] Slow but sure. Back to Hamp via the notch.[402] Mildred likes the mountains Vesper—Mr Brown of Waterbury but he didn't sow the seed.[403] The usual crowd for tea but Mrs H forgot she had invited some of them. Surprised.

---

396 Herbert Vaughan Abbott was Professor of English Language and Literature.
397 William Hamilton of Clinton and his daughter Mildred, Jennie's friend.
398 The popular Worthy Hotel at 1571 Main Street in Springfield.
399 Nelson Haynes: another Springfield hotel, also on Main Street. "[C]ampeneilled Tower": the Campanile Tower, a 275-foot clock tower in Springfield.
400 Poli's Palace was a vaudeville and movie theater on Worthington Street in Springfield.
401 Jennie's friend Isabel was apparently a student at Mount Holyoke College in South Hadley, Massachusetts. The popular Croysdale Inn on Woodbridge Street in South Hadley accommodated the entertainment needs of Mount Holyoke girls.
402 A pass on Massachusetts Route 116.
403 Mr. Brown: the Reverend Robert E. Brown, pastor at the Second Congregational Church in Waterbury, Connecticut.

*May 18 1914 Mon.* Took Mildred to chapel. Eng 4:2 and Psych. With Anna went for a walk to Allen Field.[404] Cut French and went out on Paradise Florence made 1915 archery team. Anna Mildred and I went up to Mt Tom.[405] Good time. Deceived ourselves into thinking Mrs H didn't see us get on. Anna and I went into Springfield with Mildred. Back at 9:15 Ice cream party in Marg's room.

*May 19 1914 Tues.* Routine work again after a very enjoyable bat. Dr Haines: Why do we get up and dress? Miss McL. "Social pressure" Too hot to study. Everybody restless

*May 20 1914 Wed.* Classes. Went to Holyoke with Carolyn to call on Mrs McSherry. Disappointed that she was out. Miss Slade also out.[406] Minnies three dear sisters here for 2 hr in evening. Sweet girls.

*May 21 1914 Th.* Wrote letters and studied Chemistry as usual. Nothing particularly exciting. Good weather continues Car-ride to Easthampton with Catherine

*May 22 1914 Fri.* Went to see Tetlow.[407] Same old story Cath came over and we studied all afternoon Lab 2:30-5:00. Didn't go to Senior sing. Spent most of the evening on piazza. Studied.

---

404  Smith College field for outdoor sports and events, across the Connecticut River from the main part of campus.
405  Mount Tom is a steep elevation of 1,202 feet in Easthampton and Holyoke, Massachusetts. It was and remains a destination for hikers and day trippers in the area. The Holyoke Street Railway Company (a streetcar and bus system) made it accessible by trolley in Jennie McLeod's time. Mountain Park was a popular amusement park on the east side of the mountain.
406  Teacher Madeline Slade lived at 196 Beech Street in Holyoke.
407  Elizabeth Harrington Tetlow was Instructor in English Language and Literature at Smith. The paper that Jennie worked on in the summer of 1914 to remove an academic condition for English B was submitted to her.

High Street, Holyoke, ca. 1910

*May 23 1914 Sat.* Stayed at the house all the morning and studied industriously. Anna and I spent afternoon at Allen Field. Seniors won Field Day.[408] Exciting. Took some snaps. Down town at night Marg, Euph and I met "Jim"—Wiswells[409]

*May 24 1914 Sun.* Willie Robinson & G McCanley visiting here. Called and spent part of morning  Mrs H attributes visit to excursion. Vespers with Mrs Harris. Usual Sun crowd to tea. Free evening

---

408  Field Day: a day devoted to athletic competition at the college.
409  Wiswell's: a pharmacy at 82 Main Street in Northampton.

*May 25 1914 Mon.* Classes in the morning. Hottest day ever. Reputed 98°. Anna Lolo and I went to Libe, but finally came home and sought negligée The entire house and Mrs Spencer at Plaza. Jims treat Jim's "rep" is made. Mrs H fussed him last night[410]

*May 26 1914 Tues.* Chapel with Marg on the spur of the moment. Classes. Afternoon and evening at the Libe swallowing Eng. 4:2 topics. Alma Mater Competition Sing—Prize went to Sophs.[411]

*May 27 1914 Wed.* First of week classes for last time. Mr Staines & Mme Porte-Bauer made becoming farewell speeches. Passed in 4:2 reading list Took a well-earned rest from one o'clock on Hutch to Kingsley's[412] Wonderful thunderstorm!

*May 28 1914 Th.* Shampoo. This is the life. Studied Chem. No lecture. Surprise sprung: Lab. notebooks to be handed in tomorrow. Some shock! Lab 2-5 Lecture in 10b for last time. Dippy walk with Ada 1 ½ hr

*May 29 1914 Fri.* Finished Lab notebook. Went to Lab from 10:40-1:00 and 2.-5:30. Thank fortune it's ended. That's how we all feel. No 10b. Too tired to study. House play at Ada's—fine time Florence lovesick.

---

410 "[F]ussed him": when used as a transitive verb, "fuss" means to vex or disturb with trivial matters.
411 The Smith College song: "Oh! Fairest Alma Mater" (words by Henrietta Sperry; music by Henry David Sleeper).
412 Charles B. Kingsley's pharmacy at 140 Main Street in Northampton.

*May 30 1914 Sat.* Memorial Day—No college exercises Studied for French exam more or less all day. Minnie went home. Ice cream party. Wrote C. McC birthday letter. Anna and I went to P.O. and church.

*May 31 1914 Sun.* Cath and I went down to Paradise to study. Mr Sept Morris brother May interrupted same. She was arrested. Quiet dinner Studied French the rest of the day. Anna's birthday

*June 1 1914 Mon.* French 9 exam at 9. Think I did fairly well. Crackers and milk to revive us. 8th wonder. Downtown with Min & Anna Studied in the afternoon and evening

*June 2 1914 Tues.* No exams. Finished up Seashore experiments and got them in. Studied English in P.M. and went down town with Euph. Senior step sing & Junior sing[413] House meeting!!!

*June 3 1914 Wed.* No exams. Spent part of morning and most of afternoon at Libe on Eng 4:2. Batted around the house with the kids all evening.

*June 4 1914 Th.* Eng 4:2 exam was ideal. Until to-day "Cards were superfluous here" Started out "to palliate dullness and give time a shove" Serious consequences. L & I beat A & E. E took light cut

---

413  Step singing: a college tradition of classes singing on the steps of a campus building.

*June 5 1914 Fri.* Studied Psych except for diversion of cards. We have the fever in earnest. Montana Mike entertained "de gang" from 9:30-11:00 P.M. Perfect circus

*June 6 1914 Sat.* Studied Psych all morning Started Chem 10b paper. 1915 class meeting. Voted for new permission system Card party at Sam's (that's me) The gas went out

*June 7 1914 Sun.* Finished Chem 10b paper. Lucy Brearley to dinner[414] Vina and Irene to tea. Helen came over—troubled about our mutual friend. Florence got note from "Pinky"

*June 8 1914 Mon.* Spent the morning at Adas grinding Psych. Studied the same afternoon and evening. Desperate because Anna believes I opened her letter.

*June 9 1914 Tues.* Chapel with Lolo. Psych exam. Euph came over for me and promised me her Sr. pin.[415] Lolo, Marg, Euph & I had a swell time on Mt Tom. Mrs H peeved. Miss Childs here to lunch. Euph gave swell spread. Studied for Chem!!!!

*June 10 1914 Wed.* Chemistry 2 exam—positively the worst ever. Sure I flunked. Lolo left at 12. All went to train. Went with Ada at 3:21 Jrs. took steps. Seniors stunts. Good time

---

414  Lucy Bernice Brearley was a senior who lived in Northrop House.
415  Giving someone a senior pin was a token of affection and commitment. In a coeducational situation, a young man might give his senior pin to a girl special to him.

*June 11 1914 Th.* Spent the best part of the day trying to write paper on Domestic Water to remove Eng. B condition. Marg. recoit "non" Senior Dramatics "The Tempest" better than last year

*June 12 1914 Fri.* Euph Anna and I went to Deerfield Fri right after breakfast and made a call on Miss Childs and her mother.[416] They are both so sweet. Marg and I went to Springfield. Dinner at Forbes & Wallace[417] Went to game. Spfld beat Hartford 4-0. To Holyoke by trolley—thence by train. We two had a nice bat with M. Hines & M. Martin.[418] Broke an electric car.

*June 13 1914 Sat.* Last chapel at 10:00. Thrilling!! Pres. Burton was just wonderful. Went down town with Catherine The crowds are arriving. Spent from 2-4 in S27 waiting for distribution of standing room tickets. Learned some new little willies.[419] Someone discovered a portable organ and we had a picnic. Serenaded the cast at the Academy after the play. Bed about twelve.

---

416 Deerfield: a town in Franklin County, Massachusetts, by the Connecticut River, about fifteen miles from Northampton.
417 Forbes and Wallace was a department store in Springfield.
418 "M. Hines" is probably the May Heines who appears in Jennie's diary entry for September 30, 1914. M. Martin was likely Mary Esther Martin, a freshman who lived at 134 Elm Street. Mary Martin was listed as a freshman in the Smith *Bulletin* for two years in a row, 1913-1914 and 1914-1915. In 1914-1915, she lived at 9 Belmont Avenue.
419 Little Willies: darkly humorous rhymes projecting an incongruous indifference to gruesome or sobering subjects (accidents and death, for example).

"THIS IS THE LIFE"

*June 14 1914 Sun.* Breakfast at 8:30 and that was plenty early. Anna is marvelous in the dining room. Helped Marg finish a girdle and spent 2 hr in the laundry. Dinner as usual. President Burton preached Baccalaureate sermon at exercises at 4 P.M. The Seniors looked so pretty. Organ vespers delighted many in the evening but we were tired and spent evening with Euph

*June 15 1914 Mon.* Alumnae Procession at 9:00 A.M. A perfect circus. Then Ivy Procession and outdoor and indoor ivy exercises. Indoor exercises simply greater exquisite as it were. Glad to get dinner. Marg and I went up to the job and took snapshot of the best looking man in Hamp. Rained pitchforks about six but cleared for Illumination night.[420] Serenading & stunts of all sorts. Happy but tired. F broke Min's vase

*June 16 1914 Tues.* Commencement exercises at 10:00 Everything was pretty. So glad I stayed Euph commenced. Trip to station to get tickets and baggage checks. Marg and Euph went to class supper. Anna and I went in with 1915. The prettiest sight I ever saw. Min and I serenaded 1913 with 15 and went to Gym with '13 Saw take-off on Tempest. Screaming

---

420 Ivy Day and Illumination Night are Smith traditions, described on the college website as follows: "On the day before commencement, alumnae escort the seniors in a parade around campus. Then the seniors plant ivy to symbolize the connection between the college and its graduates. On Illumination Night, the campus is lit only by colored paper lanterns."

High Street, Clinton, looking north, ca. 1905

*June 17 1914 Wed.* Got to bed after last night's gaiety followed by trunk packing about 1:30  Up this morning at six to finish packing  Ordered cab for 8 A.M. and the Taxi arrived for Euph and me at 8:20. Made 8:25. Euph hated to leave  Worc about 10:45. Lunched at Esca with Mildred[421]  Shopped. Home 2:10 and glad to be here. Went to movies with Dad in the evening.

*June 18 1914 Th.* Went down town for pattern after sleeping late—Got pattern and worked on Helen's graduation dress. Dad went to Boston and I kept office at night. Visitors.

---

421   Esca: a cafeteria restaurant at 288 Main Street in Worcester.

*June 19 1914 Fri.* Slept late and felt more rested. Downtown shopping. Finished Helen's dress. She is pleased. Dad came home at 6:30. Spent the evening talking with him

*June 20 1914 Sat.* Got pattern for Maybelle and sewed some. Miss Reilly trying to "fuss" me—looking for news about Marg I guess.[422] Carolyn P & I drove to Northboro and spent P.M. at Dora Mitchell's

*June 21 1914 Sun.* Slept until 11:30 Went to S.S. into Mr Cushman's class.[423] He is splendid Mildred and I called on M Shaw as she is sick[424] Went to Mildred's to supper and to see Ethel[425]

*June 22 1914 Mon.* Made Maybelle a pretty muslin for Helen's graduation and fussed with Helen's clothes. Nothing exciting in Clinton after Hamp. Dead

---

422 Teacher Mary L. Reilly lived at 56 Cedar Street in Clinton.
423 "S.S.": Sunday School. James Allerton Cushman lived with his wife and family on Prescott Street. Born in 1881 in Taunton, he graduated from M.I.T. in 1903 and between 1903 and 1917 worked in Clinton as a civil engineer for the Metropolitan Water and Sewerage Board on the construction and maintenance of the Wachusett Reservoir, Aqueduct and Dam and on Clinton's sewerage system. He was active in the First Congregational Church in Clinton.
424 Margaret Shaw (born 1894) was the daughter of James and Marion Shaw, Scottish immigrants who lived on Nelson Street. James Shaw was a weaver at Bigelow Carpet, his daughter Margaret a stenographer.
425 Ethel: Mildred Hamilton's older sister.

*June 23 1914 Tues.* Downtown shopping. Finally got everything done. Helen graduated from 9th grade. Didn't go to exercises. Aunt Mary McL came down and we went to Sprints High S. grad in eve.[426]

*June 24 1914 Wed.* Kept the store open as Helen went on 9th grade picnic to Whalom.[427] Spent the time reading The Promised Land[428] Spent two hr in the evening at Rd Comm. Office[429]

*June 25 1914 Th.* Town Hall 9-12 on service assessments. Went to Lancaster with Miss Reilly. Visited Industrial School.[430] It is a big problem. Store at night. Dad in Boston

*June 26 1914 Fri.* Dad in Boston Town Hall 9-12 & 2-4. In the Assessors Off. making out cards for new streets sprinkled this year. Went to Nurse's graduation at 8 with Christine.[431] R. Pickford graduated.[432]

---

426 Aunt Mary McL: George McLeod's sister, who lived in Clinton with George McLeod and his family in the 1890s and subsequently married Joseph M. Johnston, who was born in Ireland. The Johnstons had three daughters—Anna (born 1902), Christine (1907), and Mary (1909). During the period Jennie kept her diary, her Johnston relations lived in Sterling. They later moved to Clinton, where the 1920 federal census places them.
427 Whalom Park: an amusement park operated between 1893 and 2000 in Lunenburg, Massachusetts, on Lake Whalom.
428 *The Promised Land*: the 1912 autobiography of Mary Antin, who emigrated from Belarus to the United States.
429 The Road Commissioners' office in the Clinton Town Hall on Church Street, where Jennie worked in the summer of 1914, when her father was one of the commissioners.
430 The Industrial School for Girls on Old Common Road in Lancaster was the first state reform school for girls in the country. A progressive institution focused on the transformation rather than the punishment of delinquents, it ran from 1856 to 1975. Jennie's visit there reflects an interest in social issues.
431 The graduation ceremony for nurses trained at Clinton Hospital's nursing school.
432 Ruth Belle Pickford, daughter of widow Elizabeth Pickford, who lived at 124 Cedar Street.

***June 27 1914 Sat.*** Downtown in time to see Clinton Union S.S. picnic parade.[433] Brass band St. Sp. Ass. 9-12 writing names on cards.[434] Store in P.M. to write letters  Hall with Dad on school job in eve.[435]

***June 28 1914 Sun.*** Got up just in time to go to S.S. Will be in Mr. Cushman's class for summer  Mildred and I went down to Margaret's. She's better. Mildred here to supper.

***June 29 1914 Mon.*** Town Hall 8-12 and 1-5. Saw many of the 1912 people as they were preparing Bd of Trade room for reunion. Called on Anna Comaskey and F. Shutts in evening

***June 30 1914 Tues.*** Blanche McQuaid married.[436] Worked in Assessors office from 9-12 and 2-4  Finished "The Promised Land." Dad went before School Comm. about Walnut St Gram.

***July 1 1914 Wed.*** Rd Comm Office 9-12:1-2:7-11  Wrote letters and cards to eight of the girls. Feeling of something done. Members of Playground Comm. waited for quorum in Rd Comm Office

---

433  Preceded by a parade, the annual Union Sunday School picnic was attended by children from the Sunday schools of all of Clinton's churches.
434  "St Sp": street sprinkling (the management of which to keep down the dust was one of the responsibilities of the Road Commissioners).
435  George McLeod visited the Town Hall in his effort (ultimately successful) to gain the contract for heating and ventilating the Walnut Street School.
436  Listed under "Music Teachers" in Clinton directories, (Mary) Blanche McQuaid lived with her father James and her four sisters at 324 Chestnut Street. She married William Fahey of Waltham.

*July 2 1914 Th.* Rd Dept. 9-12. In the afternoon I loafed around the office and read Tennessee Shad.[437] Downtown at night. Met Marg and Anna.

*July 3 1914 Fri.* Down town shopping in the morning. Met Cath and Aunt Mary at 3:14. Uncle Andy came later.[438] Movies in the evening

*July 4 1914 Sat.* The great and glorious 4th. Cath. and I went to the parade. Sent silver candlesticks to Aunt Barbara for the wedding anniversary. Loafed all day.

*July 5 1914 Sun.* Got up and Cath and I went to Sunday School. The whole crowd went over to the woods. Read Tennessee Shad aloud. All went to church at night. I didn't want to.

*July 6 1914 Mon.* All the girls went to 8:05 train with Uncle Andy. Sent films to Niquette.[439] Rd Comm office 8:30-12:00. 1-4. Catherine and I went to Miss Stevens first Mon of year.[440] Indoors on ac of rain

---

437  *The Tennessee Shad*: a 1911 work of fiction by American writer Owen Johnson.
438  Catherine and her parents Andrew and Mary McCance were family friends rather than blood relatives. Jennie referred to Andrew and Mary as "Uncle" and "Aunt" simply as a mark of respect. The McCances lived in Roxbury.
439  E.L. Niquette & Co. at 273 Main Street in Northampton was a drug store with its own photographic department. Niquette catered to the developing and printing needs of Smith College students. Orders were processed on-site and could be sent in. Niquette also sold cameras and photographic supplies.
440  A gathering at the home of Miss Ellen K. Stevens (1860-1955), who lived at 223 Chestnut Street (the house is no longer standing). She was knowledgeable, artistic, and musical, and she wrote poetry. She ran C.G. Stevens & Son in Clinton, an insurance agency established by her father, lawyer Charles Godfrey Stevens. Jennie worked for Miss Stevens at the insurance business during the years she kept her diary, became a junior partner, and eventually took the business over under her own name. Miss Stevens was active in the Episcopal Church of the Good Shepherd and in multiple community organizations and initiatives, including the church-based Girls' Friendly Society.

*July 7 1914 Tues.* Rd Comm. 9-12 and 1-5. All went to the movies in the evening. Catherine passed for a child. Lunch at home before going to bed. Got report. Safe!!

*July 8 1914 Wed.* Went to Whalom at 9:10 Back at 7. Miss Burdett's S.S. class there. Had lunch with them and took pictures. Theatre The Red Mill.[441] Pretty fair. Called at Anna's in the evening

*July 9 1914 Th.* Dad got school contract 4th J. Pictures came back awfully good. Rd Comm office 8:30-12:00 & 1-5. Sewed all evening. Cath and I want new dresses for Sat.

*July 10 1914 Fri.* Rd. Comm. 9:30-12 1:30-4.30. Fitted Catherine's dress in the morning before leaving. Saw Anne Donlan. Got P.K for skirt.[442] Sewed all evening. Cath fitted me.

*July 11 1914 Sat.* Rd Comm. 8:30-12:00. Got up early and had skirt hung. Both pleased with our "distress making." Harry Martin won game against Shrewsbury.[443] Marg went with Cath and me. Met the Dr. Marg came to supper. Terrible storm

---

441 *The Red Mill*: a farcical operetta by Victor Herbert, with libretto by Henry Blossom.
442 P.K.: possibly a phonetic abbreviation for piqué (a type of fabric).
443 With six hundred onlookers, Clinton beat Shrewsbury in this baseball game at Fuller Field—"Proctor Was Star Player," *Clinton Daily Item*, July 13, 1914. Harry Martin pitched.

*July 12 1914 Sun.* Christine and Mamie spent the day with us.[444] Christine Cath and I went to S.S. Mother Dad and Aunt Mary went to Grandpa Johnston's funeral.[445] Cath and I called in evening. Gingerbread. Town Hall 7:00-10:00

*July 13 1914 Mon.* Aunt Mary and Catherine left at 11:08. Hated to have them leave. Mailed films for Cath. Went to Rd Comm office 11:45-5:45. Piazza party at Miss Stevens[446]

*July 14 1914 Tues.* Town Hall 9-12 & 1-5 Played cards with Sprint and Stan. Ate cherries and ice cream like mad. Forgot the danger and didn't meet it.

*July 15 1914 Wed.* Town Hall 9-12 1-2:30 Cath Carp Mrs C and 2 friends came in new machine Went up to see Marg then lunch at house. Got pay $16.75. Mother and I went to Berlin with the Paines[447]

*July 16 1914 Th.* Town Hall. 8:30-12. 1-4. Downtown shopping. Got cloth for skirts and shrunk it in the evening. Downtown with mother. Annie and Sadie crazy over stories[448]

---

444 Christine and Mamie: Jennie's Johnston cousins.
445 Joseph Johnston, age 74, who died on July 9, 1914. A retired weaver born in Ireland, he lived with his daughter and son-in-law Sarah and David Foster and their family at 23 Palmer Court. There may have been a blood relationship between Mary McLeod Johnston's husband Joseph M. Johnston and the elder Joseph Johnston of Clinton, but they were not father and son.
446 "Piazza party": outdoor party, under a veranda or porch roof.
447 Neighbors of the McLeods, automobile dealer and repairman Joseph W. Paine, his wife Ella, and their children lived at 104 Pearl Street.
448 Probably Annie Johnston, Jennie's twelve-year-old cousin from Sterling, and ten-year-old Sadie Foster, daughter of David and Sarah Foster and granddaughter of Joseph Johnston (who died on July 9).

Clinton Town Hall, ca. 1910

*July 17 1914 Fri.* 8:30-11:30 and 1-4:30 at hall  Cut out skirt. Went to store with Dad in the evening to make out bills. Terrible thunder storm in the night

*July 18 1914 Sat.* Rd. Comm 8:30-12:00 and 1-5  Terribly hot day but a nice breeze in the office. Went down to the store at night  Went shopping with Maybelle.

*July 19 1914 Sun.* My turn to take S.S. class down stairs. Someone must have put them wise as no sub was asked for  Town Hall in the P.M.  Store at night  Letters

*July 20 1914 Mon.* Town Hall 8:30-12:00 1-5 Mock trial at Miss Stevens. I was arrested on charge of forging check. Pick my lawyer vs Lewis. Jury brought in verdict of "not guilty"

*July 21 1914 Tues.* Town Hall all morning. Worked about 3 hr. Came up after lunch 1 hr but went home at 2:00. Make skirt during terrible thunderstorm. Movies with Esther T at night

*July 22 1914 Wed.* Town Hall 9-12 and 1-5 Nothing very exciting except letters from Lois and Catherine Mc. Went down to the store to help Dad in the evening

*July 23 1914 Th.* Town Hall. 8:15-11:45. Afternoon 2-5 but worked only one hour. Marg came down. Downtown with her. Uncle Allan came to the house by surprise about 8 P.M.[449]

*July 24 1914 Fri.* Town Hall. 9-12. 1:30-4:30 Called on F. Shutts on way home. Took walk with her. Made call at Merls in the evening  Met M Duncan & M Freitag.[450] Exciting bat. Park!

*July 25 1914 Sat.* Town Hall. 8-12 and 1-4 Went shopping with Mildred and then to the movies. Lucille Love bores me to death and distraction[451]

---

[449] George McLeod's obituary in the February 8, 1936 issue of the *Clinton Daily Item* lists among his survivors "a brother, Allan, of Chicago, Ill.," as well as his sister Mary McLeod Johnston. Allan does not appear in the 1881 Scottish census as then living in Findley McLeod's household.

[450] "M Duncan": Clinton directories include a Margaret C. Duncan, who was a teacher. According to the 1900 federal census, she was the stepdaughter of Joseph McKnight of Clinton, the daughter of his wife Lillias. Margaret was born in 1880 in England to Scottish parents. "M Freitag": possibly Mildred Freitag, age nineteen, daughter of Otto and Fredericka Freitag of Green Street in Clinton.

[451] *Lucille Love, Girl of Mystery* was a 1914 serial action film directed by Francis Ford, starring Grace Cunard and Francis Ford.

*July 26 1914 Sun.* Tried to get rust out of waist and back fell out so couldn't go to S.S.[452] Called on E. Maitland in the P.M.[453] Town Hall with Dad for 3 hr in the evening

*July 27 1914 Mon.* Town Hall 8:30-12 and 1-6 Varied work. Got locked in as I didn't know front door key had been changed. Went up to Miss Stevens. Allan left Pleasant evening

*July 28 1914 Tues.* 8-12 and 1-5 at the Town Hall After much plotting and planning flat rate of 4¢ per ft on sprinkling decided. Maybelle and mother in Sterling

*July 29 1914 Wed.* Town Hall 8:30-12 and 1-5 Received $10.00 pay. Work went along smoothly all day. Down to store in the evening. Edith has invited me to Bare Hill 2nd wk aug[454]

*July 30 1914 Th.* Town Hall. 8:00-12 and 1-5. Bought three new linen dresses and spent the evening altering them. No dressmaking for mine. How does she do it at .25 per

---

452 Waist: a woman's blouse or shirt.
453 E. Maitland: Esther Maitland, Clinton High School Class of 1912, was the daughter of plumber Robert B. Maitland and his wife Dolly (both born in Scotland), who lived at 285 Water Street.
454 Edith Strout—a daughter of widow Jennie B. Strout of 128 East Street in Clinton—was a member of the Alpha Club. Bare Hill Pond is a partly natural, partly man-made pond in Harvard, Massachusetts, long popular as a recreational hotspot. Some Clinton people had cottages or camps there.

*July 31 1914 Fri.* Town Hall 8-12 and 5-7 Chautauqua opened.[455] Dunbar singing band  Evolution of a city—Dr Turner  Panama Canal and Pacific Exp—Dr. Rader

*August 1 1914 Sat.* Town Hall. 9-2  Then to Chautauqua. Mrs. Oliphant against woman suffrage was splendid.  Frank Stevens in favor at night not so good.[456]  Tyrolean Yodlers

*August 2 1914 Sun.* Town Hall. 9-12. and 5:45-9:45  S.S part time. Chautauqua.  Dr Turner on The Conventional Conscience. "Culture is the opposite of absorption in the obvious"—Pres Hadley

*August 3 1914 Mon.* Town Hall. 8-2 and 5-7. Took Ruth H to Chautauqua.[457]  Dr Pierson on ["]the joy of living" and Mr Conwell on "Acres of Diamonds"  Tuskegee jubilee singers at night with F. Shutts

*August 4 1914 Tues.* Town Hall 9-2:30 and 5-8  Dr. Turner.  Cinderella—very pretty by college Players  Dr Hawkins in the evening.  Splendid animal pictures.

---

455  Chautauqua was a late nineteenth- and early twentieth-century movement promoting popular education and entertainment through a series of varied programs, often held under a large tent. Towns and cities around the United States booked talent through agencies like the Redpath Lyceum Bureau, and speakers moved from place to place on the Chautauqua circuit. Clinton's Chautauqua ran for a week and featured lectures, concerts, plays, and more. As reported in the *Clinton Daily Item* for July 31, 1914, that year Chautauqua was held between July 31 and August 6 "under the big tent on the Harris lot." The tent had seating capacity for an audience of 1200. Admission was by ticket. A "juvenile department" for children fourteen and under was a publicized feature of Chautauqua week. All of the programs were described in some detail in successive issues of the *Item*.
456  Mrs. J.D. Oliphant of New Jersey (of the National Anti-Suffrage Association) and Frank Stephens, who was a founder of the utopian single-tax colony in Arden, Delaware, as well as a suffrage advocate.
457  Ruth H.: Ruth Hamilton, one of Mildred's younger sisters.

*August 5 1914 Wed.* Town Hall. 9-11:30 12-2. 5:45-7:15 The Four Artists and Dr. Turner in the P.M. The Artists and Frank Dixon on "Taking Stock of a Town." Big day

*August 6 1914 Th.* Town Hall 8-12. 12:45-2:15 4-5:15 and 6-7:15 Adriatic Band and pretty children's play at P.M. Chautauqua Band. Judge Lindsey. The Misfortune of Mickey

*August 7 1914 Fri.* 9-12 and 2-5 at Town Hall. Went to Esther Towne's for supper. Up to tennis court and to Globe with Esther & Alice Macfarlane.[458] Pictures "swell"

*August 8 1914 Sat.* Town Hall 9-12 and 1:30-4:00 Assessments now check with adding machine. Went down to the store in the evening and went shopping.

*August 9 1914 Sun.* Hot!!! Spent day doing odd jobs for myself. Alice Mac and Esther T came to tea. Mr Stone called for them and spent the evening.[459] Everyone seemed happy!!!

*August 10 1914 Mon.* Town Hall 8-12 and 1-5. Didn't go up to the piazza party but stayed home and sewed and ironed to get my clothes ready for vacation

---

458  Alice Macfarlane was identified in a notice in the "Local Affairs" column in the *Clinton Daily Item* for August 28, 1915 (when she was a guest of Esther Towne) as "of Dedham." A Dedham directory for that year shows that she was a bookkeeper.
459  Most likely Orra (or Ora) Stone, a lawyer who lived at 22 Pearl Street.

*August 11 1914 Tues.* Town Hall 8-11:30 1:30-5 Got up after midnight to go to fire in Boston Conf. store.[460] Didn't go to Miss McDonald's party. Rain ruined my clothes, spattered twice

*August 12 1914 Wed.* A hope—postponed until to-morrow Town Hall 9-12 and 2-4. Minnie visiting Anna.[461] All at Marg's in the afternoon  Pay from department $12.25

*August 13 1914 Th.* Town Hall. 5 ½ hr. between 8:30 and 2:30. Marg, Minnie and Anna came down for a while. Met Helen Irving at 6:30. Both took 7:11 for Arlene's.[462] Pepperell at 7:43. Lawn party!

*August 14 1914 Fri.* Everybody lovely. Mrs Deware and the family are charming. Country Club all morning  Tennis at home in the afternoon. Clarence Irving (6′ 3 ½″) came.[463] LeTenas circus.[464] Pretty good.

*August 15 1914 Sat.* Slept late. Went up to Country Club  Lil and I had a "regular" nap. Crowd went to Manchester, N.H in the machine. First time I was ever out of the state. Movies in the evening

---

460  "Boston Conf. store": a fire of unknown origin in the Crown Confectionary Store in the Associates Block on High Street (owned by John B. O'Toole)—"Fire in a Stairway," *Clinton Daily Item*, August 11, 1914.
461  "Minnie" can be definitively identified as Minnie Long of Brattleboro, Vermont through a notice of this visit in the "Local Affairs" section of the *Clinton Daily Item* for August 13, 1914.
462  Arlene Deware—one of Jennie's Smith friends—lived in East Pepperell, Massachusetts.
463  Presumably the brother of Smith friend Helen Irving.
464  LaTena's Circus: a traveling three-ring circus.

*August 16 1914 Sun.* Slept until 9:30. After breakfast crowd went to see Groton Schools and Pepperell Springs.[465] Helen and Clarence left at 3 Fooled around and ate all afternoon & night

*August 17 1914 Mon.* Up at 7:30 Left Pepperell after joyous time at 9 A.M. To Nantasket via train & boat.[466] Reached Gem Rock House at 1:00. Bathed in P.M. Cards with some fellows at the house in eve.

*August 18 1914 Tues.* Spent the morning on the beach writing. Left in the middle of the afternoon to catch 3:40 boat. Reached Aunt Mary's about 5:30 and glad to get here at last.[467]

*August 19 1914 Wed.* Slept until nine o'clock. Wrote letters rest of morning. Terribly sleepy and slept all afternoon. Cath & I went down in the evening to see the new store

*August 20 1914 Th.* Didn't get up until ten. Haven't been so lazy since the baby died.[468] Wrote a diplomatic letter to dear Mother Hoagland. She ought to love me forever.

---

465 Groton Schools: Groton School and Lawrence Academy. Pepperell Springs: an extensive forested tract in the Nissitisset River watershed.
466 Nantasket Beach in Hull, Massachusetts (not far from Boston) was and remains a popular venue for ocean swimming and recreation.
467 The Boston residence of Andrew and Mary McCance and their daughter Catherine, at 32 Sherman Street in Roxbury.
468 An allusion to the death of Jennie's youngest brother Norman, who was born prematurely and died on April 6, 1904.

*August 21 1914 Fri.* Slept late—Rather unusual for us eh what Ignatz.[469] Ironed and Cath sewed. Went to Shawmut—Saw $1,000,000 mystery.[470] Played cards in the evening

*August 22 1914 Sat.* Up early 9 A.M. because we had to work. Went to Franklin Park and then in town.[471] Met Anne Marie and thereby hangs a tale—Car-ride to Dorchester

*August 23 1914 Sun.* Got up at a sensible time. Cath went to churched [church] while I wrote letters  Hester here to dinner. Went to Revere Beach and all had a lovely time—Oh you roller coaster[472]

*August 24 1914 Mon.* Restless weather. Did a little bit of everything in the morning. Played "I have a word that rhymes with["]—Worked on Eng. B. Oh that well begun were done!

---

[469] "[E]h what Ignatz": a reference to George Herriman's 1913-1944 newspaper comic strip "Krazy Kat," in which Ignatz Mouse was a character.

[470] Shawmut: the Shawmut Theatre on Blue Hill Avenue in Roxbury. *The Million Dollar Mystery* was a film serial in twenty-three parts released in 1914. Directed by Howard Hansel, it starred Florence La Badie and James Cruze.

[471] Franklin Park: a park and recreational area in Jamaica Plain, Roxbury, and Dorchester in Boston, designed by landscape architect Frederick Law Olmsted. The Franklin Park Zoo, which opened to the public in 1912, is located there.

[472] Revere Beach: a popular public beach in Revere, Massachusetts, about five miles north of Boston, home to a variety of eateries and entertainments (dance halls, ballrooms, roller skating rinks, and bowling alleys among them) and known for its roller coasters. "Oh you roller coaster": Jennie is having fun with the title of the irreverent 1909 hit song "I Love, I Love, I Love My Wife, But Oh! You Kid" (words by Jimmy Lucas; music by Harry Von Tilzer).

"THIS IS THE LIFE"

*August 25 1914 Tues.* Last chance to sleep late  Went through H.S.P.A.—a most up to the minute school.[473]  James here.  Yvonne too.  Much fun with games and problems

*August 26 1914 Wed.* Early birds.  Cath went to dentist at 9 and I worked on Eng B at Libe.  Long carride to Salem ruins[474]  Pitiful sight.  Scraps over fares[475]

*August 27 1914 Th.* Spent morning at Libe while Cath suffered at dentists.  Mrs Walker here to lunch and for afternoon.  Aunt Mary C. & I to Shawmut  Good.

*August 28 1914 Fri.* Libe and dentist in the morning.  In town in the afternoon  Met Uncle Andy.  Supper at Cafeteria  Orpheum after as last year.[476]  Good show

*August 29 1914 Sat.* Rainy.  Mailed films to Niquette's.  Mrs. Stearn, Florence and Adele here for the day.  Did errands in the evening.  Mrs Myers brot up chicken salad[477]

---

473  H.S.P.A.: the High School of Practical Arts on Greenville Street in Roxbury, opened late in 1913.
474  The Great Salem Fire of June 25, 1914 destroyed nearly 1,400 buildings, both homes and places of employment, devastating the local economy.
475  Scraps: squabbles; fights.
476  Orpheum: the Orpheum Theatre was a music, vaudeville, and movie theater on Hamilton Place in Boston, housed in the former Boston Music Hall, the first home of the Boston Symphony Orchestra.
477  Mrs. Myers: Mr. and Mrs. Harry Myers were neighbors of the McCances. "Brot": brought (Scots).

***August 30 1914 Sun.*** Mrs. Phillips and Norton came. "The boys call him nuts." That's not saying what Cath & I think of him  Hester here to dinner. Pianola pleasures[478]

***August 31 1914 Mon.*** Took Norton to Franklin Park to see the zoo. An everlasting question box. Libe in the afternoon  Cath got thru with dentist  Helen Burke to supper

***September 1 1914 Tues.*** Aunt Mary had a headache. Went to Libe in the A.M. Saw Mrs Phillips & Norton off on 5:56 and the boys off for New Orleans at 6. Went up to the store  Carride to Dor.

***September 2 1914 Wed.*** Sewed and read while Cath finished up two dresses for R.I. Niquette reports no films received. Came home on 5:05. Had a perfectly lovely vacation

***September 3 1914 Th.*** Helen in Sterling so sub'd at store. Tried to write but didn't get beyond first sentence. Better luck to-morrow when it cools off a bit

***September 4 1914 Fri.*** Spent another day at store on English B. Outlook a little more encouraging but it's nerve wracking. Two weeks will seal my fate

***September 5 1914 Sat.*** Spent the morning at the store and the evening there too. Afternoon at home. Worked all day long writing English B.

---

478   Pianola: a type of player piano.

*September 6 1914 Sun.* Worked on English B all morning. Type-wrote rough draft at Town Hall in the afternoon. Played Parcheesi with the kids in the evening[479]

*September 7 1914 Mon.* Labor Day and I labored with a vengeance. Corrected and typewrote in duplicate Eng B & outline  Mrs Taylor visiting C. Sprague. Pleasant afternoon and evening

*September 8 1914 Tues.* Had to have special envelopes made to hold paper. Sent English B. to Miss Tetlow by registered mail. P.M. at store. Movies in the evening with E. Towne

*September 9 1914 Wed.* Rec'd $6.38—Last pay from Rd Dept for the season  Typewrote 25 letters to Cedar St residents. Wrote a few personal letters. Excitement: Saw Merl, Ruth, Esther, Gladys & Edith.[480]  E.G & I went to Edith's to discuss alpha dance

*September 10 1914 Th.* Did a few odd jobs for store in between siege of calls. C.E.S. actually made a mistake and I wickedly "gloried in his shame"[481] Marg came to store about 8. Went to see school job.[482]

*September 11 1914 Fri.* Went down to the store in the morning and did quite a bit on the books  Alpha meeting at Esther's. Took snaps, ate candy. good time. Went to bed early.

---

479  Parcheesi: a popular board game, based on the Indian game Pachisi.
480  Gladys M. Howe—who attended the Alpha Club meeting on January 1, 1914—was the daughter of Nathaniel L. and Elizabeth Howe, who lived at 45 Prescott Street. Nathaniel Howe sold doors, windows, blinds, wallpaper, paint, and hardware from a store on Water Street. Gladys was a clerk.
481  "C.E.S.": Jennie is likely referring to Charles E. Shaw, who was Town Treasurer and Collector in Clinton in 1914.
482  The Walnut Street School job George McLeod had won in July.

*September 12 1914 Sat.* Sewed all day with exception of morning trip to bank and afternoon trip to pay the help. Made Helen a dress. Shopping and movies with Mildred. Stayed over night with her

*September 13 1914 Sun.* Up and having breakfast at 11. Went to S.S. Took pictures of school job but expect blanks. Alpha girls peeved because M & I went autoing to Concord instead of making favors for dance.

*September 14 1914 Mon.* Errands down town in the morning. Sewed for Helen all afternoon  Alpha Club dance. Pierce Hall—8-12.[483] Miss Stevens and Mrs Towne patronesses. I called for E.K.S.[484]

*September 15 1914 Tues.* Rec'd return of registry on Delivery of Eng B. More errands and more sewing  General rush. Telephone from Arlene. Awfully glad to hear Miriam is going to Burnham School[485] Helen & I went to piazza party. Xtra trip. Unit. Ch. lights[486]

*September 16 1914 Wed.* After much excitement left for Hamp. at 9:35. Travelled with C. Sprague M. Philbin, Arlene and Miriam Deware  met Lois and Marg Deware at train. No room at Boyden's. Went to Lonesome Pine.[487] Oh such a wait. Called on Miss Tetlow but got no decision. Stayed in all night waiting her phone call.

---

483 Pierce Hall: function and meeting space upstairs in the Pierce Block on High Street.
484 "E.K.S.": Ellen K. Stevens.
485 Miriam: Miriam Deware, younger sister of Smith students Arlene and Marguerite Deware. Burnham School: founded in 1877 as the Classical School for Girls, the Burhham School in Northampton was a prep school for Smith.
486 Unit. Ch.: Unitarian Church.
487 Boyden's: a restaurant on Main Street in Northampton. Lonesome Pine: a tea room on Henshaw Avenue.

*September 17 1914 Th.* Miss Tetlow phoned. Paper satisfactory Dieu soit loué.[488] I am free from a condition for the first time since I entered. Batted all P.M. Sings in the evening. Called on several

*September 18 1914 Fri.* No Lab. Called on Ada. Thrilled over her engagement. She is a dear girl. Fr. 7 at 2. First real class. Called on Anna after and Marg at night. Wrote letter home

*September 19 1914 Sat.* Chapel with Marg. Downtown on numerous errands. Straightened room in P.M. Freshman Frolic with Lois Evans[489] Birthday serenade to Pres Seelye. Beckmann's

*September 20 1914 Sun.* Wrote several letters and went to 1st Cong. Church. Dr Keeler was back. Called on Ada and went to vespers. Old girls called on new. I had 21 callers

*September 21 1914 Mon.* Classes promise to be largely lecture and supremely interesting  Crazy about Drama. Downtown buying books & books. Ada called in eve  Studied.

*September 22 1914 Tues.* Four classes—all lectures  Only Louise Wood and I taking Scotch.[490] Both favorably impressed. Studied all afternoon and evening. My kingdom for a fountain pen  Fire drill 9:30

---

488  "Dieu soit loué": God be praised (French).
489  Smith freshman Lois Evans from Brookline, Massachusetts, who lived in Dewey House. Lois was the daughter of "Mrs. E.A. Evans, formerly of Clinton" ("Local Affairs," *Clinton Daily Item*, September 15, 1914).
490  Louise Wood was a senior from West Newton, Massachusetts. In 1914-1915, she lived at 21 Henshaw Avenue.

*September 23 1914 Wed.* Classes from 9-12. It's insufferably hot. Anna Potter and I called on Miss Childs after school.[491] Went to bed at nine o'clock and slept well.

*September 24 1914 Th.* Chem. Lect and Lab 9-12 Miss Foster is a splendid teacher.[492] Fr. 7 in P.M. Schinz is pretty cute[493] Read "The Abbott" all evening.[494]

*September 25 1914 Fri.* Lecture and Lab 9-12:30 Tried to see osmosis in squash leaf spine and "kept looking with no avail" Discoursed with Bertha until 11:30 P.M. on atheism[495]

*September 26 1914 Sat.* Miss Paulding back for lunch My free day. Spent A.M. at Libe reading various assignments. Bat with Freshman to Cider Mill.[496] Hasty return on account of forgotten schedule. 125 on electric from Hadley[497] Made it

---

491 Anna Potter, a senior from Portland, Connecticut, was one of Jennie's Gillett housemates during her last year at Smith.
492 Miss Foster: Mary Louise Foster, Associate Professor of Chemistry. Jennie elsewhere refers to her as "M.L.F."
493 Schinz (nicknamed "Schinzie"): Albert Schinz, Professor of French Language and Literature.
494 "The Abbott": Sir Walter Scott's historical novel *The Abbot* (a sequel to *The Monastery*).
495 Bertha Hills of Burlington, Vermont was a senior living in Gillett House in 1914-1915 and, like Jennie, a member of Colloquium (the departmental chemistry club).
496 The cider mill in Hadley attracted Smith as well as Mount Holyoke students. A Hadley writer and poet wrote of it in 1907: "In the mellow autumn months the Hadley cider mill is also a favorite shrine of the college girls, and we call them 'the tin pail brigade.' Sometimes they go to the mill in squads of two or three and sometimes it is a whole company. The devices that the girls use to get the precious liquid upon the campus are most ingenious"—Clarence Hawkes, "Old Hadley, Past and Present," *The Village: A Journal of Village Life* (February 1907), 89-90.
497 Electric: electric car (trolley; streetcar).

*September 27 1914 Sun.* Went down to breakfast & prayers. Read all morning—principally Education and "The Abbott." Vespers with H. Hannahs[498] Over to 17 to our regular Sun. tea

*September 28 1914 Mon.* Classes again Ah yes and woe is me. Much jests from Wallace House pointing finger of suspicion on "Jim" and his friends. Studied drama technique with Cath all eve.

*September 29 1914 Tues.* Classes. Neither of us knew much Scotch. Crammed Scotch and Anthony and Cleo. all day. No diversion except a little rain at night to cheer us up!!

*September 30 1914 Wed.* Up at 5:45 to study. Cut breakfast to keep up chapel record. Finally squeeked thru. Eng 25 expected to find Scotch ballads. Written in Eng 12 Minnie Anna & May Heines called in the evening

*October 1 1914 Th.* Fire drill at 6:30 "It's nice to get up in the morning but it's nicer to stay in your bed" Lab from 9-12. Did French Comp. Lois and M. Deware called. Beckmann's with Lois

*October 2 1914 Fri.* Lab. 9-12 and an hr in the P.M. Got thru Fr. Comp. scrumptiously. Went to bed at 5:50. Several calls during the evening. Florence came over Poor child

---

498   H. Hannahs: Helen Elizabeth Hannahs of Watertown, New York, a junior who lived in Hatfield House.

*October 3 1914 Sat.* Spent A.M. at Libe on French  Libe in P.M. on Education. Finished Un Jeune Siberienne "Jamais encore."[499] Freshman dance at house. I took Lois Evans

*October 4 1914 Sun.* Peace Sunday[500]  Slept until 11. Enjoyed Anna Sparks piano concert after dinner.[501] Called on Carp & C. Sprague  Vespers with E Heinrich.[502]  John Bates Clark on Peace[503]  Ada & Gladys called in the eve

*October 5 1914 Mon.* Spent first hr at Libe. Classes as usual. Studied at Min's after French 12:3. Went to bed rather early and studied

*October 6 1914 Tues.* All regular classes. Pretty thick in Scotch. Miss Scott must think we're "nuts."[504]  Nice little written in Drama  Ada Bertha Elsie and I laughed all night at Libe

*October 7 1914 Wed.* Fire drill during breakfast. Attended all classes. Went to Chem Libe and reference Libe and downtown in the P.M. Went to bed early and read

---

499 *La Jeune Sibérienne* by Xavier de Maistre (originally published 1825). "Jamais encore": never again (French).
500 Peace Sunday: Sunday, October 4, 1914, was designated by President Woodrow Wilson as a day of prayer for the restoration of peace abroad.
501 A freshman from New York, New York, Anna Davenport Sparks lived in Gillett House.
502 Elsie Margaret Heinrich of New Haven, Connecticut, a freshman who lived in Washburn House.
503 John Bates Clark (1847-1938) was Professor of Economics at Columbia University between 1895 and 1923.
504 Mary Augusta Scott, Professor of English Language and Literature.

HOCKANUM FERRY, NORTHAMPTON, MASS. MT. HOLYOKE IN DISTANCE.

Hockanum Ferry, Northampton to Hadley

*October 8 1914 Th.* Mountain Day.[505] Left via 3 seater for Mt Holyoke with 12 Seniors and "A.D"[506] crossed Hockanum Ferry with a big crowd.[507] Rode to half way house. Climbed the 522 steps with Sally. Some climb  Had lunch and batted around summit until 5. came down 600 ft plane at an < of 45°. Thrilling  home through Hadley via auto. Batted with Marg in her false face. Pleasant evening. Locked out

---

505 Mountain Day: a spontaneously scheduled annual fall holiday at Smith, selected by the college president. The ringing of the college bells announces the suspension of classes.
506 A.D.: Arlene Deware.
507 Hockanum Ferry: a simple ferry across the Connecticut River between Northampton and Hadley. It consisted of a ruddered platform which the ferryman moved hand-over-hand along a rope stretched from bank to bank. The ferry was used to transport passengers, goods, animals, and vehicles.

*October 9 1914 Fri.* Chem 9-1. I have visions of my free Sat. vanishing into the thin air. The class may be divided. Made a few calls after Fr. Practically everywhere "Nobody home"

*October 10 1914 Sat.* Spent A.M. at Libe. Cut lunch to do O'Shea for Ed. and stayed until after 3[508] Went down town Met Florence. She can't decide to leave Northrup [Northrop].[509] Studied Eng at Libe in eve.

*October 11 1914 Sun.* Oh you fire truck! Breakfast in A. Potter's. Finished "Hobhouse."[510] Went over to Tyler after dinner and read A King & No King[511] The Martins & the Philbins had a scrap.[512]

*October 12 1914 Mon.* Studied from 7 A.M. to 11 P.M. Scotch lit is a bore Read another play for Drama at Libe in the afternoon. Campus is an incentive to study.

*October 13 1914 Tues.* Marvōlous surprise. Drama written postponed until Mon. Had a nice interview with Prof Townsend.[513] No rain since Aug 28. Rumor that college will close fear typhoid & fires. $H_2O$ low

---

508   "O'Shea for Ed.": Jennie is reading a title by Michael Vincent O'Shea (1866-1932) for her course on contemporary education.
509   Opened in 1911, Northrop House was a Smith residence.
510   Leonard Trelawny Hobhouse (1864-1929) was a British political theorist and sociologist who wrote a number of influential works promoting social liberalism, including *Liberalism* (1911).
511   Tyler House: a Smith residence. *A King and No King*: a tragicomic play by Beaumont and Fletcher, first published in 1619.
512   "The Martins & the Philbins": the squabble Jennie here refers to could have been either a Clinton or a Smith spat.
513   Harvey Gates Townsend, Instructor in Education at Smith.

*October 14 1914 Wed.* Ebbinghaus test in Educ.[514] I finished last. Went to Miss Dale's recital with Marg 11.[515] Studied all evening Betty Reed spoke with Bertha socially a few days ago.[516]

*October 15 1914 Th.* Lab all morning and one hour in afternoon to finish up. French prose—It beats all how I have to recite. Wrote long letter to Dad in the eve.

*October 16 1914 Fri.* Lab. all morning. Flunked right and left in lecture recitation Called on Min after 3. First rain here since Aug 28. Read "The Abbott" all eve.

*October 17 1914 Sat.* Surprise of my college career. Amy Walker pinned me into Colloquium[517] Spent morning and afternoon at Libe reading plays. Serenaded at lunch[—]unique experience

*October 18 1914 Sun.* Up for breakfast and prayers Marguerite came to dinner. Pleasant reception in Edith T's room.[518] Called on Mary Martin. Studied all evening

*October 19 1914 Mon.* Classes. Ah yes! Fiendish written in Drama. Prof Schinz cut French 12:3 Spent afternoon at Libe. Education 2a is making me reflective.

---

514  Ebbinghaus test: a gauge of memory, developed by German psychologist Hermann Ebbinghaus (1850-1909).
515  Esther Ellen Dale was Instructor in Music.
516  Elizabeth Frances Reed of Greenfield, Massachusetts, Class of 1916, lived in Gillett in 1914-1915.
517  Colloquium member and Gillett resident Amy Walker was a senior from Albany, New York.
518  Gillett resident Edith Eleanor Tierney, a senior from Holyoke, Massachusetts.

*October 20 1914 Tues.* Classes. Scotch Lit grows more interesting as I know more when called on. Went to Catholic mission with house crowd. Life is only a preparation for death!!

*October 21 1914 Wed.* Live classes all day. Missed call from Lena and Louise—also dinner invitation.[519] Ada came over in the evening. She and Bertha had a long rel. argument

*October 22 1914 Th.* Chapel—Cash record system explained by Dean[520] Had a flash light taken for Panama Pacific Exp.[521] Bacteriology will drive me to drink yet. Worse and more of it! Miss McElwain read to us for one hour while we did Red Cross work.[522] Fascinating

*October 23 1914 Fri.* Faculty flash light after chapel. Girls made a line and took Pres B. home. Serenaded before he started on western trip. Lab 9-1 Set ether on fire. Martha Wells burnt[523]

---

519  Lena: possibly Lena Mary Cesare of Latrobe, Pennsylvania, who was a junior living in Clark House in 1914-1915.
520  Ada Louise Comstock was Dean at Smith College, later President of Radcliffe College.
521  Flash light: a reference to flash photography. The Panama Pacific Exposition was a world's fair held in San Francisco, California from February 20 to December 4, 1915.
522  Mary Belle McElwain was Assistant Professor of Latin. "Red Cross work" consisted of work parties to make mufflers, towels, bandages, and pillowcases for European war relief.
523  Martha Barron Wells of Roslindale, Massachusetts, member of the Class of 1917 and resident of Tenney House.

***October 24 1914 Sat.*** Marg is a Jr. Going down? Batted around with Rose Philbin all morning.[524] Had a shampoo, studied and called on Lena in her adorable little suite  With Ada to "Bunty Pulls the Strings"[525] Rotten.

***October 25 1914 Sun.*** Got up for breakfast. Read all day except for trip to station to see Rose off. "What is it to be Educated" is splendid.[526] Worth the price

***October 26 1914 Mon.*** Little written in Drama. Spent all my waking hours in the Library and accomplished absolutely nothing. Scotch Lit is deadly. Worst bore ever

***October 27 1914 Tues.*** Have been terribly blue all day  Got 7-37 in first Educ. written. 37 being the last  I am overjoyed nit![527] I'm getting tired to death of studying

***October 28 1914 Wed.*** Classes. Miss Scott thinks I am a perfect dub.[528] I hereby pledge myself to change her opinion next week. Went to Democratic Rally. Gov. Walsh spoke.[529] Shook hands

---

524  Rose Philbin, a teacher, was the older sister of Jennie's Clinton and Smith classmate Marguerite Frances Philbin.
525  *Bunty Pulls the Strings*: a play by Graham Moffat, later (1921) made into a silent film.
526  The 1914 book *What Is It to Be Educated?*, by C. Hanford Henderson.
527  "Nit": not. Jennie may have picked up this usage from German neighbors in Clinton.
528  "Dub": slang for a clumsy person.
529  David Ignatius Walsh, Democratic governor of Massachusetts (January 1914-January 1916); the state's first Catholic governor, and a Clintonian.

*October 29 1914 Th.* Chem Lab. all morning. Cut lunch to finish French comp. Read in Chem. Libe from 3-5. Bertha spent the evening with me. We studied—occasionally.

*October 30 1914 Fri.* Great achievement. Mark it all ye scientists. I wrote jurjurol formula correct and frightened the class.[530] Read "Venice Preserved" P.M. & eve.[531] Spent night at 17 with Anna

*October 31 1914 Sat.* Breakfast at 17—Returned to Gillett to find whole floor had been disturbed at my absence over night. Many plots had been contrived to shield the sinners  Went with Arlene to White's to have her picture taken.[532] Then to Lab for 2 hr. with Bertha. Matinee "The Darling of the Gods" with Arlene & Ada[533] The most elaborate spectacle over here.  Sophs gave house a swell vaudeville show for Halloween

*November 1 1914 Sun.* Up for breakfast—Cut prayers  Studied more or less all day. Six men to dinner. Much excitement—Student volunteers. Missionary vespers  Even the organ balked

*November 2 1914 Mon.* Much Libe and much disappointment over Fr. 12:3 books. Written in MacCracken.[534] Nice letter from Dad. Studied all evening. Caught cold

---

530  Jurjurol: furfural, a liquid inorganic compound.
531  *Venice Preserv'd*: an English Restoration tragedy by Thomas Otway.
532  The photographic business of Luther S. White was located at 52 Center Street in Northampton.
533  *The Darling of the Gods*: a play by David Belasco and John Luther Long. It was made into a film in 1916.
534  Henry Noble MacCracken was Professor of English Language and Literature.

*November 3 1914 Tues.* Classes until 3 P.X. [P.M.] Paid tuition, board and room, books etc and am clear with the world Went to 5 P.M. lecture by Miss Barbour.[535] Teaching is some job

*November 4 1914 Wed.* Classes 9-12. Bertha and I had special session with M.L.F. at 12. Studied until 4. Went with Gillett girls to Dr. Cabots lecture on social work of Mass. Gen. Hospital[536]

*November 5 1914 Th.* Aside from an hour in French I didn't think much about anything but Chem all day. Thinkin' doesn't write reactions. Studied with B. in the eve.

*November 6 1914 Fri.* Main occurrence of the day—written in Bacteriology. Result:—21/11 Mrs Wilder and friends of Sterling called at Lab.[537] Afternoon and eve at Libe

*November 7 1914 Sat.* Spent all the morning, all the afternoon and part of the evening at the Libe—French 12:3. Met "Aunt Mattie" and George. Everybody's knitting for Red-Cross gray mufflers

*November 8 1914 Sun.* Slept until 11 o'clock. Irene Long called with the girls. Went to Olive's tea in honor of Miss Pickett of Wellesley Bishop Davies at vespers.[538] Studied evening

---

535 Miss Barbour: Amy Louise Barbour, Associate Professor of Greek.
536 Dr. Richard Clarke Cabot (1868-1939) was Professor of Clinical Medicine and Social Ethics at Harvard and Chief of Staff at Massachusetts General Hospital from 1912 to 1921.
537 Ella Caroline Abbot Wilder (Mrs. Arthur Silas Wilder) of Sterling, Massachusetts, Smith Class of 1889.
538 Thomas Frederick Davies, Bishop of the Episcopal Diocese of Western Massachusetts.

*November 9 1914 Mon.* MacCracken written. Cut lunch to write résumés for French. Studied all afternoon and most of the evening. Mira and Grace had spread.[539] Ice cream fell out window   Bed at one o'clock

*November 10 1914 Tues.* Classes. At last have hopes of going home for Thanksgiving as I can arrange Eng. Φ with Miss Scott. Great excitement over De Voe's diamond[540]   She glowed

*November 11 1914 Wed.* Table 5 with a clicquey gang. Abb and Louise redeem it.[541] Terribly tired and annoyingly feverish—2 hr joke on Anna Potter   "Stag Inn" and "Stagger Out"   Fun until 11 P.M.

*November 12 1914 Th.* Chemistry once more. Abbie and I confessed. Anna's a true sport! Went to my first Colloquium meeting.    Pleasant   Started penance as proctor.

---

539   Like Grace Hovey, Mira Reed of Roxbury, Maine (Class of 1917) was a Gillett resident.
540   De Voe Elizabeth Holmes of Chicago (Class of 1916) was another Gillett housemate.
541   Abb (elsewhere referred to as Ab, Abbie, Abby): possibly Abbie Mae Stanley, a junior from Beverly, Massachusetts who lived in Baldwin House, or Abbie Anne Wilson, a freshman from Catonsville, Maryland and a resident of Washburn House.

*November 13 1914 Fri.* The thirteenth. M.L.F. says I ought to know more Chem to pass course. Got transfer to Miss Scott for Eng Φ Late for Fr. Schinz will pardon all for m. gen. of personne.[542] To pie factory with Lena[543]

*November 14 1914 Sat.* Up at 7:30 after 22 hr rest. Fever gone. Morning at Libe and Telegraph Office  P.M. Read "Rehearsal"[544] Anna and I walked up Dippy & around Bay State.[545] Called on A. McQuoid[546]

*November 15 1914 Sun.* Mira and Grace gave lovely breakfast party. Reed butter.[547] Went to dinner at Arnold Hall with Marg.[548] Stayed until 6:15 Exchanged confidences as regards J.R.M.[549]

---

542   "[M]. gen. of personne": my kind of person (fractured French).
543   The pie factory was apparently a magnet for Smith students. It was mentioned as something of a local landmark in "The Freshman Class History" of the *1915 Class Book*: "If all the weighty, lurid, 'invaluable' memorabilia acquired at an early date by 1915 were placed end to end, they would reach from the pie factory to Paradise [Pond]."
544   *The Rehearsal*: a satirical play of the 1670s, skewering the excesses of English poet, critic, and playwright John Dryden and Restoration tragedy.
545   Bay State Village, a section of Northampton.
546   Anna (Annie) McQuoid—daughter of Clinton barber Samuel A. McQuoid (born in Ireland) and his wife Mary (born in Germany)—was a Smith freshman in 1914-1915. She lived at 54 Belmont Avenue at school, 104 Beacon Street at home in Clinton.
547   "Reed butter": perhaps a brand name. (The New York company of Pettit & Reed—Charles Reed, President—dealt in butter, eggs, and cheese at the time.)
548   Arnold Hall is described in the *Smith College Monthly* for April 1898 (Vol. 5, No. 7), 340: "Arnold Hall, in connection with the Arnold Houses on West Street, was opened in February. It consists of one large and two small dining rooms, a hall for dancing, fitted up with a stage, and dressing rooms at one end; and will eventually have a bowling alley. It is the first thing of the kind for the use of the students outside of the College buildings, and will doubtless prove a great convenience for small dinners and dances."
549   "J.R.M.": identity not established; possibly Jim Martin (see diary entry for February 12, 1914, and accompanying footnote). "J.R.M." also shows up in Jennie's entry for April 13, 1915.

*November 16 1914 Mon.* Lead out of chapel with Amy Walker MacCracken written on the Rehearsal Studied all day except 1 hr at song trials 1918 leader Kept office for Min from 4:30-5:30 M. went to Holyoke Light cut

*November 17 1914 Tues.* What Is It To Be Educated? Classes. Marg's birthday. Alone in Scotch Lit. Pretty soft. Batted with Marg part of afternoon Studied in the evening. Light cut.

*November 18 1914 Wed.* Classes. MacCracken written Went to hear Mr Binyon read his poems The death of Adam most drove me to death[550] Studied all P.M. and most of evening

*November 19 1914 Th.* "Three hours of uninterrupted Lab. Quality not quantity—Get a wiggle on you." Spent the rest of day in deep study. Snow. Trip to Beckmann's at 9.

*November 20 1914 Fri.* More Lab. The last before Thanksgiving. Studied and loafed turn about the rest of the day. Fell asleep at quarter past nine. Even Joney![551]

*November 21 1914 Sat.* Chapel with Mira. Lots of our girls went to Yale-Harvard game at N.H. Had shampoo and read "The Abbott" all A.M. Downtown with Marg. Studied all evening

---

550 Laurence Binyon (1869-1943) was an English poet, dramatist, and art scholar. His poem "The Death of Adam" was included in *The Death of Adam and Other Poems* in 1904.
551 Joney: Jennie McLeod's college nickname.

*November 22 1914 Sun.* Mae Mitchell & M. Poole called.[552] Breakfast party in Amy's room. "Strange what we will eat here for breakfast" says Mira. Studied all day and until 12:15 Anna Potter discloses baser instincts!!!!!

*November 23 1914 Mon.* MacCracken written. Nothing particularly exciting all day. Read all afternoon and eve. Finished everything but Plato.

*November 24 1914 Tues.* The most unkindest cut of all. No MacCracken written but written sprung on Plato. Wrote on Religion in P. School  Home at 7:45 via Sp & Worc.[553] Delighted with "117"[554]

*November 25 1914 Wed.* Up by 8:30. Went downtown  Made yellow cretonne couch cover and pillows.[555] Helen sick a-bed. Mrs Duncan called in the P.M. Miss Fiske at night[556]

*November 26 1914 Th.* Thanksgiving. Stayed home all day. Alumnae beat H.S. in football  Howard got hurt.[557] Went to Somerset minstrel show with Dad.[558] Coarsest ever!!

---

552  Mae Mitchell: Mae Kehoe Mitchell graduated from Smith with the Class of 1914. In 1914-1915, Marion Chamberlain Poole of Hudson, Massachusetts was a senior who lived at 6 Ahwaga Avenue.
553  "Sp & Worc.": Springfield and Worcester.
554  "117": 117 Pearl Street, the McLeod family's Clinton address.
555  Cretonne: a heavy cotton fabric.
556  Ella A. Fiske, a Walnut Street resident.
557  In the Thanksgiving Day Clinton High School/alumni football game, Howard Needham injured his leg.
558  Clinton's Somerset Club put on a Thanksgiving minstrel show annually.

*November 27 1914 Fri.* Looked up St Andrew for Dad at the Libe.[559] Shopped rest of morning Ironed all afternoon. Aunt Mary & Mamie came down.[560] Back to Hamp on 6:45—arrived 9:40. Beckmann's with Dewares. Bed late

*November 28 1914 Sat.* Friday at college. Ye old Chem Lab once more 9-1. Fr 7 at 2 P.M. Studied rest of P.M. Turkey supper in Neugy's room[561] Spread given by Bertha & Hutch Swell feed and time. Called on A. McQuoid

*November 29 1914 Sun.* Slept until 10:30. Got up, took bath, read Buckle's history to Mildred and Bertha until 12:30.[562] Dinner. Read "Cato" for Drama.[563] More turkey. Fired as proctor

*November 30 1914 Mon.* Lectures in all classes. Suffering with neuralgia as punishment for back-platform trip back. Studied all day.

*December 1 1914 Tues.* Classes. Didn't get to sleep last night until 4:30 this morning. Went down to Bridgmans and viewed Minstrelsy of the Scottish Border[564]

---

559  St. Andrew: patron saint of Scotland. George McLeod belonged to Clinton's St. Andrew's Mutual Benefit Society. He presumably wanted information on St. Andrew in connection with a Society event. Libe: Clinton's Bigelow Free Public Library, at the corner of Walnut and Church Streets.
560  Mary McLeod Johnston and her five-year-old daughter Mary, visiting from Sterling.
561  Neugy (also spelled Neugie): identity undiscovered.
562  Buckle's history: the unfinished *History of Civilization* by English historian Henry Thomas Buckle (1821-1862).
563  *Cato*: a tragedy by English essayist, poet, and playwright Joseph Addison (1672-1719), written in 1712.
564  Bridgman's Book Store was located at 1208 Main Street in Northampton. Edited by Sir Walter Scott and first published in 1802, *Minstrelsy of the Scottish Border* is a collection of ballads.

*December 2 1914 Wed.* Written in Drama and in Education—Some writtens!! Hutch came over to see Bertha and we talked all P.M. Attempted Fr. Prose in the eve.

*December 3 1914 Th.* Studied yeast through microscope. Heard Mrs Foster's Agazzi story about the fish for the fourth time[565] Studied afternoon and evening.

*December 4 1914 Fri.* Unknown solutions of carbohydrates!—Climax hysterics  Called on Miss Childs at Pierpont Annex[566]  Spent evening with Grace & Mira

*December 5 1914 Sat.* Spent the morning in the Libe on French. Shopped most of the afternoon. Fooled around all night and got to bed at 1 A.X [A.M.] to-morrow

*December 6 1914 Sun.* Spent the day in bed and studied off and on. Much excitement about 11. At 12 Miss Spaulding Let us go to Arnold Hall fire.[567] Back 2:30

*December 7 1914 Mon.* Got back from fire at 2:30 A.M. Big fire—big crowd. Faculty losses heavy. Miss Mann lost manuscript for German book.[568] It's a wonder we went.

---

[565] Jennie is here referring to the Swiss-born biologist, geologist, and naturalist Louis Agassiz (1807-1873), who taught at Harvard and founded the Museum of Comparative Zoology there.
[566] Pierpont Annex: possibly a residence.
[567] Martha Reed Spalding was Head of House at Gillett.
[568] Myrtle Margaret Mann, Instructor in German.

*December 8 1914 Tues.* Classes all morning  Harry Lauder in Hamp.[569] Couldn't go on account of 2 o'clock class. B & I went to Lab 3-5. M.L.F. told me I would flunk the course

*December 9 1914 Wed.* Classes 9-12. Stood in line from 12-1 to see Dr. Gilman.[570] Got prescription filled, went to bed, ordered toast & tea and got chicken ice cream dope

*December 10 1914 Th.* Lab once more. Didn't get a chance to be the goat. Cut Colloquium meeting. Spent the night at "17" Mrs H was kind in asking me—Good sleep

*December 11 1914 Fri.* Had class book picture taken[571] Lab 9-12. Dr Gilman 12-1. Went to Fr 7 with 2/3 lesson done. Finished by working every minute in class. Shampoo. Fr. 7 for next week done.

*December 12 1914 Sat.* Slept until 9:30. Went over to Lab. M.L.F. wouldn't let us work. Told me she didn't think I would flunk. Walked with B 2-4. Libe 4-9:30 except 7:30-8  Saw Jim at Marg's

*December 13 1914 Sun.* Got up for breakfast and prayers  Faith Yeaw called during the morning.[572] Went up to Aunt Mattie's 76 Franklin for supper. All went to St. A. oratorio "The Messiah"[573]

---

569  Harry Lauder (1870-1950) was a popular Scottish singer and comedian.
570  College Physician Florence Gilman, at 33 Elm Street.
571  This is the photograph that appears in Smith's published *1915 Class Book*.
572  Faith Yeaw was a member of Smith Class of 1913.
573  The *Messiah* was performed by a joint chorus of Smith and Amherst students under the direction of Henry Dike Sleeper, Professor of Music at Smith, in John M. Greene Hall. The hall was filled to capacity.

*December 14 1914 Mon.* Unique opportunity. M. Brieux talked informally to Eng 12 on Blanchette.[574] No Fr 12:3. Brieux again in the evening. Stirring lecture.

*December 15 1914 Tues.* Classes all morning. No Fr 12:3 Studied at Libe all afternoon. Down town with A. Potter. Light cut until 12:30 to study for MacCracken to-morrow

*December 16 1914 Wed.* Pres MacCracken is to leave to become Pres. of Vassar.[575] Much chapel excitement. Fair to middlin written. Batted with Aunt Mattie all P.M. 75 West fire

*December 17 1914 Th.* Lab. Examined blue mould "Kept looking" for penicillium glaucum for 2 hr.[576] Studied laboriously for Chem written.

*December 18 1914 Fri.* Chapel with Marg. Chem written. Worse than the last. Spelled "brillantes" in Fr. 7 using Eng letters Sent Eleanor off the handle.[577] Light cut

*December 19 1914 Sat.* Spent the morning doing first of week lessons to gain time for much neglected Ed. paper. P.M. at Libe Christmas dinner. Studied all evening Light cut

---

574 Eugène Brieux (1858-1932) was a French realist dramatist. His play *Blanchette* (1892) was about a peasant girl educated beyond her position in life.
575 Professor MacCracken presided over Vassar College in Poughkeepsie, New York—then a woman's college—from 1915 to 1946.
576 *Penicillium glaucum*: a mold used in making some varieties of blue cheese.
577 Eleanor: one of many Eleanors at Smith in 1914 and 1915. The most that can be determined about this one is that she was in Jennie's French class.

*December 20 1914 Sun.* Breakfast and prayers. Studied morning and afternoon. Tea in library. Hildt & Wright here. Music. Hildt's ghost story. Xmas presents

*December 21 1914 Mon.* Classes. Spent afternoon and evening at Libe reading for Education paper. Louise is as badly off. Suspense is apalling [appalling].

*December 22 1914 Tues.* Classes. Miss Scott gave us each postals with our plaids.[578] Ed paper—Libe 3-9:30 Went to bed at 1:45. Got up at 4:15.

*December 23 1914 Wed.* Up at 4:15. With much help finally got off for classes. Left for home on 12:30 Boston special} Marg / Carolyn / Anna Home 3:15. Spent the evening "at home"

*December 24 1914 Th.* Up at 10:30 Spent the day going downtown to do all Christmas shopping for household Got all except college friends settled

*December 25 1914 Fri.* Christmas. Up at 10:30. Mr. Mitchell Bradford Eng. friend of Stanley's had dinner with us. Went to Mildred's to supper. Mr. H.M & I played cards

*December 26 1914 Sat.* Slept late. Read considerably. Went to movies with Mildred Punk show.[579] Almost froze to death Started a couple of guest towels for presents

---

578 "Postals with our plaids": postcards illustrating the tartans associated with particular Scottish family names.
579 "Punk": poor; inferior.

*December 27 1914 Sun.* "Sun[day] wears away the rust of all the week"[580] Sewed on guest towels all day. Boys and dad worked all day & ½ night thawing pipes

*December 28 1914 Mon.* Sewed and read. Finished towels and consequently ended Xmas worries. Got stung on 5:15 and took 6:45 to Sterling. Left from new station

*December 29 1914 Tues.* In Sterling. Pleasant day with Aunt Mary and the kids. Came home laden with presents & goodies. Rained "pitchforks"—Bad trolley. Met C.W.S.

*December 30 1914 Wed.* Spent afternoon and morning at store on the books T.H [Town Hall] 4.-5. Made fudge, read part of the Rivals & wrote Marg in the eve.[581]

*December 31 1914 Th.* Spent the morning at the store and the afternoon at the Town Hall on balancing ledger with warrant for the yr

# — 1915 —

*January 1 1915 Fri.* Not a resolution. Spent morning and afternoon on Road Dept. accounts. Typewrote dep't letter to Finance Comm. in the evening

---

580 The adage "Sunday clears away the rust of the whole week" appears in Richard Steele and Joseph Addison's *The Spectator*, No. 112 (July 9, 1711).
581 *The Rivals*: a comedy by Irish-born English satirist, playwright, and poet Richard Brinsley Sheridan (1751-1816).

*January 2 1915 Sat.* Slept late. Then went up to the hall. Also spent P.M. there. Spent evening with Marg, who has tonsilitis [tonsillitis] in the ear.

*January 3 1915 Sun.* Slept until eleven. Then read Rob Roy until 4.[582] Mildred came then stayed to tea and most of evening  Made candy sang! hymns, popped corn

*January 4 1915 Mon.* Slept until 9 o'clock. Called on Mrs. P. to pay rent. Went to T.H [Town Hall] cut lunch & worked till 4  Called with Maybelle at Comaskeys

*January 5 1915 Tues.* Slept until 10. Washed and ironed until 4. Called at Christine's  Miss Parsons there. Got "Broken Bowl" from Miss Smart.[583] Trusting it's a treasure

*January 6 1915 Wed.* Slept late for last time. Made fudge cake.[584] Called on Maybelle's teacher. Elmer came for me, took Marg & me to Clinton Jct for 2:45. Hamp 5:30. Batted Mira 11 P.M.

---

582  *Rob Roy*: historical novel by Sir Walter Scott, originally published in 1817.
583  "Broken Bowl": a poem by Scottish poet Jessie D.M. Morton (Mrs. Morton; born in 1824). "Miss Smart": Ellen H. Smart, age about forty, offers one possibility. Born in Scotland, she came to America in 1890 with her family, with whom she lived at 56 East Street. She was a weaver at the carpet mill, where her father George also worked. There are other plausible possibilities, as well.
584  Jennie McLeod's fudge cake was a specialty in which she took some pride. She submitted the recipe for it for publication in the *Clinton First Centennial Cook Book* (compiled and edited by the Young Adult Group of the First Methodist Church in Clinton, published in 1950).

John M. Greene Hall, Smith College

*January 7 1915 Th.* Of all sad words. Bacteriology Lab to start the term. All registered in J.M. Greene  Regular Spring Day. Got Helen's & Ada's pictures  Arlene & I called on Ada. Nice call

*January 8 1915 Fri.* Chem Lab—Fr. 7—Spent afternoon with Minnie. Went to bed at 7:00 and read Rob Roy until 9:30. Then to sleep

*January 9 1915 Sat.* Stayed in bed until 11:00  Read Rob Roy until lunch. Down town to pay bills. Called on Min & Marg. Bed 8:30. Florence called

*January 10 1915 Sun.* Stayed in bed all day. Slept until noon. Read Rob Roy. Had a tray for supper. Finished Rob Roy and read rest of evening. Mildred came over, spent evening—Love affairs!

*January 11 1915 Mon.* Classes. Spent most of afternoon at Libe looking up Scotch words. Wrote music to Four Maries.[585] Ice cream party. Grace, Mira, Phin, Marje

*January 12 1915 Tues.* Classes as usual Handed in Broken Bowl Read some Rob Roy criticisms in Moulton[586] Pres MacCracken bade Eng 12 farewell Mr Dodge attended class, didn't participate[587]

*January 13 1915 Wed.* Discussed Rob Roy. Louise and I both full of comment. Disappointed that Miss Scott is to discontinue Eng 25. Did Fr 7 at Libe 2-4:30. Fooled around all eve.

*January 14 1915 Th.* Bacteriology—Told M. Munsey that "emulsion is the bane of the chemist"[588] Read Leathes at Chem Libe after Fr. 7[589] Colloquium—Mr Warrell on sugar—"eats"[590]

*January 15 1915 Fri.* Lab 9-1—Said goodbye to everything. After much deliberation made out and handed in 2nd semester course card. Theatre "Mistress Nell" with A. Potter[591]

---

585  "Four Maries": an ancient and tragic ballad about four ladies named Mary who were attendants in the court of Mary, Queen of Scots.
586  Moulton: possibly Charles Wells Moulton's multivolume reference work *The Library of Literary Criticism of English and American Authors*.
587  "Mr Dodge": Lee Wilson Dodd, who took over English 12 (Modern Drama) when Professor MacCracken departed for Vassar.
588  "M. Munsey": Margaret Munsie, a senior from Leominster, Massachusetts, who lived in Dickinson House.
589  Jennie was reading one of the writings of British physiologist and biochemist John Beresford Leathes (1864-1956).
590  "Mr Warrell": probably David Elbridge Worrall (1886-1944), then Instructor in Chemistry at Smith.
591  "Mistress Nell": likely the play *Mistress Nell*, written by George Cochrane Hazelton (1868-1941).

*January 16 1915 Sat.* Fire drill 7:45 Bell stuck Chapel with F. Hanford. Then went back to house and spent the day in bed. About noon "broke my beads."[592] Got up for dinner. Went to bed at 8.

*January 17 1915 Sun.* Got up for breakfast. Feeling fine. Studied for Fr. 7 at Eleanor's all A.M. She came over in P.M. Called on Marg after supper. Studied with Laura 7:30-9:30. Called 331-R

*January 18 1915 Mon.* Mid-Years begin. Studied for Fr 7 at Libe all morning. Took exam 2-4. Rather difficile.[593] Read School for Scandal on a 12 o'clock light cut[594]

*January 19 1915 Tues.* Chapel with Amy. Spent morning at Libe doing Education reading. Spent afternoon and evening at Libe. Studied religiously

*January 20 1915 Wed.* Spent morning reading The Gamester and The West Indian at Libe.[595] Spent afternoon and evening there on various & sundry crams

*January 21 1915 Th.* Studied for Bacteriology at Libe all A.M. With Alice Richardson in my room all P.M.[596] Went to organ recital Studied all evening. Light cut.

---

592 "Broke my beads": possibly a colloquialism for a fever breaking.
593 Difficile: difficult (French).
594 *The School for Scandal*: a comedy of manners by Sheridan.
595 *The Gamester; The West Indian*: comedies by two English playwrights, *The Gamester* (first produced in 1633) by James Shirley, *The West Indian* (originally produced in 1771) by Richard Cumberland.
596 Alice May Richardson was a sophomore from Melville Village, New Hampshire. She lived at 6 Ahwaga Avenue in 1914-1915.

*January 22 1915 Fri.* Up at 6. Studied until 9. Took Bacteriology 9-11. Think I passed. Education exam 2-4. Dead cinch. Didn't get anything done all evening

*January 23 1915 Sat.* Spent morning and lunch hour on MacCracken. Exam 2-4 Worst ever. Almost sure I flunked. Bertha, Eleanor, Mira—Catholic Belief.

*January 24 1915 Sun.* Bertha & Mira brot breakfast to me. Marg came over after church. Hutch & Babes to dinner.[597] Read Poison [Poisson] D'Or[598] On candle shades before & after.[599] D. Sykes tea 9:30[600]

*January 25 1915 Mon.* Spent morning and afternoon at the Libe reading Poison [Poisson] D'Or and working on paper for 12:3 Light cut

*January 26 1915 Tues.* Got up at 5:30 and worked on paper until 10:45. Handed it in at Libe desk at 11. Downtown with Hutch. Ab got new Vic.[601] Corridor dance

---

597 "Babes": identity undiscovered
598 *Poisson D'Or*: an 1863 novel by French novelist and dramatist Paul Féval (1816-1887).
599 "On candle shades": meaning unclear.
600 Dorothy Louise Sykes was a junior from Malden, Massachusetts. She lived in Gillett in 1914-1915.
601 "Vic": Victrola—a phonograph made by the Victor Talking Machine Company.

*January 27 1915 Wed.* Holiday. Had to get up for breakfast because Dr Jordan called at 8:45.[602] Went up to Aunt Mattie's A.M. Loafed all P.M. Dinner at 17 Orpheus concert[603]

*January 28 1915 Th.* Slept until 11. New term started. No Educ. rest of week. Townsend ill. Schinz hashed over exam in Fr 7 Went to bed at 9:30.

*January 29 1915 Fri.* Got up at 11. This is the life. Fr 7 only class. Spent rest of P.M. in telegraph office helping Min make heart favors for valentine party.

*January 30 1915 Sat.* Up for breakfast. One year older No classes. Letters from all the family, relatives & friends. Escaped being sung to. House sleighride—20 went. Nice time at Abby's

*January 31 1915 Sun.* Slept until 10 o'clock. Babes came over and we did Fr 7 for Fri. Loafed all afternoon and evening Much happier birthday season than last

*February 1 1915 Mon.* English 12 for first time with Mr. Dodd. Very favorable impression—many like him better than MacC. Miss Scott's Eng 8 swell.

---

602 Jennie seems to mean the Reverend Doctor William Jordan—Congregational minister from Clinton—rather than Professor Mary Augusta Jordan of Smith, to whom she refers elsewhere in the diary as "Miss Jordan."
603 "Orpheus concert": concert by the Orpheus Club of Springfield.

***February 2 1915 Tues.*** Like new schedule fine—much more time. Scared out of a night's sleep by note from Mary E.—Eloc. 7.[604] Expect to see M.L.F. to-morrow.

***February 3 1915 Wed.*** Saw M.L.F. Got D+ in course but she doesn't think it will be a lasting disgrace. Took Vina to "Mlle?"[605] Went to Eloc 7 for first time. 4 in class

***February 4 1915 Th.*** Slept until about 10. Prof. Gray took charge of education class.[606] O you Greek History. "Emil's the guy who put the pep in peptone"[607]

***February 5 1915 Fri.*** "F. Ehrlich wouldn't lecture—give organ grinder a mark."[608] Slept late and went to bed at 2 A.M. à cause de B's German exam to-morrow.

***February 6 1915 Sat.*** First regular Sat. chapel date with Ada. Breakfast at Chocolate Shop. Met Alice R. batted together all A.M. Bot new skirt  visited 5 & 10  Saw Gillett & Northrup frolic stunts

---

604 Mary E.: the possibilities are junior Mary Emily Erwin from Worcester, who lived at 10 Green Street, and freshman Mary Elizabeth Elder of Amherst, a resident of 18 Henshaw Avenue.
605 "Mlle?": possibly a reference to Assistant Professor Clara Belle Williams, to whom Jennie refers as "Mlle. Williams" in her diary entry for April 8, 1915; or perhaps a reference to some type of production.
606 William Dodge Gray, Associate Professor of History.
607 A reference to German chemist Emil Fischer (1852-1919), who synthetically made peptones—water-soluble products of the partial hydrolysis of proteins—*in vitro*, and who received the Nobel Prize for Chemistry in 1902.
608 A reference to German physician and scientist Paul Ehrlich (1854-1915), who also won a Nobel Prize (1908). Ehrlich's thought processes were stimulated by the music of an organ grinder in the street.

"THIS IS THE LIFE"

*February 7 1915 Sun.* Slept until 10:30. Babes came over & we corrected Fr. Babes my guest at dinner. Went to tea at "17." Reg Jones came down 10:30. Stung B. Anna & I for singing "Good night"

*February 8 1915 Mon.* Chapel with Lois Evans. Classes as usual. Spent P.M. in Browsing room reading Balzac.[609] Mira says Rob't Louis Stevenson leads vespers next Sun.[610]

*February 9 1915 Tues.* Alice R went to Eng 12 with me I like Dodd better & better all the time Read Balzac 12-1. Bacon in Dic. Nat. Biog P.M. to eve.[611] Why? was that Dic. ever written

*February 10 1915 Wed.* After much cramming had Bacon life recitation. Irene Boardman made star speech on suffrage.[612] Went to "The Country Boy" with Alice.[613] Birthday letter to dad in the eve.

---

609 Balzac: Honoré de Balzac (1799-1850), French novelist and playwright.
610 "Rob't Louis Stevenson": a joke. Scottish writer Robert Louis Stevenson died in 1894. The Reverend J. Ross Stevenson spoke at Smith's vespers.
611 Jennie was reading about English philosopher, scientist, and statesman Sir Francis Bacon (1561-1626) in the *Dictionary of National Biography*, a standard multi-volume reference source on the lives and works of British worthies.
612 Remembered as the first Smith student to complete the college's four-year degree program in three years, Irene Boardman went on to a career in medicine and public health as well as to marriage and motherhood.
613 *The Country Boy*: a play by Edgar Selwyn; made into a silent film by Paramount Pictures, directed by Frederick A. Thomson, released February 18, 1915 (eight days after Jennie and Alice saw the play).

*February 11 1915 Th.* Read at home all morning. Educ at 12. Fr 7 at 2. In libe until 6. reading Balzac's Les Maranas.[614] Reed Hovey party at 9:30.[615] Broke fountain pen

*February 12 1915 Fri.* Broke alarm clock trying to have a short morning nap. Shopped with Eleanor after Fr. Bertha Alice R. & I had Welsh Rarebit party in the evening. O you stale orange

*February 13 1915 Sat.* Did French prose for next Fr. Babes & I are little heroes in that line. Class meeting. Met Marg on way to meet her promising young Boston lawyer. Libe all eve.

*February 14 1915 Sun.* Stayed in bed all day. Slept until 12. Read Virginius in the afternoon.[616] Babes came over. Rested all evening— all alone.

*February 15 1915 Mon.* Feeling O.K. once more. Quiz in Eng 12 by Mrs Conkling.[617] She's charming. Browsed 3-5. Little Babes & Joney spent the eve together. Bertha at concert

---

614   Balzac's novella *Les Marana* (1833).
615   Reed Hovey: junior Grace Hovey of Cambridge, Massachusetts lived in Gillett. Reed Hovey may have been someone related to her. Two other Hoveys living elsewhere are also listed in the 1914-1915 Smith *Bulletin*.
616   *Virginius*: a tragedy in five acts by Irish dramatist and actor James Sheridan Knowles (1784-1862).
617   "Mrs Conkling": from 1914 to 1947, poet Grace Walcott Hazard Conkling (Mrs. Roscoe Platt Conkling) taught English at Smith, from which she had graduated in 1899.

*February 16 1915 Tues.* Started in weeklong siege of chapel. Classes. P.M. in Libe reading The War and the Chem. Industry for Eloc. 7[618] Evening at Libe on Scotch ballads.

*February 17 1915 Wed.* Ash Wed. B. made five breaks I made one. B said "What's on yr. head M.K."[619] Spent afternoon at Libe on Eng D. Called on Miss Childs with Anna. Called on Arlene

*February 18 1915 Th.* Classes and Eng D. considerations. Spent evening at Libe. Haven't been going to bed strictly according to Lenten resolves. Must reform

*February 19 1915 Fri.* Worked on Eng D from 9-12 Cut Fr. 7 Went to Educ. Went to telegraph office at 1 Wrote like mad and finished paper at 5:42. Loafed all evening. Tired to death

*February 20 1915 Sat.* Chapel—shampoo—did Fr comp & general reading. Bertha went home. Went to sing. Babes & I down town Sent B 10 postcards Nuts!!? Batted together all eve

---

618 "The War and the Chemical Industry" was a journal article by American chemist and businessman Dr. William Henry Nichols. It appeared in *Science* (Vol. 41, January 8, 1915) and in *The Journal of Industrial and Engineering Chemistry* (Vol. 7, February 1915).

619 M.K.: senior Marguerite Florence Kennedy is a possibility (she lived in Gillett in 1914-1915).

*February 21 1915 Sun.* Slept until 9:30—Babes came over, had breakfast, corrected prose & read Émile.[620] Excellentes étudiantes!![621] Babes over all P.M. Walk. Spent eve at Northrup

*February 22 1915 Mon.* Rally Day.[622] Went to J.M. Greene for commemorative Wash. exercises. Die Journalisten wired news to Beany.[623] Batted together Latter P.M. Libe all evening

*February 23 1915 Tues.* Classes all morning. Spent P.M. at Libe. Bertha got back—wanted telegram deciphered!!! Spent evening at Irene Boardman's working on debate for Eloc. to-morrow.

*February 24 1915 Wed.* Resolved: That a general college education is preferable to a specialized training for a woman whether she is preparing for domestic or vocational activities

*February 25 1915 Th.* Mr. Townsend got back. To "Man does not live by bread alone" he replied "By their fruits ye shall know them."[624] Improved the day by studying assiduously at home—at Libe

---

620 The French treatise *Émile, ou De l'éducation* (*Émile, or On Education*) by Swiss-born philosopher, writer, and composer Jean-Jacques Rousseau (1712-1778), first published in 1762.
621 "Excellentes étudiantes": excellent students (French).
622 Rally Day: a Smith College tradition featuring an all-college gathering at which the president awards medals to distinguished alumnae, and a student rally. Rally Day had its origins in the college celebration of George Washington's birthday (February 22).
623 Die Journalisten: journalists (German).
624 A little student/teacher Biblical repartee.

*February 26 1915 Fri.* Spent morning at Libe reading Balzac in Browsing Room. Libe 3-5 Went to Kimball's lecture on the achievements of the Wilson Administration at 5 with Marg.[625]

*February 27 1915 Sat.* Chapel with Ada. Read all morning. Ed. only class. Wrote Dad in the afternoon  Babes & I went with Bertha on Soc. case[626] "Emma" Played together in the evening.

*February 28 1915 Sun.* Got up for breakfast. Babes came over and did French comp. Went to dinner at 17. Lolo and Marg also there. Supper in Arlene's room at Albright.[627] Mrs D's honor[628]

*March 1 1915 Mon.* Took Mrs. Deware to Eng. 12. Regular classes. Petit critique—Le Requisitionnaire at last done.[629] Read Mikado at Libe.[630] —Dressed up in Babe's clothes—visited Libe

---

625 "Kimball's lecture": Everett Kimball was Professor of History at Smith.
626 "Soc. case": from this and subsequent entries (March 10, April 20, April 23, and May 5, 1915), it is apparent that Jennie's friend and housemate Bertha was taking a course in the Economics and Sociology Department—likely either 5b, "Present Social Problems (dealing with "certain conditions affecting the welfare of the laboring classes, as immigration, housing conditions, and social insurance") or 7b, Advanced Sociology ("a critical study of the methods of social research"). Jennie's involvement in Bertha's coursework hints at her own interest in social issues.
627 Albright: a Smith house built in 1900 on Bedford Terrace.
628 Mrs. D.: Mrs. Deware (Arlene's mother).
629 "Petit critique—Le Requisitionnaire": a little review (or critique) of Balzac's short story "Le Réquisitionnaire" (French).
630 "Mikado": perhaps the libretto to the Gilbert and Sullivan comic opera *The Mikado* (music by Arthur Sullivan; libretto by W.S. Gilbert), which was first produced in 1885.

*March 2 1915 Tues.* Went down for "Telegram" before class[631] Clinton went dry and democratic—Not a single Republican elected.[632] In ill humor all day. Went to Jameson's Lect. on "Am blood of 1775"[633]

*March 3 1915 Wed.* Classes. Took Mira's friend to Eng 12 Couldn't recite in Eloc 7 on acct of cold. Slept all P.M. thru faculty tea. Schinz disappointed not to see Miss McLeod!!

*March 4 1915 Th.* Slept until 11. Deliberately lied to Mr Townsend. Told him I hadn't read lesson. Made up with Schinz. Senior marks came—Safe. Went to votes, hear Mrs. Kelley, Sec'y nat. consumers league on morals and the minimum wage[634]

*March 5 1915 Fri.* Attended Educ and Fr. Read On Report Comm. of 10 at Libe in the morning.[635] The only thing I can recall of the days doings—Moral don't delay diary 1 wk

---

631 "Telegram": the *Worcester Telegram*.
632 This complete defeat of Republican candidates in the March 1915 town election resulted in George McLeod's failure to secure reelection as a Road Commissioner. He later regained the position.
633 "Jameson's Lect. on 'Am blood of 1775'": a lecture on the role of ethnicity in American history by John Franklin Jameson (1859-1937)—historian, author, and editor of the *American Historical Review*.
634 "Mrs. Kelley": social reformer Florence Kelley (1859-1932) was the first general secretary of the National Consumers League (founded in 1899 by Jane Addams and Josephine Lowell to promote conscious consumer spending to support labor-friendly employers).
635 "Report Comm. of 10": The Committee of Ten was a group of educators working in 1892 under the auspices of the National Educational Association to make recommendations for standardizing American high school education. The *Report of the Committee of Ten on Secondary School Studies* resulted from this effort.

*March 6 1915 Sat.* Chapel with Ada and Arlene Studied and read all morning. Ed at 12 Went to basket ball game Freshmen beat Sophs again. Loafed with Midie & Grace all eve

*March 7 1915 Sun.* Up for breakfast. Went over to Babes & did Fr. 7. She and I went to Wallace to dinner with Neugy & Edna. Jane Addams at vespers with Hutch.[636] Arlene & I wrote to H.C.A. to make peace

*March 8 1915 Mon.* Classes 10-12 Dodd quiz by Mrs C. Libe 12-1 reading—Balzac—Vendetta.[637] Class 2-3. Libe 3-5. Went to Mr. Fays lecture on probable results of the war.[638] Studied all eve Light cut

*March 9 1915 Tues.* Regular classes. Dodd commenced Ibsen lectures—Splendid.[639] Wrote letter to Dad Studied afternoon and evening. Babes was over for the evening

*March 10 1915 Wed.* Practiced A Service of Love for Eloc[640] Didn't get time to recite. Review for next time Classes 10-1. Read Venus D'Ille to Mira[641] Went with Bertha on Soc visit. Light cut. Doll's House[642]

---

636 Jane Addams (1860-1935) was a major American social reformer of the Progressive Era. She was an advocate for settlement houses and a co-founder of Chicago's Hull House; a social worker and sociologist; a supporter of suffrage and world peace; a co-founder of the American Civil Liberties Union; and a recipient of the Nobel Peace Prize.
637 *La Vendetta* (1830): a novel by Balzac.
638 American historian Sidney Bradshaw Fay (1876-1967) taught at Smith from 1914 to 1929. He explored the causes of World War I in his influential book *The Origins of the World War* (1928).
639 Ibsen: Henrik Ibsen (1828-1906), Norwegian playwright and theater director.
640 "A Service of Love": a short story by American writer O. Henry—pen name of William Sydney Porter (1862-1910).
641 "La Vénus d'Ille": a short story written in 1835 by French Romantic writer Prosper Mérimée (1803-1870). It was first published in 1837.
642 *A Doll's House*: a three-act play by Ibsen, published and premiered in 1879.

*March 11 1915 Th.* Read "Lady from the Sea"[643] Classes as usual. Wrote to Mildred & Esther. Welsh Rarebit party—Grace Bertha & I. Cheese was stringy, B. nervous!!

*March 12 1915 Fri.* Read Munro, Clinton Courant & Town Report all A.M.[644] Regular classes. At 3 Geo. W. Kirchwey Dean Columbia Law School on law of nature & law of man.[645] Evening saw Saturn Heard Mrs Marion Craig Wentworth[646] Read the Sunken Bell[647]

*March 13 1915 Sat.* Chapel with Ada. Studied all A.M. Cut Educ. to attend Dean Kirchweys lecture: Law as Perfection of Human Reason  Spent evening in Browsing Room.

*March 14 1915 Sun.* Up for breakfast. Mira had guest from Clark school to dinner.[648] Did Fr with Babes and read all P.M. Supper at H. Irving Albright. Alice R spent eve with us.

---

643 *The Lady from the Sea*: another play by Ibsen, written in 1888.
644 Munro: perhaps a reference to Neil Munro (1863-1930), a Scottish journalist, newspaper editor, author, literary critic, and writer of short stories. Munro used the pen name Hugh Foulis. Jennie also mentions the work of writer James Phinney Munroe in later diary entries (August 24, 1915, and February 8, 1916). *Clinton Courant*: another Clinton newspaper, published—like the *Clinton Daily Item*—by William J. Coulter.
645 George Washington Kirchwey (1855-1942) was a lawyer, legal scholar, law professor at Columbia (1891-1901), Dean of the Columbia Law School (1901-1910), journalist, co-founder of the New York Peace Society in 1906, and president of the American Peace Society in 1917.
646 Marion Craig Wentworth (1872-1942) was an American playwright, poet, and suffragist. Her anti-war feminist play *War Brides* was published and produced in 1915 and made into a silent film in 1916.
647 *The Sunken Bell*: an 1896 play in blank verse by German dramatist and novelist Gerhart Hauptmann (1862-1946).
648 "Clark school": perhaps a reference to Clark College, opened in 1902 as the undergraduate liberal arts component of Clark University in Worcester.

*March 15 1915 Mon.* Studied all morning. Came home after 2 o'clock. Libe 4-5. Went with Mary to Bassetts lecture—forecast of Pres. election[649] Spent evening at Libe. Bed at 10 sharp

*March 16 1915 Tues.* Classes as usual. Libe 2-4 Went down town with Marg. Libe all eve Studied Miltons life with Eunice.[650] Bed at 10. Petite scène de larmes avec Berthe.[651]

*March 17 1915 Wed.* Practiced Eloc religiously 8-10 J.R. Crawford, Yale lectured Eng 12 on Strinberg & Bjornsen.[652] Batted all P.M. with Babes Watched Glee Club Jussere 6-8. Batted around house

*March 18 1915 Th.* Shampoo Fr & Ed 9-12 Written sprung in Ed. Went to Dean Kirchwey's lecture Present Indications of Legal Tendencies. Bed at 7. Read Lady Windermere's Fan[653]

*March 19 1915 Fri.* Read The 2nd Mrs Tanqueray & Michael and His Lost Angel[654] —and Ed. in all time free from classes 8-6 Attended Lady Gregory's lecture "Ireland and the Unseen World"[655]

---

649 John Spencer Bassett was Professor of History at Smith.
650 "Milton's life": the biography of English poet and polemicist John Milton (1608-1678), perhaps as presented in the *Dictionary of National Biography* (see Jennie's entry for February 9, 1915).
651 "Petite scène de larmes avec Berthe": a teary little scene with Bertha (French).
652 "Strinberg & Bjornsen": Swedish playwright, novelist, poet, essayist and painter August Strindberg (1849-1912) and Norwegian writer Bjørnstjerne Bjørnson (1832-1910).
653 *Lady Windermere's Fan*: a three-act comedy (1892) by Irish poet and playwright Oscar Wilde (1854-1900).
654 *The Second Mrs. Tanqueray*: a play by English playwright Arthur Wing Pinero (1855-1934). *Michael and His Lost Angel*: a play by Henry Arthur Jones (1851-1929), also British.
655 Augusta, Lady Gregory (1852-1932) was an Irish dramatist and folklorist and a co-founder of the Irish Literary Theatre and the Abbey Theatre in Dublin.

*March 20 1915 Sat.* Phi Beta Kappa announced 28 made it. Hutch among them. Studied & went down town to buy hdkf [handkerchief] for Devoe.[656] Gym drill in P.M. B & I spent eve in G's room She was at theatre

*March 21 1915 Sun.* No French to do. Got up at 12. Quiet dinner— the 4 of us at table 9 Read & loafed all P.M. In the evening B, Babes & I went to P.O. Escaped hdkf shower for DeVoe as Alice R called Freshies gave mock wedding.

*March 22 1915 Mon.* Classes as usual—Quiz in Dodd on Ibsen. Paid tuition, bd, rm & all bills Babes & I solicited votes for "The Road to Yesterday"[657] Read all evening in bed

*March 23 1915 Tues.* Classes and soliciting in all free time. Got about 300 votes in all. Went to H.G.S. Bed at 2 A.M. Bertha copied Eng D. Natalie's typewriter!![658]

*March 24 1915 Wed.* Chapel at 8:30 with Vina. Called on Aunt Mattie, packed, classes etc Off for Clinton with regular crowd & Mira on Boston special. Home 3:15. Bed at 9!!

---

656  "Devoe": De Voe Elizabeth Holmes (see the diary entry for November 10, 1914).
657  *The Road to Yesterday*: a comedy in four acts and six scenes by playwright, novelist, and screenwriter Beulah Marie Dix (1876-1970) and journalist, author, and playwright Evelyn Greenleaf Sutherland (1855-1908)—both Americans.
658  Natalie: probably senior Natalie Grimes of Portland, Maine, who lived in Gillett. (Natalie Carpenter of Watertown, New York—another senior—lived at 16 Belmont Avenue in 1914-1915.)

*March 25 1915 Th.* Got up about 8. Spent A.M. sewing for Helen. Downtown with Maybelle P.M. Made fudge & helped Gordon in the eve.[659] Annie spent night with me

*March 26 1915 Fri.* Slept until 9. Went down town with Maybelle at noon and again later. Gordon came down in the evening and played "Words that rhyme"

*March 27 1915 Sat.* Sewed most of morning. Went to a tea at C. Bowers. Attacked by grippe[660] Christine brot me home and excused me from supper engagement with her & M. Bates[661]

*March 28 1915 Sun.* In bed all day—sleeping mostly in day time and waking at night. Most horrible Paradise Lost dreams[662] 'Forewarned.'

*March 29 1915 Mon.* In bed all day. Nothing to break the monotony.

*March 30 1915 Tues.* In bed until 5 P.M. Stayed up rest of evening. Feel fine  Read "The Truth"[663]

*March 31 1915 Wed.* Sewed in bed all morning  Got up and dressed in the afternoon. Feel pretty fair.

---

659  Young Gordon Needham, who shows up in Jennie's diary entry for July 24, 1915.
660  Grippe: an old-fashioned word for the flu.
661  Marjorie (Marje) Bates was a member of the Class of 1911—Jennie's class—at Clinton High School. Like Jennie, she was enrolled in the college preparatory course at the high school.
662  *Paradise Lost*: an epic poem in blank verse by John Milton. Milton's treatment of the Biblical story of the Fall of Man apparently impressed Jennie.
663  *The Truth*: a play in four acts by Clyde Fitch, first performed in 1906.

*April 1 1915 Th.* Got up in good seasoned [season] Sewed and read "Ghosts" all morning[664] Went over to Armory with Ruth P. in P.M. Played pool. Went down to store in eve.

*April 2 1915 Fri.* Sewed some more. Finished "Ghosts" Started "An Enemy of the People."[665] Went down to the store and worked on books in the evening.

*April 3 1915 Sat.* Made a fudge cake. Sewed. Went down town about 11:30. Store until 3:00 Terrible snow storm prevented Marg coming to supper. All home all evening

*April 4 1915 Sun.* Slept until 12:30. Got up & made fudge cake. Maybelle elated with new Easter gown I made her. Mil & Eliz to tea. Went to Easter concert. Then to 75 Forest[666]

*April 5 1915 Mon.* Stayed home all day doing odd jobs—sewing, ironing, reading Went down to store about 4:30 but didn't stay. Called on Mrs. Shutts & Florence.

*April 6 1915 Tues.* Rainy. Went down town early. Into Worcester on 10 o'clock. Got suit. Lunched with Mildred & Merl. Home on 3:00 Supper at Esther's. "Suffragette" movy [movie] at Globe.[667]

---

664　*Ghosts*: a play by Ibsen, written in 1881, first staged in Chicago in 1882.
665　*An Enemy of the People*: another play by Ibsen (1882).
666　"75 Forest": where Mildred Hamilton lived.
667　"'Suffragette' movy": *Your Girl and Mine,* described in a Globe Theater advertisement in the *Clinton Daily Item* for April 6, 1915 as "a dramatic photoplay in 7 acts, produced under the auspices of the National Women's Suffrage Association, by the World Film Corporation."

*April 7 1915 Wed.* Got up about nine and managed to keep busy all day. Maybelle presented me some chocolate almonds. Back with C.W.S. on 6:45. Hamp. 10:40. Bed just after 10

*April 8 1915 Th.* Registered. Still have dizzy feeling, headache and no energy. Schinzy & Mlle Williams aren't back.[668] LeDuc is a boob.[669] Bed right after dinner

*April 9 1915 Fri.* Slept until 11:00. Attended classes and loafed rest of time. Ada & Mr Fitch called in the evening. Went to bed early. Studied till 10.

*April 10 1915 Sat.* Chapel with Ev. Warren having missed both parts of regular date. Read Émile most of the day. No Ed. Down town Babes & B. at 11. Bed at 7:00. Thunder storm 11 P.M.

*April 11 1915 Sun.* Couldn't get up until 12:00  Babes Hutch & Neugy Bertha's guests at dinner  Went to hear Hugh Black at vespers.[670] Bed at 7:00  Studied until 10. Noise in bthrm about 11 scared B & me.

*April 12 1915 Mon.* My well beloved first of the week classes once more. Saw Marg in Fr. 12:3  M. Dunne saw me with my friend.[671] Libe 2-6. Fire drill 10 P.M.  Peg Jones stung "us"[672]

---

668  Clara Belle Williams was Assistant Professor of Spoken English.
669  Alma LeDuc, Instructor in French.
670  Hugh Black (1868-1953): a Scottish-American theologian and author.
671  Freshman Margaret Recardia Dunne, a Gillett resident from Derby, Connecticut.
672  Gillett housemate Margaret Norris Jones, a junior from Wellesley Hills, Massachusetts.

*April 13 1915 Tues.* Classes. Studied from 9 till 3  Didn't do much in the afternoon. Too tired after standing in line for tickets for last night  Babes took "R" instead of a box.[673]  B. mad?!!  Saw "J.R.M."

*April 14 1915 Wed.* Had the great pleasure of hearing Mr. Canbie of Yale on "Oscar Wilde" in Eng 12.[674]  Spent P.M. with Marg at 39 West  Much house meeting in Anne Bailey's room until 10:30[675]

*April 15 1915 Th.* Routine Classes. "Reussir à dans notre jeunesse."[676] Miss Spalding spoke in house meeting of visiting the home of the girl with the larger vision

*April 16 1915 Fri.* Read Education assiduously all morning. Babes & I went to Libe from 3-5. Walked & missed dinner  Went to Sing. Then to Babes. Burglars at 12:30

*April 17 1915 Sat.* Went down town and then in to Minnie's until Educ. Read in the afternoon—Went to Eng Comm. Meeting.  Spent eve first with Evelyn & her woes—then with Grace

*April 18 1915 Sun.* Slept until ten. Grace rescued me with some breakfast. Went to vespers with Marg & some week end guests of Mary Martin  Called on M Deware, Ada & Mrs H with Arlene 7-10

---

673  "Babes took 'R' instead of a box": seemingly a reference to theater seating arrangements.
674  Henry Seidel Canby (1878-1961) was an American academic, literary critic, editor, and author. He is credited with offering the first courses in American literature at Yale.
675  Anne Kimball Bailey from Ipswich, Massachusetts was a sophomore living in Gillett.
676  "Reussir à dans notre jeunesse": to succeed in our youth (French).

*April 19 1915 Mon.* Classes 10-12. Schinzy cannot meet 12:3 this week and oh you devoir ecrit.[677] Went to driving park with Babes to count seats.[678] She came over 7-9:30. Bertha at Kreisler

*April 20 1915 Tues.* Classes 10-12. Canvassed nationalities with Bertha in the afternoon.[679] Went to Senior sing with her friend Miss Cochran.

*April 21 1915 Wed.* Took Mary Louise & Margaret to Eng 12[680] Dodd quizzed. Didn't have to recite in Eloc Babes, M.L. & I went down town. Marj Alden & I had M.L & M to dinner.[681] Gabrilowitsch with Marguerite—[682]

*April 22 1915 Th.* Studied all morning until Ed. at 12 Cut Fr. 7 to go to ballgame with M.L.R. Dr. Lawyers & Clergymen beat N. Players. Big crowd. Mary L took me to dinner at Boydens. Colloquium open meeting Dr Welsh of Goucher lectured on women in science.[683]

---

677 "Devoir ecrit [écrire]": duty to write (French).
678 Driving park: the Northampton driving park (an area with a racetrack for harness racing) was originally located about where the Industrial Park is now situated. The grandstand was moved from there to the fairgrounds for the local annual agricultural fair.
679 "Canvassed nationalities": possibly an assignment related to the Sociology course Bertha was taking.
680 Teacher Mary Louise Reilly was a visitor from Clinton.
681 Gillett housemate Margery Ames Alden was a freshman from Brockton, Massachusetts.
682 Russian-born American pianist, conductor, and composer Ossip Salomonovich Gabrilowitsch (1878-1936).
683 Physician, educator, and suffragist Dr. Lillian (Lilian) Welsh of Goucher College delivered the lecture "American Women in Science" in multiple venues as part of an initiative to encourage college women to take an interest in the sciences.

*April 23 1915 Fri.* Chapel with Grace. Studied all A.M. Went canvassing with Bertha in Ward 4. Supper at Boydens. Senior sing. trip to P.O. a bath and to bed. Didn't bat with Mary L. to-day

*April 24 1915 Sat.* Breakfast at Copper Kettle with Miss Reilly.[684] Batted with her until 12 at which time she left. Spent P.M. and eve at Libe. Bertha came in about 12 P.M. and gave me all the news of the Players last night

*April 25 1915 Sun.* Pretended to do considerable French reading all day with almost no success as we spent most of the time talking and bewailing our fates.

*April 26 1915 Mon.* An exceedingly busy day from dawn till late at night. Spent much time at the Libe still apalled [appalled] at thought of French paper and dramatique critique

*April 27 1915 Tues.* Studied hard all morning and cut lunch to finish paper for Fr. 12:3 Lunched at chocolate shop. Visited Min. Eve at Libe with B & Marg—Reread "L. W's Fan"

*April 28 1915 Wed.* Classes. Cut lunch to finish: dramatic criticism of Lady Windermere's Fan Got it in at 5. Showed Mrs B & Marlitta around.[685] Went to suffrage canvassers meeting at local headquarters. Fr at Babes until 9:30 spent night with Marg. at 39 West

---

684 The Copper Kettle Tea Room at 45 State Street in Northampton.
685 "Mrs B & Marlitta": Mrs. Anton Brockelman of 105 Prescott Street in Clinton and her teenaged daughter Marlitta, who entered Wellesley College the following fall. Mr. Anton Brockelman ran a flour, feed, grain, and produce operation with his brother Henry (a grocer), at 25 Sterling Street.

*April 29 1915 Th.* Spent morning with Marg at Libe  Ed at 12 and Fr. at 2. Then to Libe some more. Carride to EHamp. postponed[686]— thunder storm  The kids went to M.P.s and the martyr to Libe[687]

*April 30 1915 Fri.* Downtown shopping. Stormed all day  C.H. tower struck.[688] Left for home via Spfld at 3:23  Arrived in dripping rain about 8. Mr. Cushman etc discussing Arabian nights.[689]

*May 1 1915 Sat.* Missed Educ—Reason?—At home!! Went shopping in the morning. Sewed most all P.M. Mary Louise Reilly called. Went downtown with Mildred. Esther T engaged to Harold Hight[690]

*May 2 1915 Sun.* Slept until 11:15. Got up and went to S.S. for pleasure of being with J.A. Cushman. Mildred & Dorothy spent P.M. with us. Dad & I went to church to hear Dr J: on Minimum Wage

*May 3 1915 Mon.* Cut Eng 8, Eng. 12 and French 12:3  Downtown shopping and doing errands in the morning. Sewed in the afternoon  Read "Emile" all eve. No particular excitement

---

686  "EHamp.": Easthampton.
687  "M.P.s": Marguerite Philbin's (the martyr being, of course, the tongue-in-cheek Jennie).
688  "C.H.": College Hall.
689  "Arabian nights": see Jennie's diary entry for June 8, 1915.
690  Harold William Hight of Somerville, Massachusetts, son of Samuel Chase Hight and Statira Althea Thompson Hight, married Esther Belle Towne in Clinton on September 1, 1915.

*May 4 1915 Tues.* Cut Eng 8, Eng. 12 and French 12:3  Amused myself variously all day.  Did a little A#1 ironing and got Maybelle ready for M. Festival.[691]  Left C at 6:45, Hamp 9:12  Marg & Anna met me. Sweet girls.

*May 5 1915 Wed.* Classes all morning.  Spent afternoon at Libe and evening at home crabbing with Bertha over map and index cards for Soc. problem  Alice's fault

*May 6 1915 Th.* Spent morning and afternoon at Libe working on Fr. 7 and Ed.  Good resolutions for evening spoiled.  Read Harpers to Bertha Babes, Neugy & Agnes at Babes[692]

*May 7 1915 Fri.* Spent the day in the Libe with the books.  This is the life.  Hung skirt & Agnes Jones garden party dress before chapel and slip after coming from Libe at night[693]

*May 8 1915 Sat.* Lusitania sunk[694]  Spent most of the day in the Libe working on Educ. report 9-12.  2-5.  7-9:30  Have read so constantly I am well nigh blind.  Portland Players here but didn't go.

---

691  "M. Festival": May Festival.
692  *Harper's* was and remains a general-interest magazine, including pieces on literature, the arts, culture, politics, social issues, and economics.
693  Junior Agnes Christina Jones of Maplewood, New Jersey lived in Northrop House.
694  Despite America's official position of neutrality regarding the European War, the sinking of the Cunard ocean liner RMS *Lusitania* on May 7, 1915 inflamed anti-German sentiment in this country. En route from New York to Britain, the ship was torpedoed eleven miles off the southern coast of Ireland by a German U-boat. Nearly 1,200 passengers and crew members were killed in the incident, 128 American citizens among them. The Germans claimed (rightfully, it turned out) that the *Lusitania* was carrying ammunition, but the fact that it was not armed for battle caused widespread indignation and some justification for America's entry into the war in 1917.

*May 9 1915 Sun.* Up for breakfast. Bertha and I hashed over all Gillett. Hutch came over and I insulted her Φ.B.K. Got a little more done in the afternoon. Went to bed early & read drama

*May 10 1915 Mon.* Libe 9-10 and 12-1 on Eng 8. Classes the rest of the time until 3. Went over to Marg's until 4:30. Libe in eve. Read Herrick.[695] E. Waterman stung B. Marg & me for noise[696]

*May 11 1915 Tues.* Much like yesterday. Marg. fears Hutch may turn Catholic. Exams posted. Loafed all P.M. Went to Senior sing and then came home and read all eve.

*May 12 1915 Wed.* Prom and I needs must attend classes all A.M. and Educ. committee meeting 3-4:30 Went down in the evening and walked around Student's & Gym. Babes looked adorable.

*May 13 1915 Th.* Went on errands for Babes & Liz & got them off batting Dubious weather Came home after 3. Read, finished Fr, dictated ward 6 to Bertha. Unprecedented Gillett dinner for Miss Jackson—marathon to station for 9, 12 more Ret'd laundry case to Mary—visited informal at Gym.[697] O you Ethel[698]

*May 14 1915 Fri.* Busy all morning. Interesting French versification!! Not so's you'd notice it. Did some more work on the voting list. Also some drama.

---

695 English lyric poet Robert Herrick (1591-1674).
696 "E. Waterman": probably 16 Belmont resident Ruth Edith Waterman of Albany, New York, a senior.
697 Informal: a dance for which formal dress is not required.
698 Ethel was a common name at Smith at the time. As a Gillett resident in 1914-1915, sophomore Ethel May Frothingham of Portland, Maine is a possibility.

*May 15 1915 Sat.* Spent morning at Libe. Fooled around with Bertha until Hutch dragged her off. Called on Marg and spent rest of evening at Libe with Babes.

*May 16 1915 Sun.* Just missed breakfast. Spent the day reading the books I brought home from Libe—Complete Angler etc.[699] Downtown Neugie & Babes. Scrap over Hutch  Merry Xmas

*May 17 1915 Mon.* No Eng 12. Spent first 2 hr at Libe on French 12:3. After class dictated ward list to Bertha. Same monotonous diversion in the evening.

*May 18 1915 Tues.* Mr Dodd sets forth amusing criticism of G. Barker's Iphegenia at Tauris at Yale Bowl.[700] Minnie gave me rehearsal of the BIG SCRAP. Marg spent P.M. with us. More ward list—P.M. and eve.

*May 19 1915 Wed.* Classes all P.M. What is eloquence? A lecture following my Eloc 7 recitation  B & I late for lunch. Public reprimand & private apology. Downtown on errands  After scrap with Hutch & Neugie more ward list

---

699  *The Compleat Angler, or the Contemplative Man's Recreation,* by Izaak Walton (1593-1683).
700  The ancient Greek tragedy *Iphigenia in Taurus* by Euripides, produced by British theater director and playwright Harley Granville Barker (1877-1946) while in America in 1915. Barker was stirred by a visit to the Yale Bowl (capacity: 70,000) to produce Greek tragedy outdoors, in theater spaces similar to those of the ancient Greeks.

"THIS IS THE LIFE"

*May 20 1915 Th.* Stood in line for tickets for Forbes Robertson in Hamlet[701]—#486—excellent seats Swell fight with Wallace contingent. P.M. and evening at reg occupation i.e. ward lists

*May 21 1915 Fri.* Breakfast at Chocolate Shop. Morning at Libe— lost borrowed green silk umbrella. Bertha left for Boston 4:35 Lonesome!! Finished Suffrage canvas. Batted with Anna Called on Marg

*May 22 1915 Sat.* House picture at 8:15. Babes & I did commencement and other errands. 2nd floor bacon bat chez Edith & Marg.[702] Lasted until 10—mat squelched us

*May 23 1915 Sun.* Made breakfast on 59 sec of last minute. Babes & I spent morning on Mt Tom. Babes my guest at dinner. I came back at 9:30 to bring her home in the dark Ab, Pat and I went up to Alice's

*May 24 1915 Mon.* An eventful day in my life. Saw Forbes Robertson in "Passing of 3rd Floor Back" in P.M. and in "Hamlet" in the evening.[703] His last appearance in Hamlet. Never have seen such acting & interpretation. Bertha & I enjoyed it together in M 7 & 9

---

701  English actor and theater manager Johnston Forbes-Robertson (1853-1937), who was renowned for his interpretation of Shakespeare's character Hamlet. Forbes-Robertson was in Northampton as part of a farewell tour of the United States.
702  [B]acon bat: although Jennie lowercases "bacon" in her diary entry, she may refer here to discussing Sir Francis Bacon, who shows up in other diary entries from the spring semester of 1915.
703  *The Passing of the Third Floor Back* was a 1908 play and short story by English writer Jerome K. Jerome. It was adapted to cinema in 1918 and again in 1935.

Summit of Mount Tom, Holyoke

*May 25 1915 Tues.* Forbes Robertson spoke in chapel about his art and made a plea for attention to spoken Eng.—Girls made gauntlet machine & serenaded.[704] Then in the evening Dr. Anna Howard Shaw gave a brilliant convincing talk on equal suffrage[705]

*May 26 1915 Wed.* Conference with H.G.T.[706] Not flattering Mr. Dodd said farewell—happy lives pleasant vacation, successful exam. Went to Libe P.M. to work on Educ speech  Wrote Fr. in evening  Last prepared recitation in Smith.  made plea for new recitation Hall in Eloc 7—Best attempt of season

---

704  Gauntlet machine: the girls formed two rows facing one another, between which Forbes-Robertson passed.
705  Born in England, Anna Howard Shaw (1847-1919) was a women's suffrage leader in the United States, a physician, and an ordained Methodist minister.
706  H.G.T.: Harvey Gates Townsend.

*May 27 1915 Th.* Worked on Ed. paper all morning and gave it in condensed form "Man does not live by bread alone" Thoughts of Fr 12:3 paper already perplex me night & day.

*May 28 1915 Fri.* No Educ. Spent morning at Libe after breakfast at Chocolate Shop. Read drama critiques & digests all eve in Per. Rm while B roamed about. Bed 8 P.M.

*May 29 1915 Sat.* Read Hamlet by Laforgue in the A.M.[707] Barbe Bleue and Balzac's Vendetta in the P.M.[708] Put the "P" in Northampton in the eve, went down town & fooled around

*May 30 1915 Sun.* Up for breakfast. Didn't do much all day save drama notes off & on. The "old girls" at supper at "17." Had a talk with Helen Irving. Pleasant reunion

*May 31 1915 Mon.* Memorial Day. Fooled with B and went to Libe for good 2 hr. work. Lunch in my room. Bertha, Hutch & Neugie— Asparagus etc. Did a few more drama notes. Sleepy

*June 1 1915 Tues.* The Big Day—by dint of cutting lunch got 12:3 paper in at 2:15. Spent ½ hr on Extempore speech—"best thing I ever did!" Went to bed immediately after dinner

---

707 Born in Uruguay, Jules Laforgue (1860-1887) was a French Symbolist poet. Written in 1885 and published in 1887, his *Moralités légendaires*—a collection of "prose poems"—included a piece titled "Hamlet ou les suites de la piété filiale."
708 Barbe Bleue: the folktale "Bluebeard" in French, likely in the version of Charles Perrault.

*June 2 1915 Wed.* Studied at home all morning for Eng 12. Exam 2-4. Nicest ever. Did various errands with Bertha and loafed for the most part as I couldn't get book

*June 3 1915 Th.* Spent morning 9-12 at Libe on Education. Discussion with R. Painter & Etta B from 12-1.[709] Exam 2-4. Studied Bacon & Milton quotations all evening

*June 4 1915 Fri.* Studied French Prose all AM while Bertha ended up exams with U.S. Hist after an all night seige [siege]. Fr 7. 2-4. Hated it Met Schinzie in Libe. Studied for Eng. 8.

*June 5 1915 Sat.* Eng 8 9-11 ended my college exams. Liked the exam very much. Went to Mt. Park with Grace—Roller coaster, merry go-round and—Penny Arcade!![710] Movies with Babes

*June 6 1915 Sun.* Went to bed at 3:15 this A.M. Got up about ten. Breakfast at 12 at Alumnae House with Bertha.[711] Left Hamp at 1:20 with M. Deware—via Spfld & Worc—home 5:30. Bed 1:45

---

709 Gillett seniors Rebecca Painter from Kittanning, Pennsylvania and Etta Taylor Boynton from Warren, New Hampshire.
710 Penny arcade: an indoor amusement venue featuring coin-operated games, booths, shows, and other entertainments. The term came into popular use between 1905 and 1910.
711 Alumnae House: in 1915, Smith's Alumnae House was on the second floor of College Hall (Lincoln and Pinto, 155).

*June 7 1915 Mon.* Went into Worcester at 10 and got out at 7. Got Commencement dress & evening dress. Lunched with Mildred. Heard O. Stone Mrs George & Miss Dorman on anti suffrage[712]

*June 8 1915 Tues.* Spent the day in Worcester. Would to my patience Commencement clothes were settled. Lunched at Louise K. Sprague's. Brotherhood play An Arabian Dey.[713] I read the prologue and served as prompter

*June 9 1915 Wed.* Didn't do much of anything all day but several errands downtown. Went to Sterling with Dad in the machine. Supper at Aunt Mary's. Esther down in the evening

*June 10 1915 Th.* Busy all day. Esther T down to lunch. Mrs Kittredge helped me all P.M. with silk slip.[714] Telegram from B—Everything O.K. Left C 6:45—Hamp. 9.27. Babes & B met me.

---

712 The Clinton branch of the Women's Anti-Suffrage Association of Massachusetts held the meeting to which Jennie refers in the Music Hall of Clinton's Town Hall on the evening of June 7, 1915. As described on the front page of the *Clinton Daily Item* for that day, the meeting was the first "of the local campaign against the adoption of the proposed constitutional amendment calling for woman suffrage." (The amendment failed when it came to a vote on November 2, 1915.) Clinton attorney Orra L. Stone (1873-1961) introduced anti-suffragist speakers Marjorie Dorman and Alice N. George (Mrs. A.J. George). At the time, Stone was private secretary to Republican Congressman Calvin D. Paige of Southbridge. Much later, he became editor of the *Clinton Daily Item* and the *Clinton Courant*.

713 The Congregational Brotherhood presented *An Arabian Dey*—a travesty in four acts by James A. Cushman and Waldo T. Davis—in the vestry of the First Congregational Church.

714 There were a number of Mrs. Kittredges in Clinton in 1915. The local directory for that year describes Mary Kittredge of 63 Beacon Street as a dressmaker, but it is doubtful that she was Jennie's Mrs. Kittredge. In the 1910 federal census, weaver Mary E. Kittredge at that address is identified as single.

*June 11 1915 Fri.* Breakfast at Boydens with Bertha & Neugie. Did errands and finished silk slip. Went to Plaza. Bertha Babes & Neugie. Bed about one o'clock. Sold dramatics tickets

*June 12 1915 Sat.* Last chapel—went with Lolo. Worked on ward lists. Miss Reilly called  Sold tickets for dramatics as Bertha had a cold & I was tired $3.00 each. Pretty soft.

*June 13 1915 Sun.* Up for breakfast. Took Mrs. Smith over campus.[715] Baccalaureate sermon in P.M. #72 with Hyla Watters.[716] Bertha couldn't go on account of her cold.  Loafed all evening

*June 14 1915 Mon.* Ivy Day. Got place #129R on the last minute. Terribly hot. Planted Ivy at Libe. Illumination night ideal. Cried myself to sleep because the family aren't coming

*June 15 1915 Tues.* Commencement Day. Got our little Dips and think we're educated.[717] #80R Spoiled solemn march by going two aisles too far. Met H.A.S. Like him ever so much  Class supper a bore.  21 engagements announced.  Bertha did not run around table

*June 16 1915 Wed.* Babes left at 8:25. Went to Boydens for breakfast with B & Neugie  N. Dead Broke  N & Hutch left 12:40. Did errands all P.M. B went to dinner with Miss Layton.[718] I went to 17. Bed 4:30 A.M.

---

715  There were six Smiths in Jennie's graduating class.
716  Hyla Stowell Watters of Atlanta, Georgia.
717  "Dips": diplomas.
718  Probably Katherine Alberta W. Layton, Instructor in German.

*June 17 1915 Th.* Awakened by thunder storm. Couldn't get Bertha to wake up and thot she was struck.[719] Up about 9:30. Breakfast at Boyden's. Packed and finished errands. Missed 4:35. Bertha and I left Hamp at 6:00 Spfld at 7:26. Had dinner on diner. Said goodbye at Worc. Hated to leave Bertha more than anyone else. Home via electric 10 P.M.

*June 18 1915 Fri.* Stayed home all day helping in cake and candy-making for neighborhood surprise party on Maybelle. Complete. Kids nearly sent insane

*June 19 1915 Sat.* Slept late. Didn't do much of anything all day. Just stayed at home Went downtown to do a few family errands in the evening.

*June 20 1915 Sun.* Slept until 12:30. Autoing with family to Hudson Bolton Lanc. "The little Ford just rambled right along"[720] Called on Philbins. Read & wrote letters all eve.

*June 21 1915 Mon. and June 22 1915 Tues.* No entries

*June 23 1915 Wed.* Went downtown and got blue linen and silk for smock for Maybelle. Cut it out and worked on it all P.M. and all evening.

---

719 "Thot": Scots variant of "thought."
720 "And the Little Ford Rambled Right Along": a song recorded in 1915 by singer Billy Murray.

*June 24 1915 Th.* Worked on baby's smock all A.M and finished it about 3 P.M. Dressed her up in it and took her down town. Read "Arms and the Man" in the eve.[721]

*June 25 1915 Fri.* Finished "Arms & the Man." Visited Maybelle's teachers to get instruction for tutoring her. Got green linen & worked on smock for Helen all P.M. and eve.

*June 26 1915 Sat.* Went down to store morning and afternoon as Helen went on Union S.S. picnic.[722] Finished smocking on H's smock Movies with Mildred at night.

*June 27 1915 Sun.* Slept until noon. Dressed up in my Commencement gown for dinner to give the family a treat. Rain prevented taking Philbins out. Spent evening there

*June 28 1915 Mon.* Spent morning and afternoon at store—Finished Helen's smock and Read 3 chapters of Wilcox "American City"[723] Read another act of "You Never Can Tell" evening at home[724]

---

721 *Arms and the Man*: a comedy by Irish playwright, critic, and polemicist George Bernard Shaw (1856-1950), first produced in 1894.
722 In 1915, the Union Sunday School festivities opened with a parade, following which some 700 day-trippers headed for Washacum Park in Sterling on a special nine-car train.
723 Delos Franklin Wilcox (1873-1928) was an authority on municipal government. His *The American City: A Problem in Democracy* was published in 1904.
724 *You Never Can Tell* (1897)—a four-act play by Shaw.

*June 29 1915 Tues.* Read The American City at store all morning. Little party P.M. at C. Bowers for L.K. Sprague. Hemmed napkins for Alice Lee.[725] H.S. grad with Eliz H. eve. Herbert Parker the speaker[726]

*June 30 1915 Wed.* Helped Mary Kittredge on sq. root[727] Bowled at Armory with Christine & K. Leeper  Finished "You Never Can Tell" and read "Mrs. Warren's Profession."[728] Dad joined B.P.O.E.[729]

*July 1 1915 Th.* It rained all day. Worked around house—dusting, hanging pictures & ironing  Read "The Philanderer."[730] Maybelle delights household by devotion to "Nicholas Nickleby"[731]

*July 2 1915 Fri.* More rain. Sewed, ironed, cooked, puttered around and read "American City."

*July 3 1915 Sat.* Downtown shopping in the morning. Helped with the finishing touches at home. Dad & I met Cath & Aunt Mary at 3:17 and Uncle Andy at 7:30 P.M.[732] Some reunion

---

725  One of two Alice A. Lees living in Worcester at the time, probably the one who was a teacher at the Oxford Street School there.
726  Herbert Parker (1856-1939) was a Lancaster lawyer and a Republican politician who served as the Attorney General of Massachusetts from 1902 to 1906.
727  Conceivably Mary M. Kittredge, teen-aged daughter of Michael A. Kittredge of 123 Franklin Street, but there are other possibilities.
728  *Mrs. Warren's Profession*—a play by Shaw (written in 1893, first performed in 1902).
729  B.P.O.E.: the Benevolent and Protective Order of Elks, a fraternal and social organization.
730  *The Philanderer*—another play by Shaw, also written in 1893, first produced in 1902.
731  *Nicholas Nickleby*: a novel by English writer and social critic Charles Dickens (1812-1870), first published serially 1838-1839.
732  As in 1914, the McCances were Fourth of July guests of the McLeods.

*July 4 1915 Sun.* Slept late—just for a unique experience. By auto to Leominster thru Clinton by Sterling—return thru Lancaster. Loafed about all evening.

*July 5 1915 Mon.* More rain. Poor Eagles.[733] Up at 9. Went to parade. Stayed home all day. Made fudge and read all P.M. General assembly in the evening for fireworks at G. Howards[734]

*July 6 1915 Tues.* Up early to say good-bye to Uncle Andy. Spent the rest of the day reading, eating and sleeping.

*July 7 1915 Wed.* Another day of sleeping, eating reading and talking. Dad took us out in the evening to relieve the monotony. Lanc—Bolton—Hudson—Berlin—Clinton

*July 8 1915 Th.* Rained hard all day long. Down street in the morning and got drenched. Sewed on white skirt for Helen while Cath smocked green middy.[735]

*July 9 1915 Fri.* Sewed almost all day. Snapshots back from Niquette's ("Can't hand them a thing") Went out with Dad Mother & Aunt Mary spent evening at Duncan's

---

733 "Eagles": the Fraternal Order of Eagles. Heavy rain reportedly did not impact the State Grand Aerie in Clinton in 1915—"Eagles Have Their Annual Field Day," *Clinton Daily Item*, July 5, 1915. The Wachusett Aerie of Eagles met regularly in Clinton.
734 "G. Howards": George S. Howard—a teller at the First National Bank in Clinton—lived on Leighton Avenue (a street located between and parallel to Pearl and Water Streets) in 1915. He was a son of Frank E. and Ella Howard of Cedar Street. Frank and his brother Walter operated a livery, hack, feed, boarding, and sales stable on School Street.
735 Middy: a woman's or child's loose blouse with a sailor-type collar.

"THIS IS THE LIFE"

*July 10 1915 Sat.* Sewed whatever part of the morning remained after we got up. Went with Dad to dble header Ladies Day baseball game. Downtown & up to Esther Towne's in the evening.

*July 11 1915 Sun.* Slept late. In the afternoon went autoing. Milkshakes at Italian store in Hudson Went to Concord. Saw historic pts.[736] Home via Littleton, Harvard & Lanc. Mildred called in the evening

*July 12 1915 Mon.* Sewed and read all day. Went to opening piazza party of the season at Miss Stevens. Doomed to serve on committee two weeks hence.

*July 13 1915 Tues.* Sewed and read most of the day. Went shopping in the afternoon Short auto trip out Shirley Road. "Beware of the Dogs."

*July 14 1915 Wed.* Catherine was sick a-bed all day. I made skirt of dress for Maybelle in the A.M. Solicited boys & girls for Chautauqua parade.[737] Agreed to serve also on Jr. Chautauqua Committee[738]

---

736  The McLeods would certainly have visited Concord's North Bridge area (now part of Minute Man National Historical Park), where Colonial resistance on April 19, 1775 marked the beginning of the American Revolution. They may also have stopped to view sites connected with Concord's nineteenth-century authors—Emerson, Thoreau, Hawthorne, and Louisa May Alcott—and their literary associates.

737  A parade on the afternoon of Monday, July 19, the opening day of the Chautauqua in Clinton in 1915. All who participated were admitted to the afternoon's Chautauqua events free of charge. About 600 children took part (200 boys and 400 girls, according to the report in the *Clinton Daily Item* for July 19). In addition to children's organizations, the Clinton Hospital and the local women's suffrage league were also represented in the parade, along with a number of prominent Clintonians in automobiles.

738  "Jr. Chautauqua Committee": Jennie was involving herself in a Junior Chautauqua program that ran through the school year ("Chautauqua Once More," *Clinton Daily Item*, July 26, 1915)—see her diary entry for July 23, 1915.

*July 15 1915 Th.* Still faithful to the quest for the 50 youths & 50 maidens. Result only about half through. Aunt Mary left at 5:18 Went for short ride. Canvassed all evening

*July 16 1915 Fri.* Catherine sewed while I scouted about for Chautauqua Brigaders in A.M. Went downtown shopping & scouting in afternoon. Went to bed early & read

*July 17 1915 Sat.* Finished up brigade canvas [canvass] interviewed comm. & Mr. Atkinson, the parade man.[739] Made skirt for mother. Went over to N. Lanc in auto at 9 P.X [P.M.] to cool off

*July 18 1915 Sun.* Cath, Dad & I took Mr. & Mrs. Irving Johnson to Bare Hill.[740] Went to SS in Mrs Donald's class. Read all P.M. Went to church in the evening. Then autoing.

*July 19 1915 Mon.* Answered telephone all morning Road [Rode] with Jr. Chautauqua committee in Tally Ho at parade.[741] P.M. Dunbar Sing. Orch Mrs Gregory "Folk lore of the South & Cabin Day in Dixie["] Eve. Dunbars & Dr Cronin "Weeds & Flowers of Literature."[742] 2 thunder storms

---

739 Mr. Atkinson: Paul G. Atkinson, an outside Chautauqua organizer.
740 In 1915, Irving E. Johnson was Superintendent of Roads in Clinton.
741 "Tally Ho": as reported in the page-three article "Receipts Are Over $1400" in the *Clinton Daily Item* for July 19, "Eight young ladies rode in Howard's brake," followed by the boys and girls.
742 As with the Chautauqua program for 1914, the program offerings for the 1915 season were covered in-depth in the *Clinton Daily Item*, in the issues for July 19 through July 26.

*July 20 1915 Tues.* Attended Jr. Chautauqua, sang, folk danced & selected cast for Jr. Play. P.M. Mr & Mrs Michitaro Ongawa in "Along the Road to Tokyo" Mrs Gregory continued subject of yesterday. Polly Parker made surprise visit. Scared out of a weeks growth for fear she would accept invitation to supper  Marg stayed. Japanese in eve gave an afternoon in Japan. Germain the magician mystified us

*July 21 1915 Wed.* Jr. Chautauqua 9-12. Afternoon Mrs Gregory read with remarkable brilliancy "In the Vanguard" Miss Lacey told Billy Brad at P.M. session[743] Sackett Florence Trio & Paul Pearson "Who Is Great"

*July 22 1915 Th.* Jr. Chautauqua 9-12. Miss Lacey & Miss Kerr have captivated the children's hearts[744] P.M. Mrs. G—"The Value of Story Telling in the Home" Victor's Italian Band & Venetian Troubadours

*July 23 1915 Fri.* Jr. Chautauqua 9-12. Winter contract well under way.[745] Mrs G's series lecture on "Prose & Poetry of Dunbar." McKinnie Operatic Co. Dr Thos E. Green "The Burden of the Nations"

---

743 Miss Lacey: Ruth Lacy was the Junior Chautauqua leader, as reported in the piece "Chautauqua Once More" in the *Clinton Daily Item* for July 26, 1915.
744 Miss Kerr: Margaret Kerr, Ruth Lacy's assistant ("Chautauqua Once More").
745 The article "Chautauqua Once More" included the following: "It has been definitely settled that there will be a Junior Chautauqua this winter, which will probably begin about the time the school sessions start ... It is hoped that some of the local young ladies will be sufficiently interested so that the children may meet oftener than once a month to listen to stories, play games and hear talks ... The purpose of the winter Chautauqua is supervised play for the children of the Junior Chautauqua throughout the year, and to carry through the year an effective organization."

*July 24 1915 Sat.* As Chas Brown says "The seven Joyous Days are almost over.["]⁷⁴⁶ Jr. Chau. all morning. "Average Town" play by children. "The Friends of Yesterday" by Mrs LaSalle Corbell Pickett. "Strollers Quartet" ["]Twelfth Night" by the College Players. Jr. Winter Chautauqua contract completed & presented to Miss Lacey by G. Needham⁷⁴⁷

*July 25 1915 Sun.* Slept until 10:30  Went to Leom to Dinner in a hurry. Chautauqua closing session 2:30.  Signed contract for winter Jr. Chautauqua in Miss Lacey's presence  Met Dr. Turner.⁷⁴⁸  He delivered address. Miss Stevens gave a Bible story. Went up to Sterling and spent the evening at Mary's

*July 26 1915 Mon.* Finished Maybelle's dotted muslin  Reported Jr. Chautauqua summer & winter proceedings to R. Finan.⁷⁴⁹  Didn't go up to Miss Stevens on account of rain. Early to bed. 9:40 P.M.

---

746  "[S]even joyous days": a commonly-used phrase in referring to Chautauqua.
747  Gordon Needham, age eleven, was a son of Charles A. Needham, Chairman of Clinton's Board of Selectmen. In 1915, the Needhams lived at 117 Pearl Street, a multi-family home where the McLeods also lived.
748  Dr. A.E. Turner was a frequent presenter on the Chautauqua circuit.
749  Ruth Finan, who was around Jennie McLeod's age, worked for the *Clinton Daily Item*. Her parents William (a blacksmith of Scottish descent) and Sarah lived on Main Street. In addition to reporting on Junior Chautauqua for the paper, Jennie also kept a record of the funds she collected for it in the "Memoranda" pages at the end of her diary.

*July 27 1915 Tues.* Ironed most of the forenoon. Hung around house all afternoon. Got Simmons Catalogue from Carolyn & studied course BII.[750] Band concert. Street roped off for dancing[751]

*July 28 1915 Wed.* Finished up odds & ends and packed Called on Mrs. Duncan on way to train. Left with Catherine at 3:29.[752] "32" about 5:30.[753] Swapped Chautauqua tales for N.Y. tales with Aunt Mary & Uncle Andy

*July 29 1915 Th.* Slept late. Mimi brot the neighborhood in to greet Cath & be rewarded by stories.[754] C & I went to Shawmut with all the Desautels.[755] Mary Watson spent P.M. & eve. here

*July 30 1915 Fri.* More visits from the kids & more stories I went house hunting with Teta.[756] Put Mimi to bed & told her stories. Played Casino with Teta Aunt Mary & Uncle Andy until Mrs Myers ret'd[757]

*July 31 1915 Sat.* Visits at intervals all day from the neighborhood children. Catherine & I did the regular Sat. errands. Batted around in the mist with the Desautels in the evening

---

750 The Simmons catalog Jennie perused describes Course BII as a one-year secretarial program—including shorthand and typewriting—for college graduates.

751 "Dancing in Clinton Street," an article on the front page of the *Clinton Daily Item* for August 30, 1915, opened with the following: "Dancing in the public street at a public concert is something new in New England but it has been most successful under the auspices of the Chamber of Commerce."

752 Catherine McCance remained with the McLeods through Junior Chatauqua, with which she—like Jennie—assisted.

753 "32": the McCance home at 32 Sherman Street in Roxbury.

754 "Mimi": four-year-old Miriam Myers (daughter of McCance neighbors Mr. and Mrs. Harry Myers).

755 Desautels: Sherman Street neighbors of the McCances.

756 "[H]ouse hunting": the McCances were looking for another apartment.

757 Casino: a card game.

*August 1 1915 Sun.* More bad weather. Read most of the morning while Cath repaired bead chains  While the elder members went to Brookline the boys took Cath & me to movies at the "Boston"[758]

*August 2 1915 Mon.* Still raining. Catherine and I went to Dorchester and spent afternoon with Annie "Shaw." Found her much better. Aunt Mary spent night in Brookline  Early to bed but talked late

*August 3 1915 Tues.* After "dearie" did her duty we dusted up and swelled with pride—then rested until we had to get supper  Aunt Mary being in Brookline Cath & I went to "The Birth of a Nation" at Tremont.[759]  Marvelous picture

*August 4 1915 Wed.* Mrs. Fleming died early this A.M. —C & I got up at 6:15 to get breakfast. Did up the work in quick time & departed for Stoughton for the day[760]  Rain!!— No pond—Played cards with Don, Helen A. & Cath

---

758  Perhaps the Boston Theater on Washington Street.
759  The 1915 epic film *The Birth of a Nation* was based on *The Clansman*, a novel and play by Thomas Dixon, Jr. It dealt with two families—one Union, one Confederate—during the American Civil War and Reconstruction. Directed and co-produced by D.W. Griffith, starring actress Lillian Gish, the three-hour movie was the first twelve-reel film ever made, requiring an intermission. It sparked black protest in Boston and elsewhere for its portrayal of African-Americans and idealization of the Ku Klux Klan, but it was nevertheless an enormous commercial success. Jennie and Catherine saw *The Birth of a Nation* at the Tremont Theatre on Tremont Street, in Boston.
760  Stoughton: a town about seventeen miles from Boston.

*August 5 1915 Th.* And still it rains. Loafed all A.M Mary Watson came & was greeted with a Scotch blessing.[761] Franklin Park movies with Cath, Mrs. Myers & Mimi. Bob & Geo. went to the wake after rehearsal[762]

*August 6 1915 Fri.* Mary, Cath & I kept house while Aunt Mary went to Fleming funeral Brookline & Lowell. Helen Burke came up. Also Mrs M. to announce intention to move. Chinatown to supper with boys, Uncle Andy & Cath—then to the movies[763]

*August 7 1915 Sat.* Took Cath to Dr. Fogg & wrote to Babes while he "excavated" 2 of her teeth.[764] Spent P.M. at home with Aunt M & M. the nurse. Went in with Cath to meet Uncle Andy & Mr. Foley took us for car-ride to Dorchester[765]

*August 8 1915 Sun.* Got up for breakfast with the family Went to Dudley St. Baptist church to hear Dr. Rees, the Evangelist.[766] Bob & Geo. took us to Nantasket. Monologue going down—Paragon Park & O you Frolic[767]

---

761 Scotch blessing: a reprimand or scolding.
762 Bob: the McCances' son Robert (Catherine's older brother), born in 1888.
763 Chinatown: in downtown Boston.
764 Frederick S. Fogg was a Boston dentist.
765 Patrick K. Foley was a bookselling associate of Andrew McCance in Boston.
766 Dudley Street Baptist Church: located at 137 Dudley Street in Roxbury. "Dr. Rees": the Reverend Milton S. Rees, D.D.
767 Paragon Park: the amusement park at Nantasket Beach in Hull, Massachusetts.

Paragon Park, Nantasket Beach, showing roller coaster

*August 9 1915 Mon.* Read "Dracula" at Dr. Fogg's for 2 hr. having finished earlier "How to Live on 24 hr a day" by Arnold Bennett.[768] Mary Fleming came over right after lunch & spent rest of the day. She is a charming girl Wrote to my daddy.

*August 10 1915 Tues.* Spent the morning doing our regular Chewsdee duties. Went to Fisk Agency & to Dr Fogg's to browse while Cath. suffered[769] Read "The Waking" to the family in the evening[770]

---

768   *Dracula*: Bram Stoker's 1897 Gothic horror novel. *How to Live on 24 Hours a Day*: a 1908 book of advice by English writer Arnold Bennett on making the most of available time to give meaning to working life—something of a twist on Thoreau's message in *Walden*.
769   Fisk Agency: the Boston branch (at 2A Park Street) of a national chain of teachers' employment agencies.
770   "The Waking": perhaps *A Waking* by English novelist Mrs. John Kent Spender (Lillian Spender; 1835-1895). The book was first published in 1892.

*August 11 1915* **Wed.** "At home" Entertained Mrs. Kelsey Don, Jr. Helen & Elsie H. for dinner at 12 and dinner at 7. Minus Don the younger set visited the Zoo. Rox Jitney Gospellers serenaded

*August 12 1915* **Th.** Aunt Mary departed early for Allston We ironed a bit, got lunch, spent the first 3 hr of the P.M. wearily at dentist. Then to Fannie's. Benny's & Minette's for dinner & evening

*August 13 1915* **Fri.** Slept late & loafed long. Went in town shopping all afternoon Fat woman insulted Aunt Mary's size!!! Uncle Andy & I beat Aunt Mary & Cath at Casino

*August 14 1915* **Sat.** Inspected Columbia Rd & Mellen St apartments & interviewed real estate agents Ironed a bit. Went in town & met Uncle Andy. Rewarded by car-ride to Dorchester

*August 15 1915* **Sun.** All up for breakfast. Boys went to Stoughton for the day. Uncle Andy, Aunt Mary, Cath & I lunched early, hunted apartments in Allston & went to Revere. Shore dinner and roller coasters

*August 16 1915* **Mon.** Up for breakfast to say good-bye to boys Aunt Mary, Cath & I pleased with 29 Wabon.[771] Uncle Andy came out and approved. Left for home on 6:05 having considered everything from 10:45 on

---

[771] The McCances subsequently moved to 29 Wabon Street, which was not far from their former Sherman Street home.

*August 17 1915 Tues.* Spent the day at the store so that Helen could entertain Annie. Wrote several letters to college mates—Also Cath. Pleased to hear of Marg's appointment.[772] Mother ill

*August 18 1915 Wed.* Spent the day at the store, wrote a few letters and worked some on the books  Went up to Sterling in the evening. Dad & Joe saw Taft & Pratt about S.H.S. vacancy[773]

*August 19 1915 Th.* Sent application to Supt Waldron for Sterling H.S. vacancy.[774] Spent day at store  Visited Marg's new room. Went to Worc. on business with Dad. Store in eve. Glad to hear that Aunt Mary will move to 29 Wabon

*August 20 1915 Fri.* Spent the day at the store. Nothing of particular moment. Had the company of travelling salesmen all afternoon  Wrote to Miss Scott & Prof Schinz for "rec's"[775]

*August 21 1915 Sat.* Spent A.M. Saw Faith Yeaw down town for a few minutes after lunch. Went to ballgame with Dad. To Star at night with Mildred to see War pictures.[776] Then Dad took us to Lanc

---

772  Marguerite Philbin landed a teaching job at Clinton High School.
773  "Joe": Joseph M. Johnston, George McLeod's brother-in-law (husband of his sister Mary McLeod), who then lived in Sterling. "S.H.S. vacancy": a teaching position at Sterling High School. "Taft & Pratt": William O. Taft and George E. Pratt were (respectively) Secretary and Chairman of the Sterling School Committee.
774  "Supt Waldron": H.C. Waldron, Superintendent of Schools for Sterling.
775  "Rec's": recommendations from two of her former Smith professors.
776  "War pictures": described in the *Clinton Daily Item* (August 19, 1915) as "the first to reach this country."

***August 22 1915 Sun.*** Slept until 11:30. Rainy day. The entire Johnston family were here for supper  Anne remains until M. Went up with Dad to take them home. Rain!!

***August 23 1915 Mon.*** At the store. Read, sewed and did some work for Dad. Took A.J.R. bill to lawyer. Went up to Sterling with Dad to take kids & Annie. Then to Miss Stevens. Swell time

***August 24 1915 Tues.*** At the store. Finished waist I started last Sunday. Read Munroe.[777] Also "The Teaching of Civics" by Mabel Hill.[778] 12-16 passenger Ford jitney causes mirth at Paines

***August 25 1915 Wed.*** At the store. Interview with C E Coyne  Promised him I would take charge of Tag Day at next concert.[779]  Read 4 nouvelles de Guy de Maupassant.[780]  Walk to Lanc with F. Shutts & her mother

---

777  Possibly the 1915 book *The New England Conscience* by James Phinney Munroe (1862-1929), an author and businessman with deep family roots in Lexington, Massachusetts, or one of the many books by American writer and conservationist Kirk Munroe (1850-1930). See also Jennie's diary entry for February 8, 1916, and the accompanying note.

778  *The Teaching of Civics*: a 1915 book reflecting a focus promoted by a committee of the National Education Association on community civics.

779  Charles E. Coyne was General Secretary of the Holyoke Chamber of Commerce. Tag Day: a day on which donations are collected for a charity or cause and donors are given tags in recognition. Next concert: the Clinton Chamber of Commerce was sponsoring a series of band concerts, which were attended by people from surrounding towns as well as local residents.

780  Guy de Maupassant (1850-1893) was a French novelist, short story writer, and poet.

*August 26 1915 Th.* At the store. Spent greater part of day on Chardenal's French Grammar.[781] Letter from Cath M. in the morning & one from Miss Scott in the afternoon. Sewed all evening

*August 27 1915 Fri.* At the store. Telephoned several girls begging aid for tag day. Poor response. Note from Prof Schinz. Spent a couple of hours on my beloved French. Loafed in the evening

*August 28 1915 Sat.* At the store in the morning. Sewed & ironed at home all afternoon. Dad & Sprint had auto accident. Car landed in brook at Power House.[782] Girls spent evening at Esther Towne's

*August 29 1915 Sun.* Got up about 10 A.M. Almost finished a shirt waist. Esther T. & Alice Macfarlane spent afternoon & evening here. Wrote to Fisk Agency Aunt Mary McLeod & Catherine M. Bed about midnight

*August 30 1915 Mon.* Got up in time to dress Dad's hand. Cut out and practically finished a blue & white stripe school dress for Maybelle. Party of thirteen at Miss Stevens. Splendid time.

---

781 "Chardenal's French Grammar": one of the standardly used, much-republished French grammar and composition books by C.A. Chardenal.
782 A brief piece on the front page of the *Clinton Daily Item* for August 30, 1915 revealed that the accident took place in Berlin, by "the culvert near the power plant of the Worcester Consolidated Street railway." Five boys had hitched a ride with George McLeod and his son George. Only three fit in the car, but the remaining two jumped on the running board once McLeod started his car again. George, Jr. tried to shoo them off. George, Sr. was momentarily distracted by the interaction, and the car swerved.

*August 31 1915 Tues.* Did several errands for Daddy & saw Mr Coyne in the forenoon. Sewed after dinner. Went up to Mrs. Custance to organize tag day.[783] Took Mary's gift to Esther. $78.14 from tags

*September 1 1915 Wed.* Esther married at 10 A.M. Errands for Dad. Interview with Mr Coyne. Bowled with Marje Bates & party 10-12. Sewed a few hr. Walk to Dam with Christine.[784] We're thinking of going to C.H.S.[785]

*September 2 1915 Th.* Finished pink chambray school dress for Maybelle spending morning and afternoon thereon.[786] Went down to the store with Dad in the evening. Lunch at 12 P.X [P.M.]—Bed 1 A.M.

*September 3 1915 Fri.* Went down and did a few errands for papa. Sewed latter morning and until 4 P.M. Made 10 Jr. Chautauqua calls but no one was in. Started Alice Lee's gift. Mary & Joe called in eve.

*September 4 1915 Sat.* Embroidered on "Hot Rolls" for Alice Lee all A.M. at home.[787] Did more of the same thing all P.M. at the store. Finished scalloping Spent evening at C.W.S's rewarded by loan of S.C. Quarterly[788]

---

783 Mrs. Custance: Adin and Lilla Custance lived at 65 Prescott Street with their family.
784 The Wachusett Dam—a local destination.
785 Jennie is referring here to the coursework (stenography, in particular) that she and Christine Beck took at Clinton High School as postgraduates.
786 Chambray: a lightweight plain woven fabric.
787 "Hot Rolls": presumably lettering embroidered on a cloth for a bread basket.
788 The *Smith Alumnae Quarterly*.

*September 5 1915 Sun.* Slept until ten forty-five. Spent rest of morning & all P.M. embroidering. Went to church with Dad in the evening. Mildred & Geo. came home with us. Sewed 10-12 & finished "Hot Rolls"

*September 6 1915 Mon.* Labor Day. Slept until 9:30. Laundered and crated Hot Rolls for transportation after trip to Morrill's for cardboard.[789] Delivered to C.A.B. in time. Read newspapers & browsed afternoon & evening

*September 7 1915 Tues.* A.M. at store with chief occupation smocking green smock for Annie  P.M. at Christine's sewing & discussing plans. At home all eve after trip to Libe.

*September 8 1915 Wed.* A.M. at store still smocking. Registered with Christine at C.H.S. as special student. Worcester on 12:50. Miscellaneous shower for Alice Lee at L Sprague's[790]. Delightful day. Home 10:10

*September 9 1915 Th.* Letter from Cath inviting me to Hamp via auto  Substituted at C.H.S. for Guy Jordan.[791] Had 4 Latin classes. My début as a school marm  Afternoon at Christines telling experiences & discussing shorthand. Evening preparing Latin for emergency call

---

789  "Morrill's": Frank W. Morrill sold stationery, newspapers, candy, cigars, and other items at 73 High Street.
790  Louise Sprague and Caroline Bowers hosted the shower in Louise Sprague's Worcester home (notice, "Local Affairs," *Clinton Daily Item,* September 10, 1915).
791  Clinton High School teacher Guysbert B.V. Jordan was the son of the Reverend William W. Jordan and his wife Elizabeth.

Mildred Hutchinson (Hutch),
from Smith College
*1915 Class Book* (yearbook)

***September 10 1915 Fri.*** Smocked at the store until time for school. Appeared for first time in Stenography III—5 min. late. Smocked all afternoon. Went to bed early & read Alice in Wonderland.[792]

***September 11 1915 Sat.*** Darned stockings & smocked all day. Hutch sailed for Spain on Cetric.[793] First communication from Fisk. Lincoln N.H.[794] Went down to meet Dad in the evening.

---

792 The 1865 novel *Alice's Adventures in Wonderland* by Lewis Carroll (pseudonym for Charles Lutwidge Dodgson).
793 The *Cetric* was a White Star Line steamer that sailed to Mediterranean ports.
794 Lincoln, New Hampshire is more than 135 miles from Clinton—a long distance for Jennie to move from home for a teaching job.

*September 12 1915 Sun.* Did housework all morning as mother did not feel well. Smocked all afternoon and completed smocking before supper  Church with Dad. Dr. Chandler of India here[795]

*September 13 1915 Mon.* Wet day so treated myself to some high black shoes. Store errands & school filled A.M. Globe in P.M. with Christine & Carolyn  Indoor Mon. night at Miss Stevens.

*September 14 1915 Tues.* Store & school as usual. Terribly hot. Went collecting for Jr. Chautauqua and spent a couple of hours making up smock. Did shorthand the balance of the hot evening

*September 15 1915 Wed.* Store, school and store. Had to go to the board in Stenog III—Mr. Matthews having kindly asked if we objected to class work.[796] Roasting hot for fair.[797] Finished Ann's smock.

*September 16 1915 Th.* No school on account of the fair  Spent morning, afternoon and evening at the store. Insufferably hot. Spent most of the day writing Spanish.

---

795 The Reverend John S. Chandler, Secretary of the American Madura Mission in India, spoke at all services at the First Congregational Church on September 12 ("Church Meetings," *Clinton Daily Item*, September 10, 1915).
796 "Mr. Matthews": Clinton High School teacher William S. Matthews.
797 The twenty-seventh Worcester East Fair in Clinton was held on Wednesday, September 15 and Thursday, September 16, 1915. The annual event attracted not only local citizens but thousands from all over Worcester County. The fair offered both agricultural and livestock displays and competitions and a variety of other exhibits and entertainments. A severe heatwave interfered with attendance at the 1915 Clinton Fair. As reported in the article "The Heat Kept Crowds Away" in the September 17, 1915 issue of the *Clinton Daily Item*, "The attendance on the second day was affected at least 2000 by the intensity of the heat … The Fair was not a financial success, but in all other ways it was a success."

*September 17 1915 Fri.* Written sprung in Shorthand. Wrote to Arlene & Carp. Spent the afternoon and evening at home mending my clothes

*September 18 1915 Sat.* Bowling party postponed. Washed, ironed and mended all day. Went down to the store with Dad in the evening. Bed at 11 for 1 hr. beauty sleep

*September 19 1915 Sun.* Slept until 11. Went to S.S. Rally Day.[798] Attendance 648. Wrote letters all P.M. Went to church at night. Finished Shorthand. Wrote more letters. Bath, & bed.

*September 20 1915 Mon.* Store & school as usual. Mr Votes in town most of day. Christine & I called on Marlitta Brockelman. Collected for Jr. Chautauqua. Last Mon. night of season.

*September 21 1915 Tues.* Rainy day. Store and school in A.M. Helped preserve peaches all P.M. Did a couple of hours sewing in between  Tutored Cameron in Algebra[799]

*September 22 1915 Wed.* Clear and cold. A rare autumn day yet postponed a long walk  Went down to 6:44 to see Arlene, Marg & Minn after tel. from Lil. Walked with F. Shutts

---

798  Rally Day at the First Congregational Church in Clinton. Rally Day was a celebration of the resumption of regular Sunday School classes and the normal church schedule after the summer—a reuniting of the congregation.
799  Cameron Duncan, age 13, son of Alexander C. Duncan (born in Scotland).

*September 23 1915 Th.* School and store. Christine Miss Kent and I walked to Sterling to Cattle Show, stayed there an hour and walked home.[800] Ten or eleven miles

*September 24 1915 Fri.* Routine day until 3 P.M. Then went to Christine's for first Spanish conference with her & Helen Plummer.[801] Studied Spanish all evening.

*September 25 1915 Sat.* Spent morning washing, ironing and cooking. Vivian Atkinson of Ipswich wanted me to sell religious book for children  Barbara & Davy came for week end. Wrote to Babes

*September 26 1915 Sun.* Slept until ten, went to S.S. and church at night. Called on Mrs Towne with Barbara. Spent wakeful nervous night upstairs on account of high wind.

*September 27 1915 Mon.* Dad set Barbara & D [to] watch Boston train pull out  Store and school. Made a new nightgown which is a blessing not in disguise. Crowning feature of life since June 15 John Cowper Powys on "Why Russia is in the War"[802]

---

800 "Miss Kent": Clinton High School teacher Nellie Kent, who lived on Chestnut Street. The 54th annual Sterling Cattle Show and Old Home Day in 1915 was attended by some 6,000 people ("Cattle Show Big Success," *Clinton Daily Item*, September 24, 1915).

801 Helen Plummer (age twenty-six) was housekeeper to postmaster Charles Stevens, who lived at 106 Cedar Street (near Christine Beck's home).

802 The first of seven public lectures on the European War, offered as the Weeks Institute lecture series in 1915. John Cowper Powys (1872-1963) was an English poet, novelist, philosopher, and lecturer.

*September 28 1915 Tues.* Cut Stenog to finish transcribing Powys lecture.[803] Called on Dr. French.[804] Mr. Gibbons said Winter Chau. may have school hall if janitor is paid to [for] lights.[805] Called on Dr. Morse.[806] Nice talk with her

*September 29 1915 Wed.* Announced written in Stenography. Read some French and wrote some Spanish. Letter rec'd with Winter Chautauqua schedule. Bolton Fair?[807]

*September 30 1915 Th.* School and store. Christine went to investigate position at Whiting Hall, South Sudbury.[808] Much excitement. Read French and loafed all evening.

*October 1 1915 Fri.* School and store and so forth. Spanish class at Christine's followed by sewing bee and supper prepared by Christine. Letter from Carp. Bed 10:30

*October 2 1915 Sat.* Bowled 2 strings at Armory with Christine, Carolyn, Dot Davis & Marion Graves[809] Had Law & Order Comm. write invitations for Winter Jr. Chau.[810] Store with Dad in the evening

---

803 Jennie reported on the lecture for the *Clinton Daily Item*. The article appeared in the issue for September 28.
804 Physician Charles L. French was president of the local Chautauqua association.
805 Teacher Thomas F. Gibbons became Superintendent of the Clinton School Department in 1915.
806 Dr. Morse: Irene M. Morse was a physician at 153 Water Street.
807 Bolton Fair: an annual agricultural fair held in Bolton beginning in 1874 (now held at the Lancaster Fairgrounds).
808 Whiting Hall: a private school for girls in South Sudbury, Massachusetts.
809 Dot Davis & Marion Graves: Dorothy Smith Davis and Marion Edson Graves (both from Northampton, Massachusetts) were members of Smith College Class of 1915.
810 The Junior Town Law and Order Committee—a committee of young Clintonians involved in Junior Chautauqua—made and enforced rules for managing participation in the program.

*October 3 1915 Sun.* Stayed at home all day. Read, slept, studied Spanish  Dad and Sprint worked all day

*October 4 1915 Mon.* Store, school and a long letter from Babes the extent of morning interest  Prof Powys discussed "Why England is in the War"[811]  Went with Dad & Maybelle

*October 5 1915 Tues.* Letter from Grace  Usual morning pursuits. Cashed check, bot cloth for bathrobe for Dad and sewed thereon all P.M. When dressed to go to pastor's reception found out it is to be Thur

*October 6 1915 Wed.* Store and school in the morning. Winter Jr. Chau. club had first meeting  Children overjoyed. Christine, Ruth & Gladys permanent assistants. Miss Marr spent night here[812]

*October 7 1915 Th.* Breakfast at 8. with Miss Marr  Took her to P.O and train. Tutored Florence S in German. Finished Dad's bathrobe. Waited on table at pastor's reception. Some rain!!

*October 8 1915 Fri.* Another week gone. Never a dull moment with all the irons C & I have in the fire. Spanish class met with Helen. Getting along well. Spent evening with Ibsen's Peer Gynt[813]

---

[811]  The second lecture in the Weeks Institute series on the European War.
[812]  Miss Marr: Helen Marr, Junior Chautauqua supervisor.
[813]  Ibsen's *Peer Gynt* is a five-act play in verse. It was first published in 1867 and first produced in 1876.

"THIS IS THE LIFE"

*October 9 1915 Sat.* Washed, ironed and mended all day. Went down to the store in the evening, straightened things out, filed accounts and paid bills and sent out bills

*October 10 1915 Sun.* Slept until 11:30. Aunt Mary & Joe called. Went with Mildred to 1911 reunion discussion meeting at Marje Evans[814] Musical at church with Dad.[815] Then Did Stenog. letter Finished Babes—Bed 12 P.M [A.M.]

*October 11 1915 Mon.* A long, long day. Worked on shorthand all A.M. Letters from Babes, M. Crawford & Ada Hill. Christine came down to store to hear acc of game.[816] Called on Alice Lee. Prof Levermore's lecture on The European Conflict. Took notes to report.[817]

*October 12 1915 Tues.* Columbus Day—a holiday. Wrote up last night's lecture. Walked to Felton observatory in Bolton with Miss Kent.[818] Wrote football songs.

---

814 Jennie's Class of 1911 classmate Marjorie Anne Evans also took the college preparatory course at Clinton High School.
815 "Musical at church": a musical service by the choir of the First Congregational Church, accompanied by piano and violin.
816 Game: a local baseball game—"All Stars Win Again. Bigelow-Hartford Team is Defeated at Hands of Pick of Other Teams. A Benefit Game," *Clinton Daily Item*, October 11, 1915.
817 Charles Herbert Levermore (1856-1927)—Professor of History at the Massachusetts Institute of Technology—was a peace activist. Jennie's report of his Weeks Institute lecture ("Lecture in Grammar Hall") appeared in the *Clinton Daily Item* for October 13, 1915.
818 "Felton observatory": the Felton family owned Prospect Farm in Bolton, on the east side of Wattaquadock Hill—a location offering a view toward Boston. Jennie here refers to an observation tower on the property.

*October 13 1915 Wed.* Rec'd 75¢ for lecture report. Store and school. Went over to Chem Lab for a while in the afternoon.[819] Ironed in the evening. Telephone call from Margaret C.

*October 14 1915 Th.* Store and school. Tutored Florence Much excitement over to-morrow's plans Washed & ironed all P.M. Heard Miss Helen Todd in favor of Woman Suffrage.[820] Great.

*October 15 1915 Fri.* Up early. Met Christine at station in rain. Left 8:30. Natick car leaked! Storm cleared before we reached Wellesley. Tramped all over campus, met faculty, saw buildings lunched at Agora with C & Connie Billings Attended Miss Vida Scudders Lit 7. Called on C.A.B. Met Marlitta called on Jean Stimets. Left 3:44 Met Margaret in S. Station.[821] Fine reunion dinner. Spent evening at Macfarlane's.[822] Locked out.

---

819  Probably the chemistry laboratory at Clinton High School.
820  Helen M. Todd (1870-1953) was an American suffragist and an advocate for workers' rights. She spoke for an hour and a half to a crowd of 600 in Clinton. The account of her talk ("Speaks for Suffrage") in the *Clinton Daily Item* for October 15, 1915 included the assessment, "Miss Todd is not only a convincing speaker, but she has a sense of humor and a broad sympathy which make her speeches for the cause appeal to her audience."
821  Agora House was built on the Wellesley College campus in 1901 as the meeting place for Agora, a society devoted to the consideration of political issues. Constance Billings: Wellesley College Class of 1916. Vida Dutton Scudder (1861-1954): Professor of English Literature at Wellesley College, writer, and social reformer. C.A.B.: Caroline Adams Bowers of Clinton, Wellesley Class of 1917. Marlitta Brockelman, also of Clinton, Wellesley Class of 1919. Jean Stimets: Wellesley Class of 1916; formerly a member of Smith Class of 1915. Opened in 1898, South Station was and is a busy train terminal and transit hub in Boston.
822  The Macfarlane household in Dedham.

*October 16 1915 Sat.* Slept until nine o'clock. Went up to Memorial Hall and Mr Hines, Supt of Schools[,] granted an interview.[823] Watertown 12 Dedham 3 football. Movies at Hyde Park. M. Mrs. C, Mrs Parsons

*October 17 1915 Sun.* Up about nine. Went to Medford for the day. Dinner at Mrs Alexander's, supper at Mrs. Smith's. Lovely view Grand day. Home at 9. Aunt Bess from Webster my roommate

*October 18 1915 Mon.* Slept late once more. After lovely visit left Margarets at 11:25 for 29 Wabon. Lunched with Aunt Mary, Cath & Mary Fleming Inspected new house and approved it. Cath went to 6:05 train with me. Home 7:46. Went with Dad to hear von Mach—Why Austria & Germany are in the War[824]

*October 19 1915 Tues.* Back to ye old routine—Store & school Entered active service of Membership Campaign Committee of Chamber of Commerce and trotted around all day—Small results[825]

---

[823] Roderick W. Hine was Superintendent of Schools in Dedham.
[824] Born in Germany, art historian and lecturer Edmund von Mach (1870-1927) taught at Harvard, Wellesley College, and Bradford Academy (in Haverhill, Massachusetts). During World War I, he wrote and lectured to increase understanding of the German perspective.
[825] The Clinton Chamber of Congress was engaged in an intensive campaign to increase membership in October 1915. Ellen K. Stevens headed one of the groups engaged in the effort, and Jennie McLeod was a member of her team: "Miss Ellen K. Stevens' team secured the greatest number of members, she having 21 to show from her campaigners, Miss Jennie McLeod of this team being the high individual with 8 to her credit" ("Campaign Is Success," *Clinton Daily Item*, October 29, 1915). The winning team took in a performance at the Globe at the expense of the losers.

***October 20 1915 Wed.*** Store, school am [and] Chamber of Commerce campaign. Had two members to report. Tutored Cameron in French. Did Shorthand after 10 P.X [P.M.]!!

***October 21 1915 Th.*** Two more members for Chamber of Commerce. Went to Luncheon, this being Ladies Day.[826] Solicited all day. Written translation test sprung in Stenog

***October 22 1915 Fri.*** School, store, canvassing. Went to luncheon with Mr Cleveland and reported two new members. Christine down for Spanish. Walked and talked more than we did Spanish

***October 23 1915 Sat.*** Handed in report to Foster Kinnear[827] Bot Helen new coat. Worc on 11:50. Spent 7 hr with Midie. Called on Spragues. Joined Smith College Worc. Club. Meeting at Amy Greene's.[828] Supper at M's Lodge

***October 24 1915 Sun.*** Slept late. Had 1911 class meeting here in the afternoon.[829] Ten present. Wrote letters and embroidered in the evening. Bed at 9:30.

---

826 Jennie is referring to one in a series of luncheons that formed part of the Chamber of Commerce effort to increase membership ("Luncheons End Today," *Clinton Daily Item*, October 22, 1915).

827 Foster Kinnear: in 1915, a clerk at 77 High Street, where several law offices were located. Kinnear lived at 93 Highland Street. The report Jennie passed along to him was undoubtedly related to the Clinton Chamber of Commerce membership drive.

828 "Amy Greene's": Amy Whitney Greene, Smith College Class of 1915, lived at 21 West Street in Worcester.

829 "1911 class meeting": members of the committee planning the first reunion of Clinton High School Class of 1911, which took place on December 30, 1915.

*October 25 1915 Mon.* Letter from Hutch from Madrid  Store and school in the morning. Store all P.M. as Helen had to go back for having insulted Marg. Weeks Lecture Prof Wilkenson Why France and Italy Are In the War[830]

*October 26 1915 Tues.* Heard from Mr. Matthews of night school Spanish job after Jan 1. Store, school and Spanish chief interests. Cut out housedress for mother. Evening Clef Club Concert with Dad and Maybelle.[831] A#1 concert

*October 27 1915 Wed.* School and store. Substituted in Vergil for Guy—period VI. Sewed in the afternoon & collected for Chamber of Comm. Studied Spanish in eve. Early to bed

*October 28 1915 Th.* Big monthly written in Stenog. Morning at store. Sewed all afternoon on new house dress for mother. Went down to meet Dad at 9:00. Got McCracken's pledge[832]

---

830  Louis K. Wilkenson spoke to some 600 people in Clinton's Town Hall ("Diplomats Cause War," *Clinton Daily Item*, October 26, 1915).
831  Clef Club: a musical organization devoted to providing Clinton "music of a high order at a low price" ("Captivated by Concert," *Clinton Daily Item*, October 27, 1915). The October 26 concert was held at the First Congregational Church. Mrs. William W. Jordan (wife of the Congregational minister) was commended in the newspaper for her work with the club: "[T]he voices of the members blending beautifully in chorus and the promptness of attack and fine shading and expression given each number proved abundantly that she had her musical forces well in hand."
832  Alpha McCracken's pledge to the Chamber of Commerce (noted in Jennie's list of Chamber receipts at the end of her diary). McCracken ran a fish market at 170 Church Street and lived at 32 Pierce Place.

Carolyn W. Sprague,
from Smith College
*1915 Class Book* (yearbook)

*October 29 1915 Fri.* School and store. Spent afternoon at Christine's embroidering and reading some wierd [weird] H.G. Wells.[833] Embroidered all evening

*October 30 1915 Sat.* Sewed all morning and practically finished mother's dress. Shopped with C.W.S. & helped her make favors. Made rules with Law and Order Comm. for Jr. Chau. Down town all eve.

---

[833] English writer H.G. Wells (1866-1946) is remembered largely for his science fiction.

***October 31 1915 Sun.*** Slept until 10:30. Then embroidered until about 2:30. Dad & I went to Sterling to spent [spend] P.M. with folks. Church at night Darius Cobb's painting of Christ.[834] Wrote to Babes.

***November 1 1915 Mon.*** School and store. Bot 54" linen to make table napkins. Cut them out in the afternoon. Sewed on them all evening as there was no lecture.

***November 2 1915 Tues.*** Store and school. Fearfully windy day. Climbed up to John St about 3:30. Had supper with Marg.[835] Watched election return at Item Off. Suff. lost[836]

***November 3 1915 Wed.*** Store and school. Second meeting of Jr. Chau. Winter Club.[837] Fine day. Big crowd. Sylvia W jumped 5'9." Local assistants spent evening at Gladys', she entertaining Miss Marr

---

[834] "The Mission of the Master," a presentation at the First Congregational Church by artist Darius Cobb and the Reverend C.F. Hill. Cobb's painting "The Master" was a feature of the program ("Mission of the Master," *Clinton Daily Item*, October 28, 1915).

[835] Marguerite Philbin lived at 179 John Street.

[836] Jennie here refers to the failure of a proposed amendment to the Massachusetts constitution that would have granted women the right to vote.

[837] This meeting of the Junior Town Committee was held in the high school assembly hall. The business session featured committee reports and the election of officials. The Law and Order Committee presented the rules that Jennie had helped to formulate on October 30; these were voted on and accepted. Arthur Brockelman, Cameron Duncan, and Carol Gibbons were appointed "assistant police" and entrusted with enforcing the rules. Stories, games, and athletics followed the business meeting. "Miss Helen Marr, the Junior Chautauqua leader, was present and she was assisted by the Misses Jennie McLeod, Christine Beck, Gladys M. Howe, Ruth Dias, and Lelia M. Finan"—"Affairs of Junior Town. Officers Are Elected to Enforce the Laws and Reports Are Given. Food Sale Later," *Clinton Daily Item*, November 4, 1915.

*November 4 1915 Th.* Store and school. Sewed on table napkins in all of my spare time. Inspected Gordon's heating plant[838] Spent evening at the store.

*November 5 1915 Fri.* No school due to teacher's convention in Worc. Washed windows at store & cleaned shelves. Spanish lesson at C.L.B.'s Sewed all evening except when I ironed

*November 6 1915 Sat.* Up early. Cleaned my room, cooked, sewed, ironed, did errands. Midie arrived at 3:10. Came to the house, then downtown Movies at Star after supper Bed about 11:30

*November 7 1915 Sun.* Up. about 9:15. After breakfast loafed around, read Sunday papers and wrote letters until dinner. Midie had to leave at 3. Did Sten & Sp. rest of P.M. and all of evening.

*November 8 1915 Mon.* Store and school. All afternoon meeting at Gladys making plans for Jr. Town foodsale.[839] Lecture by Prof Grosvenor "Attitude of Turkey & the Balkans"[840] je ne l'aimait pas[841]

---

838 Likely the heating system of the store of Lewis S. Gordon at 338 High Street. Gordon sold newspapers and other reading matter, stationery, candy, and cigars.
839 "Jr. Town foodsale": a fundraiser for the winter Junior Chautauqua, held at the Walnut Street School on November 12, 1915. There was a competition between boys and girls as to the quantity and quality of their respective contributions and the amount of money raised by each. Jennie recorded the proceeds in the accounts section following her diary.
840 Edwin Augustus Grosvenor (1845-1936) was Professor of History at Amherst College.
841 "[J]e ne l'aimait pas": I didn't like it (French).

*November 9 1915 Tues.* Store and school. Spent P.M at CLBs sewing & entertaining callers. Stayed to supper with Christine. All evening meeting at Mrs. Powers of Xmas Church fair candy committee[842]

*November 10 1915 Wed.* Store & school. Substituted for Mr Jordan 6th per. Oh you written translation!! Slept most of P.M. Read ["]The Inside of the Cup" all evening at home.[843]

*November 11 1915 Th.* Store & school. Made cake & nut bread for foodsale. Christine came down & we did 10 lesson in new Sp. book. Tutored Cameron in Fr. 4:30-6:15. Read all evening.

*November 12 1915 Fri.* School and store and last but not least all afternoon at Jr. Chautauqua foodsale. Girls table won. Netted exactly $24.00

*November 13 1915 Sat.* Slept late, busied myself around the house, deposited Jr. Chau. foodsale money  Went down to pick out wall paper with Chr  Started guest towel for Marg's birthday

*November 14 1915 Sun.* Up in time to go to German church with Christine.[844] Very enjoyable  Got the general sense to everything. Sewed P.M & eve until I finished guest towel

---

842  Mrs. Powers: Ann Powers of 79 Park Street, widow of John Powers, foreman of the Clinton Water Works.
843  *The Inside of the Cup*: a bestselling novel by popular American writer Winston Churchill (1871-1947), serialized in 1912 and 1913 and published in book form in 1913. The book fictionally explores religious doctrine, faith, and spirituality.
844  German church: Clinton's German Evangelical Congregational Church initially met in 1887 in the First Congregational Church on Walnut Street, opening its own building at 109 Haskell Avenue in 1889. It offered services in German until 1944. It is now the United Church of Clinton.

*November 15 1915 Mon.* Store and school. Letter from Babes. Much interesting theatre gossip. Embroidered lingerie clasps for Marg.[845] Read and studied in the evening.

*November 16 1915 Tues.* Store and school. Went down to Lister's with Christine & then up-town[846] Maybelle accompanied. Bought her a guest towel & padded it for her in the eve.

*November 17 1915 Wed.* Same as last year. Marg's birthday Store & school. Kept Miss Stevens office open from 2-5:30 preparing my Spanish at same time.[847] Home all evening.

*November 18 1915 Th.* Started dictation in Stenog III What we have been longing for. Spent P.M at Christines on Spanish & trying to tat & evening in actually tatting at home[848]

*November 19 1915 Fri.* Store & school. Terribly wet day. Marg. came home from school with the kids & spent balance of day. Called on Blanche and we escorted her to 179 John St. Home 11 P.M

*November 20 1915 Sat.* Sent my shoes to the cobbler & was imprisoned all day thereby. Embroidered an M on a large bath towel, made a cake, worked on a new guest towel, tatted & read.

---

845 Lingerie clasps: fasteners to hold together lingerie straps.
846 Lister & Sorenson Co., a dry goods store run by Minnie Lister and Mrs. Isabelle M. Sorenson at 449 High Street. Daughter of James and Margaret Lister, Minnie (who was in her early thirties in 1915) was also a music teacher.
847 The C.G. Stevens & Son insurance office, then at 205 Church Street.
848 Tatting: a kind of handmade lace formed by looping and knotting cotton or linen thread with a small shuttle.

*November 21 1915 Sun.* Up in fair time. Aunt Mary & Joe here from 10-12 en route to Mamie Johnston's funeral.[849] Worked on towel and finished reading "Inside of the Cup" Wrote to Babes

*November 22 1915 Mon.* Store & school. Christine recovered from cold sufficiently to resume school. Made pajamas for Helen. Went to last lecture of series by Brooks Adams. Positively N.G.[850]

*November 23 1915 Tues.* Routine morning. Puttered around in the after noon. Read a little Spanish, a little French, a little German. Wrote to Anna, made up diary bathed & retired

*November 24 1915 Wed.* Made a fudge cake before going to the store. School as usual until 11:30 Made 3 loaves nut bread in the afternoon Spent evening at Mildred's

*November 25 1915 Th.* Thanksgiving. Went to Marlboro with the Hamilton's to CHS vs M.HS football game. Disputed issue.[851] Home afternoon and evening. Read & slept. Bed at 9:00.

---

849 Mamie Johnston: Mary Elizabeth Johnston of 83 Forest Street in Clinton died on November 19, 1915, at the age of forty-one.
850 Brooks Adams (1848-1927) was an American historian, political scientist, and critic of capitalism. "N.G.": no good.
851 "Clinton football enthusiasts are still discussing the Marlboro-Clinton game on the holiday which Referee Coyne declared forfeited to Marlboro 1 to 0, but which Clinton rooters say was won by Clinton 6 to 0. Just what will be done to straighten out the wrangle is not known as yet. But the outcome may affect the agreement made this season to play this game annually"—"Challenge to Marlboro," *Clinton Daily Item*, November 27, 1915.

*November 26 1915 Fri.* Sewed all day long. Made three pairs of pajamas, 2 coats and 1 shirtwaist Went down to train at 6:45. Saw Arlene, Marg & Miriam for about 3 min. Bed at 8:30!!!

*November 27 1915 Sat.* Worked around house and sewed in the A.M. Went to HS. vs Alumni with Ruth H. HS. won. Then shopping—to Coggswell's mill & up town.[852] At store in the evening

*November 28 1915 Sun.* Slept until 10:30. Went to Miss Stevens SS class with Christine.[853] Went up to Aunt Mary's with Dad & the girls. Church in the evening. Wrote to Babes. Bed at midnight

*November 29 1915 Mon.* No letter from Babes  Store & school. Spent P.M at 111 Cedar learning fancy tatting & meeting Make-Goods.[854] Tatted all the evening and seem to have mastered it.

*November 30 1915 Tues.* Store and school. Spent afternoon making up Junior Chautauqua scrap book. Sewed all evening. Bed early

*December 1 1915 Wed.* Store and school. Jr Chau. Splendid meeting. Clean-Up & Make-Good reported. The five assistants & Miss Marr supped at Episcopal Fair[855]

---

852  Coggswell's mill: Jennie may mean the Belle Vue Mills, the treasurer of which was William A. Cogswell, who lived at 295 Church Street.
853  Ellen Stevens's Sunday school class at the Church of the Good Shepherd.
854  111 Cedar: the address of the Becks. Make-Goods: members of the Junior Chautauqua Make-Good Committee (see also Jennie's entry for December 1).
855  The fifth annual fair and supper at the Church of the Good Shepherd, organized by the Women's Guild. Christine Beck's mother and a number of Jennie's friends participated in running it.

*December 2 1915 Th.* Busy at store with salesmen  Reported Chau & cut Stenog not knowing the time of day.  Sewed afternoon & evening on Xmas effects

*December 3 1915 Fri.* Store & school.  Went to foodsale for Chestnut St Grammar  Victrola fund  Women's Club—["]Novel of 20th C" by Mrs. True Worthy White.[856]  At home in the evening

*December 4 1915 Sat.* Canvassed Chace & Oak Sts with Christine for Red Cross Xmas seal committee.[857]  Spent P.M and evening tatting after weary walk of A.M.  Was called a French lady

*December 5 1915 Sun.* Up at 11:30  Sewed on guest towel  Mr & Mrs Shaw called.[858]  Wrote to Hutch & Babes.  Bed 11:30.

*December 6 1915 Mon.* Store and school.  Bitter chill it was  Christine & I finished Red Cross work.  Total 7.43 more than dble last years.  Went to Historical Soc. with Dad.  Gov Walsh on Humanitarianism in Govt.[859]

---

856  Mrs. True Worthy White: Martha Evelyn Davis White, a writer, lecturer, and advocate for women's clubs. In her address before the Clinton Women's Club, Mrs. White—"the chairman of the State committee on literature, and a member of the committee on literature in the general federation of Women's clubs"—traced the evolution of the twentieth-century novel from the Elizabethan to the contemporary period ("Novel of the Present Day," *Clinton Daily Item,* December 4, 1915).
857  "Red Cross Xmas seal committee": beginning in 1907, the American Red Cross ran a highly successful nation-wide campaign to raise money to fight tuberculosis through the sale of decorative Christmas seals for use on holiday gifts and cards. The initiative was taken over by the National Tuberculosis Association.
858  Mr. and Mrs. Shaw: James and Marion Shaw (Margaret Shaw's parents).
859  Governor David I. Walsh, speaking at a quarterly meeting of the Clinton Historical Society at the Holder Memorial on Church Street.

*December 7 1915 Tues.* Rested once more altho it seemed impossible last night. School & store. Made candy for church all afternoon  Sewed and read at home in the evening

*December 8 1915 Wed.* Regular morning program. Spent afternoon at Christines sewing for Xmas working eye blind & finger sore  Made more candy in the evening

*December 9 1915 Th.* Morning at store & school. P.M. and evening at church working on candy table which table took in $26.15. Marg & Blanche came to supper & Marg stayed for the entertainment

*December 10 1915 Fri.* Store, school and sewing all the day long. Ante-Xmas excitement all over the house. The kids are sewing with wild interest. Will it last?

*December 11 1915 Sat.* Slept a little later than usual  Busy all morning sewing and cooking and doing errands down town. At home all P.M & evening sewing and reading

*December 12 1915 Sun.* Slept until noon. Stayed home all day and sewed most of the time principally on tatted guest towel—is a "thing of beauty a joy forever?"[860]

*December 13 1915 Mon.* Another day of "all alone" in Stenography III, Christine being still at Wellesley. Letter from Babes. At home in the evening. The wood for fireplace came!!

---

860  Jennie here plays with the oft-quoted first line of *Endymion* (1818) by English Romantic poet John Keats (1795-1821).

*December 14 1915 Tues.* Just like every Tuesday.—store and school—Christine returned. Sewed P.M & eve and read with interest Annual Rept of Pres of Smith College.

*December 15 1915 Wed.* Store and school. Went with Christine in the afternoon to the Victrola concert for the Vic fund and both of us were greatly annoyed by some bad boys

*December 16 1915 Th.* Regular routine in the morning  Did a little Xmas shopping and sewing  Went to meeting of Christmas Tree Committee.[861]

*December 17 1915 Fri.* Kept store and attended school. Big written in Stenog. Wet day. Went up to Christines, sewed, read Beltane the Smith, had supper, sewed and slip [slipped] home in a London fog[862]

---

861  As reported in the article "Christmas Tree Plans" in the *Clinton Daily Item* for November 27, 1915, the Clinton Chamber of Commerce initiated the arrangements for a municipal Christmas tree on Central Park and for appropriate observances on Christmas Eve and Christmas Day. The Clinton Gas Light Company offered to decorate the tree with electric lights.
862  *Beltane the Smith*: a 1915 novel by British writer Jeffery Farnol (1878-1952), who wrote dozens of romance and adventure novels.

*December 18 1915 Sat.* P.M at Globe— Chau. Fly Pest[863] My constant cry  Sewed most of the day and accomplished considerable. Trip to bank and a few errands about noon  1:30 A.M. Moran-Casey fire.[864] I did not go.

*December 19 1915 Sun.* Slept until eleven. Spent the day making a night gown for a Xmas present. Had a shampoo. Wrote to little Babes and retired about 11 P.M.

*December 20 1915 Mon.* Store and school. Sewed all morning all afternoon and part of evening. Attended Municipal Tree Comm. meeting  Called at dancing school and paid Auntie Jones[865]

*December 21 1915 Tues.* Called upon to sub for Mr. Jordan but could not respond due to pressure of work. Christine filled the vacancy. Filed bills etc all A.M  Chau. carol practice 4-6. H.S. Hall. Sewed all eve.

*December 22 1915 Wed.* Spent A.M at store chiefly sewing  With C.A.B as Miss MacNab's guest at noon to hear L Sprague read Dickens Xmas carol to 9th grade.[866] Met Anna & Smith people 3:15. Shopped rest of P.M. Did up out of town pkgs in eve.

---

863  A short 1910 documentary consisting of a series of pictures of flies up close, personal, and larger than life, suggesting the threats they pose to hygiene and health, which would likely have fascinated some in the Junior Chautauqua group.

864  "Moran-Casey fire": a serious fire on Mechanic Street, which started in the drug store of Peter J. Moran and spread to the bakery of Thomas H. Casey, causing some $12,000 worth of damage—"Contents Destroyed," *Clinton Daily Item*, December 18, 1915.

865  Mrs. Eda J.H. Jones (sixty years old in 1915) lived on Main Street in Lancaster and operated a dancing school in the Music Hall in Clinton. Apparently one of Jennie's younger sisters was enrolled.

866  Alice B. MacNab taught the ninth grade in Clinton and lived on Walnut Street.

*December 23 1915 Th.* Made a 9 o'clock trip to the PO to mail pkgs & cards. Did a little shopping for Sprint. Had Jr. Chau at house from 1:45-3:30 for carol practice  Went downtown with Maybelle after supper. Bed 12:45

*December 24 1915 Fri.* Finished Sprints shopping by an A.M & P.M. trip. Gladys & I took Jr. Chau out from 5:30-7:00  It micht hae been worrsse but not much. Kept house while Helen & mother went to municipal tree exercises.[867]

*December 25 1915 Sat.* Christmas & presents galore. M, H, & I opened ours in bed. Sterling folks here most of A.M. Dad & I went to Philbins to take gift, spent P.M., & got heating contract  Tree in eve with Mildred. Germans didn't show up.[868]

*December 26 1915 Sun.* Dad went to Boston at 8:30. I stayed in bed until 11:45. Tatted considerably for Rose in the afternoon & evening. Bed fairly early. Quite a blizzard & high wind in early P.M.

*December 27 1915 Mon.* Kept office in the morning and tatted, thereby finishing one half of my task  Pressed my net dress and sewed. Went to "The District Attorney," H.S. play[,] with Christine[869]

---

867  About eight hundred people gathered around the Christmas tree on Central Park on Christmas Eve in 1915. School children sang under the direction of music teacher Martha Linton and the Carol Singers under that of Mrs. George S. Estes—"Singing at the Tree," *Clinton Daily Item*, December 27, 1915.

868  The dense fog and rain of Christmas night kept people away from Central Park, and a miscommunication suggesting weather-related postponement led the local German Turnverein Singers not to show up for their part in the program.

869  *The District Attorney*: a play by American journalist, playwright, and theatrical producer Harrison Grey Fiske (1861-1942). The play was made into a movie in 1915.

*December 28 1915 Tues.* Went into Millbury & talked with Supt. Ferguson & Prin Keyes of H.S. relative to H.S. vacancy[870] Had lunch at the Esca with Mildred. Home 3:10 Wrote to Miss Eastman. Home all the evening

*December 29 1915 Wed.* Went downtown for a pattern, cut out heavy skirt and fretted about the trouble it caused me the rest of the day. Finished guest towel even to laundering.

*December 30 1915 Th.* Sewed most of the morning. Mrs. Duncan called. Had P.M. tea. Letter from Mr Lyman Sup't of Hudson Schools.[871] 1911 Reunion Pierce Hall 8-12 26 present. Fay's Orchestra.[872] Best time ever in Clinton

*December 31 1915 Fri.* Up at 8:50. Took 9:15 to Hudson Liked Mr. Lyman who quizzed for 1 ½ hr. Home 12:40 Sewed & wrote to M. Poole. Spent evening at Christine's, Pauline being here for a visit.[873]

---

[870] Millbury: a town in Worcester County, a little more than twenty miles from Clinton. C.C. Ferguson was Superintendent of Schools there, Charles H. Keyes the principal of the high school.
[871] Cassius S. Lyman.
[872] The first reunion of Clinton High School Class of 1911 featured dancing until midnight and catered refreshments. During intermission, a business meeting was held at which a vote was taken to approve another reunion in 1916 (notice, "Local Affairs," *Clinton Daily Item*, December 30, 1915).
[873] Pauline: Christine's cousin Pauline Cole, a teacher who lived in Worcester.

# — 1916 —

*January 1 1916 Sat.* Cooked and sewed in the morning and ironed and tatted in the afternoon  Anna and Marg came down to supper.  Marg late as usual.  Grand reunion

*January 2 1916 Sun.* Slept until half past eleven  Wrote thank-you notes all afternoon  Finished my new brown skirt and now breathe more regularly.  Then to bed.

*January 3 1916 Mon.* Miss Stevens ill and I kept office for her with doubtful success.  Did some Shorthand and review [reviewed] Spanish  At home all evening.  Bed at 11:30

*January 4 1916 Tues.* A busy day at Miss Stevens office  Miss Jewett and I after much labor succeeded in accomplishing several tasks[874]  Wrote to Babes in the evening.  Also to Grace

*January 5 1916 Wed.* All day at Miss Stevens office.  Things rather quiet.  Wrote letter to Bertha and did some Spanish.  Marg & I saw Smith people at 6:45.  Then to Tarbell's.[875]  Waitresses.  M. Towne with Hudson party

*January 6 1916 Th.* On duty as per schedule at insurance office.  C. Sprague called and brot Weeklies & S.C. Quarterly.  Enjoyed that literature as I was not very busy

---

874  Miss Minnie Jewett (age around fifty in 1916) boarded with Ellen Stevens at 223 Chestnut Street.
875  Airmet Tarbell's confectionery, ice cream, and catering establishment at 154 High Street.

*January 7 1916 Fri.* Morning at insurance office. Miss Jewett made regular semi-daily call. & I carried out instructions. P.M. at Christine's once more dutiful Spanish students.

*January 8 1916 Sat.* A very busy day for Miss Jewett and me, not to mention Miss Stevens. We worked as best we could and finished our many "emergency" tasks about 7:30 P.M. Earned night's repose

*January 9 1916 Sun.* Spent the day in bed, sleeping most of the time in an effort to escape the grip[876] Read some of Paul Shivell's poems, dreamed and wrote to my little sister in Hamp.[877]

*January 10 1916 Mon.* After a day of rest took up once more my duties at 205 Church. Miserable day so Miss Stevens postponed her return for a day. Read & studied in the evening.

*January 11 1916 Tues.* I came down and worked hard all the forenoon. Am beginning to learn a little bit. Worked away all afternoon. Made up Shorthand in the evening.

*January 12 1916 Wed.* Mittwoch. Just like Dienstag and Donnerstag.[878] C.L.P. had a "coming out" party!! She invited whom she chose. I spent a quiet evening at home knitting

---

876 "Grip": grippe.
877 Paul Shivell (1874-1968) was an American poet and operator of the Stillwater Press. "[L]ittle sister in Hamp.": possibly Lois Evans, with whom Jennie had attended Freshman Frolic on September 19, 1914.
878 Mittwoch, Dienstag, Donnerstag: Wednesday, Tuesday, Thursday (German).

*January 13 1916 Th.* At Miss Stevens office "per coutume" assisting her in the morning & struggling along in the afternoon alone.[879] Spent the evening at Florence Shutts

*January 14 1916 Fri.* A cold, cold day. Morning at Ins office & afternoon at plumbing office. Went to Box 46 alarm—Bartlett's house[880] No excitement. Read "Candida" again[881] ???

*January 15 1916 Sat.* Morning and afternoon at Miss Stevens during regular hours. Miss Jewett called latter P.M. Downtown shopping in the evening accompanied by Mildred.

*January 16 1916 Sun.* Slept late and loafed around half grippy all day. Read "Sentimental Tommy" and wrote to Babes.[882] Via telephone adjusted Alpha Club. Chautauqua guarantee

*January 17 1916 Mon.* My last day at the insurance business after a pleasant two weeks. Went to Auntie Jones reception in the capacity of patroness.[883] Big fire at Clinton Concrete plant[884]

*January 18 1916 Tues.* Slept until ten. Finished up Shorthand and returned to C.H.S. after absence of 4 wk. Did miserably in the dictation. Spent P.M. at the store on annual accounts. Home all eve

---

879 Per coutume: as usual (French).
880 The alarm brought both the fire department and a crowd of bystanders to the High Street home of Mr. and Mrs. Joseph F. Bartlett. There was no fire.
881 *Candida*: a comedy by George Bernard Shaw, written in 1894, published in 1898.
882 *Sentimental Tommy*: an 1896 novel by Scottish novelist and playwright J.M. Barrie (1860-1937), the creator of Peter Pan.
883 A ticketed event, Mrs. Jones's dancing party was held at Morrill's on High Street.
884 The Clinton Concrete Co. on Brook Street sustained heavy damage (estimated at $3,000) in the fire.

*January 19 1916 Wed.* Got up about nine-thirty, transcribed notes & went to school. Christine & I called on Miss C and found her some better. Dr. Goodwin called to see Maybelle & prescribed for me also.[885] Bed early

*January 20 1916 Th.* A day just as good as lost. Spent it in bed. When I wasn't sleeping I was sneezing

*January 21 1916 Fri.* After a miserable night of sneezing called Dr. Goodwin again and spent another day in bed growing better gradually. Tatted while family went to Scotch Ball[886]

*January 22 1916 Sat.* Another one in bed for the most part  Tatted and read and did two Spanish lessons dealing with staggering verbs.

*January 23 1916 Sun.* All day in bed but feeling much better. Read, sewed, did Spanish and Shorthand and wrote my weekly to Babes

*January 24 1916 Mon.* Up in time to get to school and spend a routine day. "Reverence is a virtue too often lacking in the youth of to-day etc."[887] Went to bed right after supper

---

[885] Dr. Goodwin: physician and surgeon James J. Goodwin, who lived at 202 Church Street.
[886] The annual concert and ball held by the St. Andrews Mutual Benefit Society in celebration of the birthday of Robert Burns (Scotland's national bard, born January 25, 1759). The well-attended event was held in the Town Hall.
[887] "Reverence ... etc.": a shorthand exercise.

"THIS IS THE LIFE"

*January 25 1916 Tues.* Nothing unusual. Find Sketch Book dictation somewhat advanced and it angers us.[888] Went early to bed and read Paul & Virginie[889]

*January 26 1916 Wed.* More Rip Van Winkle and more ill humor.[890] Jr Chautauqua in the P.M. Pageant discussion in eve and no one appeared. Adjourned to Tarbell's

*January 27 1916 Th.* Routine morning. Aunt Mary came down in the afternoon having walked most of the way from Sterling  Evening at store on annual accounts

*January 28 1916 Fri.* Weekly written in Shorthand  Christine substituting for Guy. P.M at Christines  Spanish, mite boxes delivered, supper and movies, both feeling the batting spirit[891]

*January 29 1916 Sat.* A day full of domestic duties cleaning, baking, sewing & ironing  Went down town in the evening, landed at store. Discussion with Dad & Waldo until 10:00

*January 30 1916 Sun.* Slept until about ten. Went to Sunday School—Miss Stevens class. Wrote to Babes. Mother Maybelle & I had supper together—Birthday cake etc

---

888  Dictation from Washington Irving's *The Sketch Book*.
889  *Paul et Virginie*: a 1788 novel by French writer and botanist Jacques-Henri Bernardin de Saint-Pierre (1737-1814).
890  "Rip Van Winkle": dictation from Irving again.
891  Mite boxes: small boxes distributed to church members for collecting special offerings of money.

*January 31 1916 Mon.* Christine still at it for Guy  Spent the day about as usual.  Wrote paper on the "Schauffler Missionary Training School" for Wed. Miss meeting[892]

*February 1 1916 Tues.* School once more all alone  Spent recess with Christine hearing wild tales of misdemeanor.  Went down town together.  Bought pink waist

*February 2 1916 Wed.* Store and school.  Read paper at Missionary meeting on Ruth's anniversary  C.A.M. rejoiced at 2 recruits to infant class having previously been sole.  Chamber of Commerce reception to Sec & Mrs Osgood.[893]  A.O.H. Hall.  Snow.

*February 3 1916 Th.* Store and school.  Spent the rest of the day in various and sundry ways.  Letters and embroidery and read a bit of French.

---

892  *The Schauffler Missionary Training School*: a book by Henry Martyn Tenney about the Schauffler Missionary Training School of Cleveland, Ohio. Jennie reported on it to a meeting of the Women's Missionary Society of the First Congregational Church. Caroline Bowers (mother of Jennie's friend Caroline Bowers) was in charge of the program.

893  Edward G. Osgood, the new Secretary of the Clinton Chamber of Commerce, and his wife Florence, who came to Clinton from Nashua, New Hampshire. Originally envisioned as a ticketed event, the reception for the Osgoods was in the end free and open to the public. It was held in the Ancient Order of Hibernians Hall at 198 High Street. The arrangements for it were made by a Chamber committee. Ellen K. Stevens was in charge of decorating the hall. Light refreshments were served, and Calvin Coolidge—then Lieutenant Governor of Massachusetts—spoke at the event ("Reception Is Planned," *Clinton Daily Item*, January 31, 1916).

*February 4 1916 Fri.* Routine morning with reg. weekly written. Shopped P.M. with C.L.B. Spanish at my house. Chau. meeting at Gladys'. Voted: no pageant. Blanche worried quant à M.F.P.[894] Miss Kent called

*February 5 1916 Sat.* Rec'd Senior Pin with rose from Agnes Sewed most of the day In the evening went with Mildred to B.B. games at Armory.[895] Married men escorts cause much amusement.

*February 6 1916 Sun.* Up in time to go to Sunday School Walked to the Dam and back with Blanche after dinner. Wrote to Babes and retired early.

*February 7 1916 Mon.* Christine back as a student of C.H.S. once more. Wrote several letters, sewed and read. Letter from Babes full of news.

*February 8 1916 Tues.* Routine morning. P.M. C.L.B's Sewing and bridge. Gladys read The Eternal Feminine.[896] Mrs. Latin died.[897] Went to cantata King David in German Church with Miss Kent.[898] All German. Birthday picture from Marg

---

894 Blanche was worried about Marguerite Frances Philbin—quant à: about (French).
895 Basketball between Clinton and Lancaster girls, followed by league games.
896 "The Eternal Feminine": perhaps a reference to a chapter by that title in the 1915 book *The New England Conscience* by James Phinney Munroe.
897 Keziah W. Latin, wife of David F. Latin, who operated a lunch business at the corner of Church and High Streets. The Latins—both of Scottish descent—lived at 98 Walnut Street. Jennie associated with Mrs. Latin at the First Congregational Church and the Clinton Women's Club.
898 The church choir of the German Evangelical Congregational Church on Haskell Avenue performed the oratorio *King David*. The event was described in the *Clinton Daily Item* for February 9, 1916 as "one of the finest musical and vocal programs which the choir ever presented."

*February 9 1916 Wed.* Store & school. Thanked Marg. Bought several pieces of embroidery having finished hemming 29 feet of table napkins. Called on Mrs Smart about shortbread.[899] Found her ill

*February 10 1916 Th.* Delivered pageant tickets at school. Visited with Marg. at recess. Called on Miss Stevens. Sewed all evening. Borden's milk episode with Brockelman clerk.[900]

*February 11 1916 Fri.* Spent the morning at the insurance office. Went to movies with C.L.B. and party. M. Pickford in "A Girl of Yesterday"[901] Read Felix O'Day all evening[902]

*February 12 1916 Sat.* Snowed all day. A.M. & P.M. at Ins. Office. Worked on expiration book. At 5:30 went to C. Bowers where I remained until 9:30 Caroline Fletcher and Helen Strong guests from Wellesley. C.L.B & Ruth also present. Cards, supper, picture puzzle.

*February 13 1916 Sun.* Snowed all day long. Was the only girl in S.S. class. Embroidered in the afternoon. Read articles on Education in the evening

---

899 There were a few Mrs. Smarts of Scottish birth in Clinton in 1916.
900 Borden's milk: a brand of condensed and evaporated milk. Brockelman clerk: an employee at one of Henry Brockelman's local grocery stores.
901 *A Girl of Yesterday*: a 1915 comedy film directed by Allan Dwan, starring actress Mary Pickford.
902 *Felix O'Day*: a 1915 novel by American author, artist, and engineer Francis Hopkinson Smith (1838-1915).

"THIS IS THE LIFE"

*February 14 1916 Mon.* Went to school alone, C.L.B being at Wellesley. Regular doings all day  Went with Helen and Ruth to drill and had a miserable time carrying a gun[903]

*February 15 1916 Tues.* Busy until 3 P.M keeping track of 15 freezeups.[904] Spent afternoon at Ruth's sewing. Went down to meet C.L.B 7:46. Embroidered rest of eve.

*February 16 1916 Wed.* Finished the last of the dozen table napkins commenced last Nov. 1  School as usual.  Spent P.M. at Libe reading lives of illustrious women[905]

*February 17 1916 Th.* Store and school. Spent afternoon shopping for mother and myself. Eve downtown at Libe. Then up until 12:30 selecting quotations with Dad on "The Ladies"

*February 18 1916 Fri.* School in the morning. Big test  Went to Pageant of Heroines given by S.C. Worc. Club with Marg, Mira, Miss Kent, Miss Smith & Miss Walsh[906]  Home 11:30. Spent night at Marguerite's

---

903 Drill: likely an exercise of the Clinton Rifle Club, which held regular drills at the armory (see "Spectators Not Wanted," *Clinton Daily Item*, January 19, 1916).
904 Freezeups: thawing frozen pipes in the winter formed a regular part of George McLeod's work as a plumber.
905 "[L]ives of illustrious women": possibly *Lives of Illustrious Women of All Ages* (1860) by American poet and editor Mary Elizabeth Hewitt (1818-1894). Jennie likely consulted the book in connection with the program she mentions in her entry for February 18.
906 A notice in the "Local Affairs" section of the *Clinton Daily Item* for February 19 reveals that Christine Beck and her mother also attended the Smith College pageant in Worcester. Miss Smith: high school teacher Susan D. Smith, daughter of lawyer and judge Jonathan Smith and his wife Elizabeth. The Smiths lived at 66 Cedar Street. Miss Walsh: Hannah Walsh, sister of lawyer David I. Walsh (then former Massachusetts governor, later a United States Senator). In 1916, Hannah—a teacher—lived at 176 Water Street with her siblings.

*February 19 1916 Sat.* Got up at twelve o'clock  Terribly cold walk from the hill to the valley.  Just missed Miss Merrick.[907]  Maybelle & I kept house while "ma" chaperoned H & R to BB.

*February 20 1916 Sun.* Slept until S.S. time. Cut out waist and made most of it

*February 21 1916 Mon.* Miss Merrick's 9-12  Went up to Christine's to see her new room or rather furniture  Spent the evening reading.

*February 22 1916 Tues.* Washington's birthday and a stupid day it was. Sewed most of the day. Mary Joe & Mamie came down

*February 23 1916 Wed.* Miss Merrick's 9-12. Jr. Chau in the P.M. Chicken pie supper at Episcopal Ch. Committee meeting at Gladys.[908] Voted to give Robin Hood May Festival

*February 24 1916 Th.* Miss Merricks 9-12. Marg came to lunch. Read Kipling all P.M.[909] Went to Cong Ch. supper. Entertainment by Louise Sprague[910] Called on Blanche. Bed at 11:30

---

907 Elizabeth F. Merrick of the S.R. Merrick insurance business at 104 High Street (later incorporated into the C.G. Stevens company). Miss Merrick—for whom Jennie kept office during the second half of February 1916—was a Lancaster resident.
908 "Chicken pie supper": the annual parish supper of the Church of the Good Shepherd. Helen Marr was at Gladys Howe's for the Junior Chautauqua meeting (notice, "Local Affairs," *Clinton Daily Item*, February 24, 1916).
909 Jennie is reading English writer Rudyard Kipling (1865-1936) in advance of a Kipling program in Clinton on February 25.
910 Congregational Church supper: organized by the Congregational Ladies' Benevolent Society. Louise Sprague was a graduate of the Leland Powers School in Boston (notice, "Local Affairs," *Clinton Daily Item*, February 23, 1916).

*February 25 1916 Fri.* Bad day—no school. Marg slept until noon while I kept office for Miss Merrick 9:15-12. Loafed all P.M. Ushered at Kipling lecture.[911] Met Marg's DR friend[912]

*February 26 1916 Sat.* At Miss Merrick's 9-12. Answered Fisk letter reg. position as governess. Sent application for summer Jr Chau. work  Note to Miss Marr. C.L.B. & I registered voters[913]

*February 27 1916 Sun.* Very cold. Went to Sunday School. Wrote to Babes and went to P.O. to mail letter. Sewed on dress for Helen in the evening.

*February 28 1916 Mon.* Downtown in the morning on numerous business errands. Kept office for Miss Stevens in the PM. Military Whist, Music Hall for Dist Nurse eve[914]

---

911  "Kipling lecture": a program of readings from Kipling by Seldon L. Brown (Principal of Wellesley High School and formerly of Lancaster High School). Titled "An Evening with Kipling," held in the Music Hall of Clinton's Town Hall, the program benefited the free bed fund of the Hospital Circle of King's Daughters.
912  "DR friend": doctor friend?
913  From the "Local Affairs" column in the *Clinton Daily Item* for February 26, 1916: "Today is the last day for registration to vote at the annual town election. The registrars are to be in session throughout the afternoon and evening in the office of Town Clerk [James H.] Carr." Christine Beck, her mother Josephine Beck, Jennie McLeod, and Ellen K. Stevens were among ten newly-registered women voters ("Ten Women Registered," *Clinton Daily Item*, February 28, 1916). The ten brought the total number of Clinton women able to vote to one hundred and eleven. It was believed that the town's female voters would take a special interest in the upcoming School Committee election, "as this is the only part of the election in which they can participate."
914  A military-themed whist party to raise funds for the District Nursing Association.

*February 29 1916 Tues.* An extra day. Kept office for Miss Stevens all day. Evening at home tatting & trying to solve Alg. prob. Dad in Worc at Central Supply banquet[915]

*March 1 1916 Wed.* Called at Miss Stevens office on errand trip in P.M. Attended social meeting of Young People's Club at Miss Stevens home in the evening

*March 2 1916 Th.* Kept office for Miss Stevens all day.

*March 3 1916 Fri.* Went up to Christine's and helped her make fudge for Wellesley play in the morning.[916] Sewed for Helen rest of the day.

*March 4 1916 Sat.* Sewed, cooked and did my regular Saturday duties. Christine & I spent pleasant evening at Miss Stevens. Marg. Melcher visiting.[917] Evening of psych exp's.

*March 5 1916 Sun.* Up in time for S.S. 3 Smith guests present. Mary Louise Reilly called in the afternoon. Smocked some in the evening.

---

[915] The Central Supply Co.—a distributor of plumbing and heating parts and equipment—advertised as "the largest concern of our kind in central New England." In 1916, it was located at "Commercial Corner"—Foster, Commercial, and Mercantile Streets—in Worcester.

[916] Wellesley's sophomores presented two one-act plays on Friday, March 10 and again on Saturday, March 11.

[917] Margaret Sybil Melcher, Smith College Class of 1916.

*March 6 1916 Mon.* Store and school per usual. Cast my first vote all alone.[918] Went to card party at C. Sprague's—honor Pratty Met Christine's friend Rupy. Dad lost election[919]

*March 7 1916 Tues. No entry*

*March 8 1916 Wed.* Store and school. Spent afternoon at Christine's and we both cut out striped linen waists. Had supper and reached home about 9:30 Blizzard

*March 9 1916 Th. No entry*

*March 10 1916 Fri.* Sewed most of the day. Ironed and got ready for Scotch supper[920] Attended concert and waited on tables Mother poured

*March 11 1916 Sat. and March 12 1916 Sun. No entries*

---

918 Jennie was one of thirty-four Clinton women who voted in the School Committee election. Leading up to the election, there was some contention centering on the need to rise above party politics in electing School Committee members—"The School Situation" (political advertisement), *Clinton Daily Item*, March 2, 1916; "Democrats Are the Victors," *Clinton Daily Item*, March 7, 1916. The two non-partisan candidates—both Republicans—prevailed on voting day.

919 Republican George McLeod once again missed reelection to Clinton's Water Commission. He received 1,067 votes to the Democratic winner's 1,134. (He was reelected in 1917.)

920 "Scotch supper": the annual Scotch Night at the First Congregational Church. The entertainment consisted of "readings and musical selections in the Scotch dialect," the refreshments of shortbread, cake, and tea. About 300 people attended ("Has Annual Scotch Night," *Clinton Daily Item*, March 11, 1916).

*March 13 1916 Mon.* Evening at the Historical Society. "The Nile Country" illustrated by stereoptican [stereopticon] views[921]

*March 14 1916 Tues. through March 16 1916 Th. No entries*

*March 17 1916 Fri.* Dad and I went to see Marguerite as leading lady in Innesfail[922]

*March 18 1916 Sat. and March 19 1916 Sun. No entries*

*March 20 1916 Mon.* First of readings. Miss Stevens Lenten course Rupert Brooke[923]

*March 21 1916 Tues. through March 26 1916 Sun. No entries*

*March 27 1916 Mon.* In Readings from Modern poets—Robert Frost[924]

*March 28 1916 Tues. No entry*

*March 29 1916 Wed.* Bible class social at Miss Stevens. Farewell party to Percie and Nellie. P.M at Ruth's on costumes[925]

---

921 A world traveler, Mrs. Ellen M. Arnold of the Ashland Public Library was the presenter ("Oriental Life and Scenes," *Clinton Daily Item*, March 14, 1916).
922 "Innesfail": The play *Innisfail* was presented by members of St. John's Catholic Parish in Clinton on March 17, 1916 (St. Patrick's Day). Inis Fáil is a poetic name for Ireland.
923 English First World War poet Rupert Brooke (1887-1915), who died while serving in the British Mediterranean Expeditionary Force.
924 New England poet Robert Frost (1874-1963), who was awarded four Pulitzer Prizes in Poetry between 1924 and 1943 and the Congressional Gold Medal in 1960.
925 Costumes: for the upcoming Junior Chautauqua May festival.

*March 30 1916 Th. and March 31 1916 Fri. No entries*

*April 1 1916 Sat.* Spent the day in Pepperell. Arlene announced her engagement at a luncheon.[926] Awfully nice time

*April 2 1916 Sun.* Dad and I spent afternoon and evening at Marg's Rose and Mame both at home[927]

*April 3 1916 Mon.* Called in to substitute for Miss Fury at C.H.S.[928] 3 classes in Algebra, one Social Science and one alas! English History.

*April 4 1916 Tues.* Strenuous day in C.H.S. Rec'd instructions from John O'Malley as to my rendition of the Our Father[929]

*April 5 1916 Wed.* Another day at C.H.S. with its attendant joys and sorrows.

*April 6 1916 Th.* Once more in the role of substitute. Christine released once more.

*April 7 1916 Fri.* Last day at C.H.S. and gave tests to all my classes. P.M. at Ruth's on Chautauqua costumes.

*April 8 1916 Sat. and April 9 1916 Sun. No entries*

---

926 Arlene Deware married Lindol French.
927 Rose and Mame: Marguerite Philbin's two older sisters, Rose and Mary.
928 Miss Fury: teacher Elizabeth I. Fury, who lived at 93 Summit Street with her family. Her father was carriage painter Lawrence Fury.
929 Multiple John O'Malleys lived in Clinton in 1916. "[M]y rendition of the Our Father": presumably a reference to the difference between the Catholic and Protestant versions of the Lord's Prayer, reciting which formed part of the morning routine in public schools at the time.

*April 10 1916 Mon.* Began substitute duties at Peters High, Southboro, in Latin and English for Faith Carleton.[930]

*April 11 1916 Tues.* At Southboro

*April 12 1916 Wed.* At Southboro

*April 13 1916 Th.* At Southboro. P.M. at Christines with Ruth and Gladys to celebrate completion of costumes

*April 14 1916 Fri.* At Southboro.

*April 15 1916 Sat.* Sewed on Maybelle's coat all A.M. Went up to Ruth's, packed & shipped trunk to Helen. To Christine's for birthday supper which she enjoyed (?) from couch.[931]

*April 16 1916 Sun.* Went over to Lancaster to Unitarian Church with Miss Kent.[932] Walked home.[933] Studied P.M and evening.

*April 17 1916 Mon.* Southboro once more. Miss Stevens in the evening Song of War by Lincoln Colcord.[934] Its boredom recalling Binyon's Death of Adam[935]

---

[930] Southboro (Southborough): another Worcester County town, about twelve and a half miles from Clinton as the crow flies.
[931] Christine Beck was born April 15, 1894.
[932] Unitarian Church: the First Church of Christ, Unitarian at 725 Main Street in the center of Lancaster, on the common. Jennie visited the fifth meeting house of the church, which was designed by famed architect Charles Bulfinch and is still standing.
[933] A distance of close to three miles.
[934] "Song of War by Lincoln Colcord": Lincoln Colcord (1883-1947) was a journalist and writer of short fiction. His epic poem *Vision of War* was first published in 1915.
[935] "Binyon's Death of Adam": See Jennie's diary entry for November 18, 1914.

273

"THIS IS THE LIFE"

*April 18 1916 Tues.* At Southboro

*April 19 1916 Wed.* Holiday. Worked most of the day on Maybelle's coat

*April 20 1916 Th.* At Southboro

*April 21 1916 Fri.* At Southboro.

*April 22 1916 Sat.* Finished Maybelle's coat and worked rest of the day on party dress for Helen

*April 23 1916 Sun.* Fine wet Easter. Stayed in all day. Waldo came up and spent evening on matters pertaining to Brotherhood play[936]

*April 24 1916 Mon.* Left at 8:30 for Southboro once more much to my surprise and chagrin, Patsy being the herald.

*April 25 1916 Tues.* At Southboro. Called on Christine. Finished Helen's dress. Studied all evening

*April 26 1916 Wed.* At Southboro Bible class party at Miss Stevens' Christine and I went part time

*April 27 1916 Th.* At Southboro. Had a gay roughhouse in main room after departure of state inspector which Mr McSherry kindly quelled[937]

---

936 The play was presented by the Brotherhood at the First Congregational Church on April 28.
937 Mr. McSherry: Henry J. McSherry, Principal of the Southborough High School.

*April 28 1916 Fri.* At Southboro. Called on Supt Marlboro H.S en route for home.[938] Brotherhood play with CLB Shanghaied by Davis and Cushman[939]

*April 29 1916 Sat.* Sewed all morning. Went to C.H.S. ballgame with Christine P.M. Kept store open in evening.

*April 30 1916 Sun.* A day's excitement over hose for Crossman. George finally coming successfully to the rescue bringing duplicate order from Boston[940]

*May 1 1916 Mon.* Commenced substituting in French in Marlboro High, still commuting. First impressions favorable

*May 2 1916 Tues.* Mr McDougall offered me English in M.H.S. for rest of year as soon as released from French assignment[941] Accepted position. Home with Dr MacKay.[942]

*May 3 1916 Wed.* Dad went to Marlboro for me, missed me & picked me up at Hudson. Reason. Jr. Chau rehearsal. Miss Marr with us. Paid me $40. for rental of costumes. We called on C.L.B who is ill

---

[938] Jennie was still looking for a teaching position. Marlborough is about twelve miles from Clinton, in Middlesex County.
[939] "Shanghaied": the Congregational Brotherhood play *Shanghaied*, presented at Ladies' Night at the First Congregational Church. The play was written by Waldo Davis and James Cushman. George McLeod was a cast member ("Culver was Shanghaied," *Clinton Daily Item*, April 29, 1916).
[940] Jennie's brother George took care of Crossman's emergency.
[941] "Mr McDougall": W.J.B. MacDougall, teacher at Marlborough High School.
[942] "Dr MacKay": Clinton physician and surgeon Edward H. Mackay, who lived at 92 Walnut Street.

"THIS IS THE LIFE"

*May 4 1916 Th.* Excused to catch 12:40. Home 1:40. Frosted cake dressed and went to play.⁹⁴³ A success. Packed trunk, adjourned to Cedar Hill for picnic⁹⁴⁴ Said goodbye all around. Limousined to Worc with Helen

*May 5 1916 Fri.* Caught Jct electric by trip on pay car. Pretty tired but lived thru the day. Farewell part [party] to Miss Claflin at recess.⁹⁴⁵ Home at 4:00 Early to bed.

*May 6 1916 Sat.* Got up about 9. Went to bank deposited Chau. funds, went to movies with C.W.S. Paid Ruth and Gladys. Called on Christine Sorry to find her still sick.

*May 7 1916 Sun.* Spent the day preparing French and English lessons, ignorant of what tomorrow has in store for me.

*May 8 1916 Mon.* My fate: English, commenced. Met all five classes 2c2; 2Lf; 3Lf; 1c2; 1L2

*May 9 1916 Tues. through May 12 1916 Fri. No entries*

*May 13 1916 Sat.* Spent the [entry unfinished]

*May 14 1916 Sun. and May 15 1916 Mon. No entries*

---

943 See "Robin Hood May Festival. Junior Chautauqua Winter Club Gives Dramatization of This Story This Afternoon" (*Clinton Daily Item*, May 4, 1916). The article notes that the costumes were "furnished by the Clinton Chautauqua Costuming Co.," of which Jennie was part.
944 Cedar Hill afforded a scenic Clinton overlook.
945 Marlborough High School teacher Rachael Claflin.

Main Street,
Worcester,
ca. 1912

*May 16 1916 Tues.* Short time classes  Adjournment to Assembly Hall for Shakesperian rehearsal before school  Home at 2 P.M.

*May 17 1916 Wed.* More rehearsal.  Went to lunch and supper with Miss Watson  Dad came over for Shak. celebration  Home via fliver at 12 at night[946]

*May 18 1916 Th. and May 19 1916 Fri.* *No entries*

---

946   Fliver (flivver): slang word for a cheap, battered, or old car.

"THIS IS THE LIFE"

*May 20 1916 Sat.* Spent the day in Worcester  Maybelle went with me, her first experience in a city.  Got new suit  Spent P.M. at Mira's

*May 21 1916 Sun. through May 25 1916 Th.  No entries*

*May 26 1916 Fri.* Memorial Day exercises at Marlboro High.  Got home at 11:40.  First teacher's [teachers'] meeting after exercises

*May 27 1916 Sat.* Ironed cooked etc all A.M  Went to the ballgame in the afternoon with Mr Sprague, W Davis and M. Graves.

*May 28 1916 Sun.* Slept late.  Went to Bible class.

*May 29 1916 Mon.* A restless day of regular work

*May 30 1916 Tues.* Decoration Day.[947]  Hung around correcting papers all day.

*May 31 1916 Wed. and June 1 1916 Th.  No entries*

*June 2 1916 Fri.* Home in good time.  Went up to CLB's, downtown with her, then met Marg and we went for a long deferred walk to the Dam.

*June 3 1916 Sat. through June 13 1916 Tues.  No entries*

---

947  Memorial Day.

*June 14 1916 Wed.* After a day of review work played around all afternoon and evening with Christine selling balloons at Epis fête at Swinscoe grounds[948]

*June 15 1916 Th.* Last day of regular work  Gave 2c2 study period. 3Lf lecture on A Tale of Two Cities.[949]  Checked book accts & gave out exam threats

*June 16 1916 Fri.* Just made the train. Finals commenced. Eng 2c2 in Room 9  Went looking for coat and grad dress for Maybelle. Home at 12:40

*June 17 1916 Sat.* Rain. Corrected 2c2 papers. Everybody passed Downtown. Bought waist etc for next week's events

*June 18 1916 Sun.* Rain, rain, rain  Made out average for year and examinations for Marlboro cherubs.

*June 19 1916 Mon.* English 3Lf room 12 at 10:45. Proctored ninth grade 8-10  Shopping in Marlboro & Clinton. Made cake and packed for visit at Miss LeBrun's[950]

---

948  Swinscoe grounds: the property of Charles Swinscoe (1833-1909) on Bourne Street, off Cedar Street. Swinscoe was manager and, from 1903, consulting engineer of the Clinton Wire Cloth Company, with which his son Henry was also involved. Charles Swinscoe was active in the Church of the Good Shepherd.
949  *A Tale of Two Cities*: Charles Dickens's historical novel of the French Revolution.
950  "Miss LeBrun's": Cecile R. LeBrun was a teacher at Marlborough High School. She lived at 171 West Main Street in Marlborough.

*June 20 1916 Tues.* English 1L2 and English 1c2 in Room 4 Then adjourned to Imperial. Supper at Miss LeBrun's. Class night exercises

*June 21 1916 Wed.* English 2Lf exam 9-1 in Miss Dalton's.[951] Corrected in Miss LeBrun's all P.M. Graduation with faculty & Mr O'Halloran at night[952]

*June 22 1916 Th.* Up at 4:50 correcting and grading papers. Teacher's [teachers'] meeting, book accts. Everything. Supper at M O'Halloran's. Reception. Stayed up until 4:30 to see sunrise

*June 23 1916 Fri.* Up in time to get breakfast and catch 10:20 for Chauncy—Jr class picnic[953] Fine day, fine lunch, fine time. Bowling pool etc. Conference with Anna Hayes.[954]

*June 24 1916 Sat.* Felt like sleeping but got up in time to catch special for Union Picnic at Sterling Camp Grounds.[955] Played with kids all day

*June 25 1916 Sun.* Slept until S.S. time. Last meeting of Bible class this year. Spent early P.M. at Christine's and we adjourned to inspect Water St house & barn.[956]

---

951 Miss Dalton: Marlborough High School teacher Grace Dalton.
952 Mr. O'Halloran: Marlborough lawyer Thomas O'Halloran, brother of local high school teacher Mary E. O'Halloran.
953 Chauncy: perhaps Lake Chauncy in Westborough, which is not far from Marlborough.
954 Anna Hayes: possibly Anna M. Hayes of Marlborough (a daughter of John and Mary Hayes), who was eighteen in 1916.
955 Blessed by perfect weather, the Union Sunday School Picnic drew about 1,500 people. The Sterling Camp Grounds offered ample opportunity for sports events.
956 Jennie's first mention of 244 Water Street in Clinton—her family's new home.

*June 26 1916 Mon.* Spent the morning altering Maybelle's graduation dress. Went into Worcester with dad in the fliver Spent A.M with Dorothy. pocketbk O.K. Home 8

*June 27 1916 Tues.* All morning getting Maybelle's clothes adjusted. Went to graduation of 9th in PM and HS at night. Card from Stanley announcing enlistment[957]

*June 28 1916 Wed.* Chaperoned the ninth grades [graders] on picnic to Whalom with Miss Linton.[958] Fine time from 9:10 to 8:50. About fifty in party

*June 29 1916 Th.* Had a long lie and a slim breakfast. Played at tennis with Christine and spent P.M with her applied for Stonington Ct. position[959]

*June 30 1916 Fri.* Generally busy all A.M. Mother & I went on 12:51 to Camp Whitney.[960] Spent PM with Stanley. Home via Hudson reaching Clinton 11:40

*July 1 1916 Sat.* Cooked, ironed etc. Errands and call at Miss Stevens office PM Downtown with Baby and Florence Archambeault. Sewed quite a bit.

---

[957] Stanley McLeod—Jennie's brother—officially enlisted June 28, 1916. He served in Company K, 101st Infantry Regiment.
[958] Miss Linton: Clinton music teacher Martha M. Linton (daughter of Samuel and Mary Linton). She lived at 37 Grove Street.
[959] Jennie's application for an out-of-state job in Connecticut suggests that she understood that she would probably not secure a permanent position close to Clinton.
[960] Camp Whitney: a state military camp in South Framingham that served as a mobilization station for Massachusetts.

*July 2 1916 Sun.* Up in fair season. Cath Aunt Mary & Uncle Andy arrived for annual reunion at 2:10. Inspected house, ate, talked, made up diary

*July 3 1916 Mon.* Generally lazy all day except for household aids. First piazza party of the season at Miss Stevens. Eight present Good time

*July 4 1916 Tues. through November 23 1916 Th. No entries*

*November 24 1916 Fri.* Hospital Day.[961]

*November 25 1916 Sat. through November 29 1916 Wed. No entries*

*November 30 1916 Th.* Thanksgiving. Poker at Christines in the evening with Jack & Pauline.[962]

*December 1 1916 Fri. through December 25 1916 Mon. No entries*

---

[961] Several speakers presented at this public relations and fundraising event at the grammar school hall on subjects relating to the Clinton Hospital. The wet weather kept attendance light.
[962] Jack: possibly John Philbin, a younger brother of Marguerite, Rose, and Mary (Mame) Philbin.

*December 26 1916 Tues.* Bible class attend S.S. tree "Cuentos Alegres" my gift for keeps.[963] Then visited Road Comm about Barn policy and attended Elks "Mock Trial" in which Dad had a part.[964]

*December 27 1916 Wed.* Christine & I went to the H.S. play "The Dutch Detective," well done for its kind but it lacks central interest.[965] Marje Bates with us.

*December 28 1916 Th. No entry*

*December 29 1916 Fri.* Called at C.W.S's in the evening—Bridge Anna Hayes came over for lunch & to reune. Marg. & Anna Comaskey also guests at lunch which Maybelle served. Visited Auntie Jones dancing class party

*December 30 1916 Sat.* Card party at Christines in the evening—Marje & Doris Bates, Ethel G. & Betty Osgood.[966]

---

963 *Cuentos Alegres*: a book (*Joyful Tales*) by Spanish author Luis Taboada (1848-1906).

964 Dad had a very big part, indeed, in the Brotherhood of Elks mock trial, which was held in the Town Hall. George McLeod was the defendant in the case of Bastian v. McLeod, in which Mrs. Minot V. Bastian was suing for breach of promise. (Emily P. Bastian was the wife of a local dentist with an office at 48 High Street; the Bastians lived at 68 Prescott Street.). Mrs. Bastian's lawyers prevailed in the trial, which spread out over two hours, after which several shorter cases were also presented. The *Item* offered the understated assessment, "Many local jokes were sprung."

965 "The Dutch Detective": the high school senior class play, produced to defray commencement costs.

966 "Doris Bates": Marjorie's younger sister. "Ethel G.": conceivably Ethel Gannon, stenographer in the office of Clinton's Superintendent of Schools. The nineteen-year-old daughter of Martin and Elizabeth Gannon of 216 Stone Street, she is listed in the Clinton directory for 1916 as Ethel M. Gannon at Stone Street, in the 1910 federal census as Mary E. Gannon at the same address. "Betty Osgood": daughter of Edward G. Osgood, Secretary of the Clinton Chamber of Commerce, and his wife Florence. The Osgoods lived at 302 Chestnut Street. Elizabeth (Betty) went to Wellesley College.

***December 31 1916 Sun.*** Met J.I.M & Jack with Marg & Mame just before S.S. "Jim" is as grand & young as ever and may yet fulfill his mission as a cathedral builder   Read "Just David"[967]

— 1917 —

***January 1 1917 Mon.*** New Year resolution—To keep my diary regularly henceforth—Wrote remaining thank you notes. Read The Contagion of Character & Spanish reader[968]

***January 2 1917 Tues.*** Work and its pleasures once more. Spent the evening at home. Studied Spanish and read "What is it to be Educated?"[969]

***January 3 1917 Wed.*** Much snow—a veritable foot of it. Spanish club met with me. All present except Marg. Usual jovial time. Miss Stevens the teacher the questions most difficult

---

967   *Just David*: a 1916 children's novel by Eleanor H. Porter, author of Polyanna. Christine Beck had presented the story at a meeting of the Girls' Friendly Society on December 26.
968   *The Contagion of Character*: a 1911 book by Congregational minister, writer, and philosopher Newell D. Hillis (1858-1929).
969   "'What is it to be Educated?'": C. Hanford Henderson's book *What Is It To Be Educated?* (see Jennie's diary entry for October 25, 1914).

*January 4 1917 Th.* C.L.B. called at office latter P.M to talk G.F.S. Lit.⁹⁷⁰ Miss Stevens & I elected to see "Under Cover" at Star—no seats available.⁹⁷¹ Saw Salvation Joan at Globe—Very good.⁹⁷² Read a chapter of Henderson before retiring

*January 5 1917 Fri.* Wet and slushy. Took Maybelle to Woman's club to hear Lucia Hutchins of Leland Powers in Daddy-Longlegs.⁹⁷³ Extremely well done. L.K.S. in town. Spent the evening at home, read G.B.S's "Major Barbara" and revelled in it and the associations it aroused.⁹⁷⁴ Believe my first impression is that GBS is sincere & not satirical in estimate of Salv. Army

*January 6 1917 Sat.* Per usual. Called on Bessie Burns latter P.M.⁹⁷⁵ Went to Christine's to supper. Read with her Strindberg's "Pariah," reviewed shorthand⁹⁷⁶ Did Bible class review.

---

970 "G.F.S.": Girls' Friendly Society, which was apparently organizing a reading course.
971 *Under Cover*: a film released by Paramount on July 20, 1916, directed by Robert D. Vignola, starring Hazel Dawn and Owen Moore.
972 *Salvation Joan*: a 1916 film directed by Wilfrid North, starring Edna May.
973 Miss Lucia Hutchins of Fitchburg recited the story told by Jean Webster in her 1912 novel *Daddy-Long-Legs*.
974 George Bernard Shaw's play *Major Barbara* is about a young woman involved with helping the poor through the Salvation Army and whose father is a munitions maker. It was written in 1905 and first published in 1907.
975 Teacher Bessie D. Burns lived on East Street in 1916. She was a daughter of William and Emma Burns, parents of Irish and German descent, respectively.
976 "Strindberg's 'Pariah'": a one-act play (written 1888-1889).

"THIS IS THE LIFE"

*January 7 1917 Sun.* Up early. Prof Foote of Harvard at Unit Ch on "Our Thought of God"[977] went with Christine. Then to Bible class at Epis. Ch—Late!! Spent afternoon at Marg's and went to vespers at R.C. Church with her & Mary Philbin. They came home with me. Read some Henderson, retired before ten.

*January 8 1917 Mon.* Spent A.M. soliciting accident insurance Special Aid class met at Miss Stevens for first lesson.[978] 22 present. Letter from Bertha. Discussed religion with Miss Stevens with much satisfaction Studied Spanish grammar in the evening

*January 9 1917 Tues.* Wrote Bertha pledging meeting at Worcester in Feb. Tutored Carl in Latin. No letter from Babes, no letter to Babes. Read for an hour before retiring.

*January 10 1917 Wed.* Typewrote G.F.S. booklists for C.L.B. all afternoon. Weekly Spanish at Miss Stevens. Full attendance. Marg. spent the night with me.

*January 11 1917 Th.* Devoted early evening to Latin with Carl. Read for a while, Retired early but slept very little on account of the intense cold.

---

977  On Unitarian Revival Sunday, the Reverend Henry Wilder Foote (a professor at Harvard Divinity School) spoke on "The Unitarian Thought of God."
978  A multi-session program on elementary hygiene and home care of the sick, sponsored by the local branch of the Special Aid Society for American Preparedness and under the supervision of the Red Cross. Hazen Gammon and Bessie Upham of the Clinton Hospital staff were instructors. The European War was clearly taking on greater significance in the local consciousness by this point.

*January 12 1917 Fri.* Friend John came into office in the morning and went off without his shed for his glasses  Went to movies with C.L.B. & Aunt Isabel.[979]  Had a shampoo and tatted in the evening

*January 13 1917 Sat.* Kept office for Dad in the snowy evening.  Studied Spanish grammar

*January 14 1917 Sun.* Up in time for study & S.S. which was dismissed on account of wind & rain.  Read Spanish and dreamed in the afternoon.  Letter to Babes in the evening.

*January 15 1917 Mon.* Practical lesson in Prep. course at Mrs. Fuller's on bed-making.[980]  Chamber of Comm annual meeting in evening.

*January 16 1917 Tues.* No letter from Babes.—Naughty darling!!  Spent the evening on Algebra with Carl.

*January 17 1917 Wed.* More or less social day at office.  Read Jettatura to Miss Stevens while she carved[981]  Full Spanish class at Christine's but no roommate afterwards

---

979 "Aunt Isabel": Isabelle T. Beck, sister of Christine's father Louis G. Beck. Isabelle Beck lived on Water Street in Clinton before moving into the Cedar Street home of her brother and his family.

980 "Mrs. Fuller's": likely Mrs. Eben S. Fuller (Cora A. Fuller), who offered classes for girls on sewing and millinery. The Fullers lived in South Lancaster. The elderly Eben Fuller had operated the Clinton Wood Yard at 354 High Street.

981 *Jettatura*: a novel by French poet, writer, and critic Théophile Gautier (1811-1872), first published in 1856. Miss Stevens was an artist, so "while she carved" probably means as she was sculpting.

*January 18 1917 Th.* Expected Carl so couldn't follow impulse to go to High School fire which lasted but a short time.[982]

*January 19 1917 Fri.* Went back to office early part of afternoon. Called on Christine and found her with the grippe. Took Ethel to Woman's Club. Havrah Hubbard operalogue Falstaff[983]

*January 20 1917 Sat.* Went down town in the evening & bought cretonne for Co. K donation[984] Ice cream party with mother & the baby

*January 21 1917 Sun.* Bible class at noon. Sewed on Co. K. Bazaar articles. Called on C.L.B., took sandwiches to G.F.S. supper for her, then called some more. Personal analyses etc

*January 22 1917 Mon.* Spent the evening dutifully studying Spanish and did a lesson in advance.

*January 23 1917 Tues.* Spanish class at Ethel's. Christine absent on account of grippe & wedding to-morrow, Marg at whist party.[985] The remaining four of us made merry as usual

---

982  High School fire: the origin of the fire was unknown, the damage it caused minimal.
983  A Clinton Women's Club program by Havrah Hubbard (William Lines Hubbard) of Boston. Operalogue: a lecture on opera presenting a summary of the particular subject (in this instance, Verdi's comic opera *Falstaff*). The Women's Club event featured piano selections performed by Claude Gotthels.
984  Co. K donation: the fabric purchase was probably made for use in advance of the Company K bazaar opening on January 31. Jennie's diary entry for January 21 shows her busy sewing for the event.
985  Christine Beck and her family attended the wedding of Janet Camrie Rodger and J. Ramsay Davidson at the Congregational church in Brighton. Christine—whose father was a cousin of the groom's father—was a bridesmaid.

*January 24 1917 Wed.* Looked up games for Bible class party and served on entertainment Comm. Lost my Senior pin for the third time en route for the social. Nice evening

*January 25 1917 Th.* Went downtown with Helen to get dress material. Met R.I.D on way home and went home with her for the evening. Engagement felicitations

*January 26 1917 Fri.* Attempted to make a blouse for Helen  Gave up. Called with Christine on Mildred Donnelly & Ruth.[986]

*January 27 1917 Sat.* Bible class at noon. Read and sewed on K. Co. gift in the afternoon  Letters & books in the evening.

*January 28 1917 Sun. and January 29 1917 Mon.  No entries*

*January 30 1917 Tues.* Twenty-fourth birthday, nice letters, cards, congratulations and gifts. Tutored Carl in the evening.

*January 31 1917 Wed.* Kept office alone all A.M, busy as could be. Jr. Chau. in the P.M. Entertained Dot Powell. Attended K. Co. Bazaar with party in evening.[987] Talk philosophy with Dot until morning

---

986 "Mildred Donnelly": born about 1894, Mildred Donnelly was the wife of James M. Donnelly (who worked in the administrative office of the carpet mill) and the mother of two small children. The Donnellys lived at 82 Haskell Avenue.

987 "K Co. Bazaar": the well-attended opening night of a fundraising event at the armory. The bazaar and festival featured a drill, booths with sale items and amusements, and dancing. James T. Duane served as the master of ceremonies. Jennie's brother Stanley was involved with organizing the event.

*February 1 1917 Th.* Spanish club met with Miss Stevens and under her discipline  Marg. Ethel & I became well-versed in the elusive counting system.  Marg with me over-night

*February 2 1917 Fri.* Odds & ends in the morning. Tutored Carl at 2. Took Maybelle & Dorothy to Woman's Club. Arthur Fisher in "Borrowed Spectacles"[988]  Called on the Spragues in the eve.

*February 3 1917 Sat. through February 8 1917 Th. No entries*

*February 9 1917 Fri.* Enjoyed a birthday supper at Christine's in honor of my 24th yr. Cake with lighted candles and everything to make one happy.

*February 10 1917 Sat. and February 11 1917 Sun. No entries*

*February 12 1917 Mon.* Went to Historical Soc. Annual party with Dad. "The Sunbeams" gave pleasing entertainment.[989]  Palled with C.L.B, M.F.P. & E.K.S.

*February 13 1917 Tues. No entry*

*February 14 1917 Wed.* Spanish at Ethel's. All present. Business sessioned [session] adjourned to celebrate Ethel's 27th birthday with feast and song.

---

988 "Borrowed Spectacles": likely *A Pair of Spectacles*, a three-act comedy adapted from the French by English dramatist Sydney Grundy (1848-1914).

989 "The Sunbeams": Hannah Baird of Kentucky and Bertha McDonough of Massachusetts, who, as subsequently reported in the *Item*, presented the program: "In their readings, recitations, dialogue, and songs, the former illustrated the negro dialect of the sunny south and the latter that of the Irish of the snowy north."

*February 15 1917 Th.* Carl and Algebra in the evening.

*February 16 1917 Fri.* Mrs. W.S. Duncan read interesting paper at the Club. Meeting in charge of Ec. Comm. Mrs. Dowling the speaker told food truths[990]

*February 17 1917 Sat.* Took Mildred to a 10-20-30 at the Star.[991] Verdict as usual "Never Again"—but?!!

*February 18 1917 Sun.* Bible class at noon. Heated discussion on Relation of Church & State  Spent the afternoon at Mrs Hubbards.[992]

*February 19 1917 Mon.* Special Aid class at Mrs. Fuller's in charge of Miss Gammon  Subject: Baths.

*February 20 1917 Tues.* Miss Stevens guest at Girls' Friendly Musical at her home. The ever charming Mrs. Stratton gave an Arthur Sullivan program.[993] Splendid music.

---

990  The February 17, 1917 issue of the *Clinton Daily Item* includes a full account of this meeting of the Clinton Women's Club, which was held in the Music Hall ("Household Economics. Women's Club Hears Practical Suggestions on the Subject").

991  "10-20-30": refers to the tiered price of admission at cheap playhouses offering vaudeville and other popular entertainment. As advertised in the *Clinton Daily Item*, the Star was featuring a slate of vaudeville acts on February 17, 1917.

992  Mrs. Hubbard: Grace G. Hubbard, who was married to William L. Hubbard, a dealer in dry goods on High Street. The Hubbards lived at 116 Walnut Street.

993  "Mrs. Stratton": possibly Mrs. Arthur M. Stratton of South Lancaster. "Arthur Sullivan": English composer known for his collaborations with W.S. Gilbert.

*February 21 1917 Wed.* Ash Wednesday. School visiting Day. Spent 6th period visiting Helen's & Maybelle's Eng. classes. 6th Grade 1:30-2:00. Church in eve. Kelly the Boyologist after church.[994] C.L.B.

*February 22 1917 Th.* Slept until noon, due to headache Read Ivanhoe in bed in the afternoon[995] Got supper for Helen & mother. Carl in the evening.

*February 23 1917 Fri.* Met Marg. at close of school. Went home with her and spent afternoon & early evening. Went up to get book from Mrs. Beck. Christine in Boston at Netta's

*February 24 1917 Sat.* Took back "The Girl & Her Religion" to Mrs. Beck, having read it.[996] Tempted to go to Wellesley to-morrow to hear Pres Burton—but didn't.[997]

*February 25 1917 Sun.* Went to church with Mrs Beck much to Dr Jordan's chagrin.[998] Bible class. Read The Spirit of Youth & The City Streets by Jane Addams.[999] Wrote at length to Babes & studied Special Aid

---

994 "Kelly the Boyologist:" L. Stanley Kelly of New Haven, who talked at the grammar school hall about the guidance and management of boys.
995 *Ivanhoe*: a historical novel by Sir Walter Scott, first published in 1819.
996 *The Girl and Her Religion*: a 1913 book by Margaret Slattery.
997 On Sunday, February 25, 1917, between leaving the presidency of Smith College and assuming that of the University of Minnesota, Marion LeRoy Burton preached at the morning chapel service at Wellesley College.
998 Clinton's Congregational pastor clearly noticed Jennie's increasing interest in the Episcopal Church of the Good Shepherd.
999 First published in 1909, Jane Addams's *The Spirit of Youth and the City Streets* explores the damaging effect of city life on the young and the need for programs to encourage the development of urban youth.

*February 26 1917 Mon.* A wet day. Had lunch with Miss Stevens and Miss Russell at Miss Russell's bidding[1000] No Special Aid class. Evening at 223 Chestnut Masters' Spoon River Anthology[1001]— Marg spent night here

*February 27 1917 Tues.* C.L.B. spent P.M at office telephoning Spec Aid Jr. Chau early P.M, then kept office while Miss Stevens conducted meeting addressed by Lt Jas A. Sullivan on Plum Island.[1002] Carl in the evening

*February 28 1917 Wed. through December 31 1917 Mon. No entries*

— 1918 —

*January 1 1918 Tues. through April 17 1918 Wed. No entries*

*April 18 1918 Th.* Write Marg, Arlene, Helen

*April 19 1918 Fri. through December 31 1918 Tues. No entries*

---

1000 Miss Russell: Sarah L. Russell, cousin of Ellen Stevens. Miss Russell lived with Miss Stevens at 223 Chestnut Street.
1001 *Spoon River Anthology*: a 1915 collection of free-verse poems by American lawyer, poet, novelist, and playwright Edgar Lee Masters (1868-1950). The book paints a picture of small-town life—a subject that may well have resonated for readers in a close-knit community like Clinton.
1002 Ellen K. Stevens presided over a program sponsored by the Special Aid Society in the Music Hall. Lieutenant James Sullivan spoke about community preparedness and about the military training camps at Plattsburg and Plum Island, showing lantern slides as part of his presentation, and spoke again that evening at the armory as the guest of the Clinton Rifle Club ("Training in Summer Camps," *Clinton Daily Item*, February 28, 1917).

"THIS IS THE LIFE"

# MEMORANDA[1003]

### WINTER JR. CHAUTAUQUA RECEIPTS

| | | |
|---|---|---|
| Fri. July 23 1915 | W.I. Jenkins | $1.00 cash |
| | Caroline Shaw | $1.00 cash |
| | Geo. Sutherland | $5.00 cash |
| | C.M. McCance | $1.00 cash |
| | Eliz. J. Fox | $1.00 cash |
| | W.W. Wallace | $1.00 cash |
| | Geo. Gibson | $5.00 cash |
| | Frank Byrne | $1.00 cash |
| Th. July 29 1915 | Adelaide Fuller | $1.00 check |
| Th. August 19 1915 | F.G. Stowers | $1.00 cash |
| Fri. August 27 1915 | W.R. Dame | $1.00 cash |
| | Jennie S. Dame | $1.00 cash |
| Sat. August 28 1915 | Mrs. E.F. Bemis | $2.00 cash |
| Sun. August 29 1915 | Esther Towne | .50 cash |
| Th. September 2 1915 | Mrs. A.W. Newhall | $1.00 cash |
| Fri. September 3 1915 | Chas. A. Needham | $1.00 cash |
| Th. September 9 1915 | Mrs. L.G. Beck | $1.00 cash |
| Fri. September 10 1915 | Mr. C.A. Buttrick | $1.00 cash |
| Tues. September 14 1915 | E.K. Stevens | $1.00 cash |
| | Mrs. R.R. Stevenson | $1.00 cash |
| | Christine Stevenson | $1.00 cash |
| | Cameron Duncan | $1.00 cash |
| Sun. September 19 1915 | Marguerite Burdett | $1.00 cash |
| Mon. September 20 1915 | Mrs. Warren Goodale | $1.00 cash |
| | Mrs. J.C. Duncan | $1.00 cash |
| | Mrs. W.M. Lee | $1.00 cash |
| | Dr. J.J. Goodwin | $1.00 cash |
| | Mrs. Geo. A. Whitney | $1.00 cash |
| Wed. September 22 1915 | Mrs. McCracken | $1.00 cash |
| | Mrs. A.F. Brockelman | $1.00 cash |
| | Mrs. Jaquith | $1.00 cash |
| Tues. September 28 1915 | Dr. C.L. French | $1.00 cash |
| | Mrs. J.M. Gibson | $1.00 cash |
| Wed. October 6 1915 | Mary P. McQuaid | $1.00 cash |
| | Miss Carr | $1.00 cash |

---

1003 "Memoranda" is the printed heading for the pages following those formatted for diary entries. Jennie used this final section of her five-year diary for financial records.

|                      | Mrs. Alfred Wiesman   | $1.00 cash |
|                      | Mrs. Carrie Hudson    | $1.00 cash |
| Fri. November 12 1915 | Foodsale             | $24.42 |
| Tues. January 18 1916 | Mrs. Hamilton (Alpha) | $4.58 |
| Fri. February 18 1916 | May Leahy             | $1.00 |

## JR. CHAUTAUQUA—PAID OUT

|                      | Food sale ad—Item    | $00.30 |
| F. W. W.             | paraffin paper (.05) |        |
|                      | twine (.05)          |        |
|                      | pins (.02)           | $00.12 |
| Th. December 23 1915 | cherry tree (.75)    |        |
|                      | Rev. st. Fly         |        |
|                      | Film (.01)           | $00.76 |
|                      | Cards (.20)          |        |
|                      | Postage (.06)        | $00.26 |
| Wed. January 26 1916 | Advt. Item           | $00.30 |

## CHAMBER OF COMMERCE RECEIPTS

| Mrs. Bemis        | $5.00 Pd. |
| John Gutman       | $5.00 Pd. |
| David Wagner      | $1.00 Pd. |
| Chas. F. Martin   | $5.00 Pd. |
| Dupuis Bros.      | $5.00 Pd. |
| Elie Corbeil      | $5.00—Jan. 1 |
| Fred Whitcomb     | $5.00 Pd. |
| Alpha McCracken   | $5.00 Pd. |
| Wm. Reisner       | $5.00 Pd. |

# ACKNOWLEDGMENTS

A project like *"This Is the Life"* is deeply satisfying not only because piecing together a life story requires skill and creativity, but also because it provides opportunities to connect meaningfully with others who find local history and primary documentation interesting. This book has benefited significantly from the generosity of such people.

For various kinds of assistance, I am grateful to Terrance Ingano and his comrades at the Holder Memorial of the Clinton Historical Society; Clinton Town Clerk Holly Sargent and Assistant Town Clerk Becky Schoolcraft; the staff at the Assessors' Office in Clinton; Smith College Archivist Nanci Young and her colleagues; Archivist and Digital Initiatives Librarian Lauren Loftis at Simmons University; Sara Ludovissy, Assistant Archivist in the Wellesley College Archives; the librarians at Clinton's Bigelow Free Public Library; Joe Mulé and his staff at the Thayer Memorial Library in Lancaster; Barbara Gugluizza and her Reference staff at the Concord Free Public Library; Benjamin Kalish and Dylan Gaffney at the Forbes Library in Northampton; David W. Gibbs at the Sterling Historical Society; Mary Ciummo at the Bolton Historical Society; Lisa Bergman at Clinton's Church of the Good Shepherd; and, for facilitating access to *HeritageQuest Online*, to staff at the Leominster Public Library.

Special thanks to biographer Megan Marshall, social historian Rob-

ACKNOWLEDGMENTS

ert A. Gross, Lancaster Historical Commission Chair Heather Lennon, and public historian Jayne Gordon for agreeing to read and comment on *"This Is the Life"*.

Robert and Judith McLeod (Jennie McLeod's nephew and his wife) were gracious beyond expectation in inviting me into their home to talk about Jennie and her family, as was my Water Street neighbor Frances Mahan. Two helpful gentlemen at Charles M. Moran Plumbing & Heating in Clinton talked informally with me about the McLeod plumbing business. And Ken Lizotte of the emerson consulting group inc. provided friendly advice and encouragement.

I deeply appreciate the hands-on efforts of Crystal Wright of Moonglade Press, whose sound editorial instincts improved the original manuscript of this book; Thomas Osborne of Thomas Osborne Design in Redmond, Oregon for copyediting the manuscript and laying out the book; Steve Collins of Collins Artworks in Clinton and Anni Wilson of Charlottesville, Virginia for scanning and editing images for the illustrations; and Jocelyn Kelly for taking an awesome author's photograph.

Even the most engaging research venture is more satisfying when someone else shares the thrill of exploration and discovery. I have been able to count on the interest of my husband Michael in every breakthrough in Jennie McLeod's story. I owe him a lot for his lifelong encouragement of my enthusiasms.

L.P.W.

# SOURCES

This list does not include every source consulted in the preparation of *"This Is the Life."* It represents nearly all of those cited in the footnotes to the introduction but not all used for the editor's annotations to Jennie McLeod's diary. It would take a very long list, indeed, to account for every one of the many notices and articles in the *Clinton Daily Item* and the numerous reference and Web resources accessed in the hunt for information for diary annotations. Moreover, many sources tapped for factual information for a single diary entry are peripheral to Jennie McLeod's story overall.

"**The Allan Line.**" *Norway Heritage—Hands Across the Sea.* http://www.norwayheritage.com/p_shiplist.asp?co=allan (accessed October 16, 2019).

**(Alpha Club reunion.)** Newspaper notice of Alpha Club reunion on January 1, 1914 in Clinton, Massachusetts. *Clinton Daily Item.* January 3, 1914: 3.

"**Auto Goes Into Brook.** George McLeod Cuts His Hand in Accident at West Berlin Saturday." *Clinton Daily Item.* August 30, 1915: 1.

"**Billy Murray (singer).**" *Wikipedia.* https://en.wikipedia.org/wiki/Billy_Murray_(singer) (accessed December 17, 2019).

**Blake, Warren Barton.** "America's Only Municipal Theatre." *The Theatre Magazine.* Vol. 20, No. 164 (October 1914): 166-70, 188.

**Bolton (Massachusetts).** "History of Bolton Massachusetts: Settlement Pattern: Late Industrial Period (1873-1914)." *Town of Bolton Massachusetts* (website). https://www.townofbolton.com/discover-bolton/pages/history-bolton-massachusetts (accessed April 6, 2020).

**(Bolton observation towers.)** Typed transcript of information published in the *Clinton Courant*, August 26, 1876, regarding observation towers on Wattaquadock Hill in Bolton. Bolton Historical Society, Bolton, Massachusetts.

## SOURCES

"**Boston and Worcester Street Railway.**" *Wikipedia.*
https://en.wikipedia.org/wiki/Boston_and_Worcester_Street_Railway
(accessed December 16, 2019).

*Boston Passenger and Crew Lists, 1820-1943.* Ancestry.

*Brattleboro Vermont Directory 1917.* Greenfield, Massachusetts: H.A. Manning Company, copyright 1917.

**Burton, Marion LeRoy.** "The New Curriculum." *Smith Alumnae Quarterly.* Vol. 7, No. 1 (November 1915): 1-8.

"**Campaign Opens Tonight:** Mrs. George and Miss Dorman to Address Anti-Suffragists Meeting in Music Hall." *Clinton Daily Item.* June 7, 1915: 1.

"**Central Massachusetts Railroad.**" *Wikipedia.*
https://en.wikipedia.org/wiki/Central_Massachusetts_Railroad
(accessed December 21, 2019).

**(Chautauqua.)** Newspaper articles covering Chautauqua in Clinton in 1914 and 1915. *Clinton Daily Item.* July 31-August 7, 1914, July 19-July 26, 1915.

**Church of the Good Shepherd (Clinton, Massachusetts).** Parish Register, Volume B (manuscript volume). Church of the Good Shepherd Office, Clinton, Massachusetts.

**Church of the Good Shepherd (Clinton, Massachusetts).** Girls' Friendly Society. Secretary's Book, 1919-1931 (manuscript record volume). Church of the Good Shepherd Office, Clinton, Massachusetts.

**Clinton (Massachusetts).** *By-Laws of the Town of Clinton, Massachusetts, 1914.* Clinton: W.J. Coulter Press for The Town, 1914.

**Clinton (Massachusetts).** Printed annual municipal reports for 1890-1930. Reports of particular importance to this project:

*Sixty-fourth Annual Report of the Town Officers of Clinton, Mass., for the Year Ending January 31, 1914.* Clinton: W.J. Coulter Press for The Town, 1914.

*Sixty-sixth Annual Report of the Town Officers of Clinton, Mass., for the Year Ending December 31, 1915.* Clinton: W.J. Coulter Press for The Town, 1916.

*Seventy-sixth Annual Report of the Town Officers of Clinton, Mass., for the Year Ending December 31, 1926.* Clinton: W.J. Coulter Press for The Town, 1927.

SOURCES

Clinton (Massachusetts). Assessors. Assessors' abstract for 244 Water Street (manuscript card). Assessors' Office, Town Hall, Clinton, Massachusetts.

Clinton (Massachusetts). Assessors. Valuation list (manuscript commitment book). 1917. Assessors' Office, Town Hall, Clinton, Massachusetts.

Clinton (Massachusetts). Bigelow Free Public Library. *Forty-second Annual Report of the Directors of the Bigelow Free Public Library of the Town of Clinton, Mass., for the Year Ending December 31, 1915.* Clinton: W.J. Coulter Press for The Town, 1916.

Clinton (Massachusetts). School Department. Printed annual school reports for the years 1905-1920. Reports of particular relevance:

*School Report, Clinton, Mass., for the Year Ending January 31, 1908.* Clinton: W.J. Coulter Press for The Town, 1908.

*School Report, Clinton, Mass., for the Year Ending January 31, 1911.* Clinton: W.J. Coulter Press for The Town, 1911.

*School Report, Clinton, Mass., for the Year Ending January 31, 1912.* Clinton: W.J. Coulter Press for The Town, 1912.

*School Report, Clinton, Mass., for the Year Ending December 31, 1915.* Clinton: W.J. Coulter Press for the Town, 1915.

*Sixty-seventh Annual Report of the School Department, Clinton, Mass., for the Year Ending December 31, 1916.* Clinton: W.J. Coulter Press for The Town, 1917.

*Seventieth Annual Report of the School Department, Clinton, Mass., for the Year Ending December 31, 1919.* Clinton: W.J. Coulter Press for The Town, 1920.

*Seventy-first Annual Report of the School Department, Clinton, Mass., for the Year Ending December 31, 1920.* Clinton: W.J. Coulter Press for The Town, 1921.

Clinton (Massachusetts). Town Clerk. Registered Births, Clinton, Massachusetts (manuscript records). Volumes 2 (1882-1898) and 3 (1899-1910). Town Clerk's Office, Town Hall, Clinton, Massachusetts.

*Clinton Centennial Volume, 1850-1950: The Story of Clinton, Massachusetts, Incorporated March 14, 1850, and the Clinton Centennial Celebration.* Clinton: The Town, copyright 1951.

SOURCES

*Clinton Daily Item* (Clinton, Massachusetts). Many issues from the period 1914-1918 and some for subsequent years into the 1990s were consulted. Individual notices and articles most significant in the preparation of *This Is the Life* are listed by title.

*Clinton Directory* (title varies—also published under the titles *Clinton and Lancaster Directory* and *Clinton Lancaster Directory*). Fitchburg (later Fitchburg and New Haven or New Haven alone): Price & Lee Co. Directories from 1893 through the 1990s were consulted.

**Clinton High School (Clinton, Massachusetts).** Classes of 1914, 1918, and 1920. *Memorabilia* (yearbooks). Clinton: Clinton High School, 1914, 1918, and 1920 (respectively).

*Clinton Military Case History.* Volume 2 (Works Project Administration typescript compilation). 1937. Clinton Historical Society (Holder Memorial), Clinton, Massachusetts.

**Clinton Women's Club (Clinton, Massachusetts).** *Yearbook of the Clinton Women's Club, Clinton, Massachusetts, 1899-1900 ...* Clinton: W.J. Coulter for The Club, 1900. "Social Organizations" pamphlet and ephemera box, Clinton Historical Society (Holder Memorial), Clinton, Massachusetts.

**Davis, Waldo T.** "Clinton at the Turn of the Century, 1900-1910." *Clinton Centennial Volume, 1850-1950: The Story of Clinton, Massachusetts, Incorporated March 14, 1850, and the Clinton Centennial Celebration.* Clinton: The Town, copyright 1951. 18-38.

**"Dr. E. Irene Boardman never stopped Serving the Public."** *Connecticut History.org.* https://connecticuthistory.org/dr-e-irene-boardman-never-stopped-serving-the-public/ (accessed February 2, 2020).

**Dorenkamp, John,** with addenda by Allan Mueller. *History of the "Germantown" Area in Clinton, Massachusetts (circa 1850-2000): A Collection of Photographs, Historical Research, and Recollections.* Clinton: The Germantown Historical Preservation Project, 2017.

**Duane, James T.** *Dear Old "K."* Boston: Thomas Todd Co., 1922.

**Education Scotland.** "Migration and Empire: Emigration and Scottish History." *NQ Scottish History.*
http://www.sath.org.uk/edscot/www.educationscotland.gov.uk/higherscottishhistory/migrationandempire/migrationofscots/emigrationandsociety.html
(accessed October 16, 2019).

**"Euphemia Lofton Haynes Biography."** *Biography.com.*
https//www.biography.com/scientist/euphemia-lofton-haynes
(accessed August 30, 2019).

SOURCES

**Facebook group "You know you're from Clinton, MA if ... "** Posts by Elaine Marino, Ann Whalen, Cathy Porter Mahan, and others in response to request for McLeod family information.
https://www.facebook.com/groups/276577909182016/ (September 14, 2019).

*Find A Grave.* https://www.findagrave.com/ (accessed frequently in 2019 and 2020 for information on many people associated with Jennie McLeod's diary).

**First Methodist Church (Clinton, Massachusetts).** Young Adult Group. *Clinton First Centennial Cook Book.* Clinton: Young Adult Group, First Methodist Church, 1950. Includes several submissions by Jennie McLeod, among them her recipe for fudge cake.

**"Fitchburg and Worcester Railroad."** *Wikipedia.*
https://en.wikipedia.org/wiki/Fitchburg_and_Worcester_Railroad
(accessed December 16, 2019).

**Flexner, Eleanor, and Ellen Fitzpatrick.** *Century of Struggle: The Woman's Rights Movement in the United States.* Enlarged edition. Cambridge: The Belknap Press of Harvard University Press, copyright 1996.

**Ford, Andrew E.** *History of the Origin of the Town of Clinton, Massachusetts, 1653-1865.* Clinton: Press of W.J. Coulter, Courant Office, 1896.

**Gavin, Lettie.** *American Women in World War I. They Also Served.* Niwot, Colorado: University Press of Colorado, copyright 1997.

**"Germans Will Not Vote for Wilson:** Resolution to That Effect Passed at Worcester Meeting." *Clinton Daily Item.* October 25, 1915: 6.

**Gibbons, Thomas F.** "Peace, Prosperity, and War, 1910-1920." *Clinton Centennial Volume, 1850-1950: The Story of Clinton, Massachusetts, Incorporated March 14, 1850, and the Clinton Centennial Celebration.* Clinton: The Town, copyright 1951. 40-66.

**Gordon, Lewis S., Jr.** "The Old Order Changes, 1920-1930." *Clinton Centennial Volume, 1850-1950: The Story of Clinton, Massachusetts, Incorporated March 14, 1850, and the Clinton Centennial Celebration.* Clinton: The Town, copyright 1951. 68-95.

**Graves, Karen.** *Girls' Schooling During the Progressive Era: From Female Scholar to Domesticated Citizen.* New York; London: Garland Publishing, 1998.

**"Greenock."** *Wikipedia.*
https://en.wikipedia.org/wiki/Greenock
(accessed November 4, 2019).

SOURCES

**Hawkes, Clarence.** "Old Hadley, Past and Present." *The Village: A Journal of Village Life.* February 1907: 86-90.

**Haynes, Euphemia Lofton.** Oral history interview with Mary Jo Deering. October 26, 1972 (typed transcription February 7, 1973). Smith Centennial Study, Smith College Archives, Northampton, Massachusetts. Transcript in the Smith College Archives is accompanied by supplementary materials: curriculum vitae; Euphemia Lofton Haynes, "The Identity Crisis" (typescript address given by E.L.H. at Smith Class of 1914 Class Reunion, May 30, 1969); Nancy Weiss, "Leader for the Public Schools, *Smith Alumnae Quarterly*, November 1967: 12-14).

**"In District Contests.** Whitney and Tyler for Representatives and Hobbs for the Senate. The Suffrage Vote." *Clinton Daily Item.* November 3, 1915: 1.

**Ingano, Terrance.** *Images of America: Clinton.* Dover, New Hampshire: Arcadia Publishing, 1996.

**"Johnston Forbes-Robertson."** *Wikipedia.* https://en.wikipedia.org/wiki/Johnston_Forbes-Robertson (accessed December 30, 2019).

**Kennedy, David M.** *Over Here: The First World War and American Society.* New York: Oxford University Press, copyright 2004.

**Leidholdt, Alexander S.** *Battling Nell: The Life of Southern Journalist Cornelia Battle Lewis, 1893-1956.* Baton Rouge: Louisiana State University Press, 2009.

**Lincoln, Eleanor Terry, and John Abel Pinto.** *This, the House We Live In: The Smith College Campus from 1871 to 1982.* Northampton, Massachusetts: The College, 1983.

**"McCance, Andrew."** Dickinson, Donald C. *Dictionary of American Antiquarian Bookdealers.* Westport, Connecticut: Greenwood Press, 1998. 139.

**McCarthy, Molly.** "A Pocketful of Days: Pocket Diaries and Daily Record Keeping among Nineteenth-Century New England Women." *The New England Quarterly.* Vol. 73, No. 2 (June 2000): 274-96.

**McLeod, Jennie C.** Five-year diary (pre-printed lined volume, with daily entries recorded in manuscript). 1914-1918. Personal collection of the author, Clinton, Massachusetts.

SOURCES

**McLeod, Jennie C.** Lecture reports by Jennie C. McLeod in the *Clinton Daily Item:*

"Lecture in Grammar Hall. Prof. Levermore Talks on 'The European Conflict' Before Crowded House." October 13, 1915: 3.

"Prof. Powys' Lecture: 'Keats,' or 'The Cult of the Beautiful,' His Theme on Monday Evening. Judge Smith Presides." January 6, 1914: 1, 3.

**McLeod, Robert and Judith.** Personal interview with the author. September 20, 2019.

**McLeod family obituaries in the** *Clinton Daily Item* (listed chronologically):

"Death of Former Rep. George McLeod Occurred Last Night." February 8, 1936: 1.

"Stanley M. McLeod, Sr." October 6, 1955: 4.

"Private Services for Miss McLeod [Jennie C. McLeod] Are Held Today." July 29, 1968: 1.

"George McLeod." May 2, 1984: 2.

"Helen W. McLeod." March 13, 1996: 2.

"Maybelle McLeod." March 9, 1999: 4.

**Mahan, Frances.** Personal interview with the author. December 19, 2019.

**Massachusetts. Bureau of Statistics.** *The Decennial Census, 1915. Taken Under the Direction of Charles F. Gettemy, Director of the Bureau of Statistics.* Boston: Wright and Potter Printing Co., 1918.

**Massachusetts. Bureau of Statistics of Labor.** *Census of Massachusetts: 1895. Prepared Under the Direction of Horace G. Wadlin, Chief of the Bureau of Statistics of Labor. Volume I. Population and Social Statistics.* Boston: Wright & Potter Printing Co., 1896.

**Massachusetts. State Board of Health.** *Monthly Bulletin of the State Board of Health of Massachusetts.* Vol. 7, New Series (February 1912).

**Massachusetts Historical Society.** "Massachusetts Woman Suffrage Victory Parade: Instructions for Marchers." *Massachusetts Historical Collections online.* https://www.masshist.org/database/1892 (accessed February 2, 2020).

*Massachusetts Marriage Records, 1840-1915.* Ancestry.

SOURCES

*Massachusetts Passenger and Crew Lists, 1820-1963. Ancestry.*

**(Massachusetts town directories.)** *Family History Books and Directories. HeritageQuest Online.* Published directories were consulted for multiple Massachusetts towns and cities in addition to Clinton—among them Boston, Dedham, Hadley, Marlborough, Northampton, Southborough, and Worcester.

**Massachusetts Water Resources Authority.** "1897—Wachusett Reservoir."
http://www.mwra.com/04water/html/hist4.htm
(accessed January 12, 2020).

**"Miss Ellen K. Stevens" (biographical note).** *Clinton Centennial Volume, 1850-1950: The Story of Clinton, Massachusetts, Incorporated March 14, 1850, and the Clinton Centennial Celebration.* Clinton: The Town, copyright 1951. 2.

**"Model T Music and Lyrics."**
https://www.fordmodelt.net/music.htm#The_Little_Ford_Rambled_Right_Along
(accessed December 17, 2019).

**Moffat, Mary Jane, and Charlotte Painter, editors.** *Revelations: Diaries of Women.* New York: Vintage Books, 1975.

**(Niquette, Northampton, Massachusetts.)** Anastigmat (pseudonym). "From Nothing to $150 a Week. How New England Druggust Built up Photo Department." *The Pharmaceutical Era.* July 1916: 283.

**Notice of award to George McLeod of contract** for the heating and ventilating system of the Walnut Street School in Clinton. *The Heating and Ventilating Magazine.* Vol. 11, No. 9 (September 1914): 70.

**Notice of award to George McLeod of contract** to install plumbing in Lancaster Mills apartments in Clinton. *Domestic Engineering.* May 18, 1918: 265.

**Notice of sale by Mrs. Elizabeth M. Pope of her interest in the Clinton insurance agency of S.R. Merrick & Co.** to C.G. Stevens & Son. *The Standard.* Vol. 87. December 4, 1920: 687.

**"Pauline Vera Bartlett."** *Haskell Family History: the Haskell Family Tree genealogy database.*
http://www.haskellfamilyhistory.com/haskell/4/82599.html
(accessed January 11, 2020).

**"Peace Sunday Sermon."** *Clinton Daily Item.* October 9, 1914: 5.

## SOURCES

**Pocumtuck Valley Memorial Association (Deerfield, Massachusetts).** "The Hockanum Ferry, Northampton to Hadley" and "Hockanum Ferry, Northampton, Mass., Mt. Holyoke in Distance." Both part of *Memorial Hall Museum Online: American Centuries.* http://www.americancenturies.mass.edu/collection/itempage.jsp?itemid=4567 and http://www.americancenturies.mass.edu/collection/itempage.jsp?itemid=5618 (both accessed April 3, 2020).

**"Prof. Powys' Lecture."** *Clinton Daily Item.* January 6, 1914: 1, 3.

**Prescott Club (Clinton, Massachusetts).** *By-Laws of the Prescott Club of Clinton, Mass., Incorporated April 2, 1886 ...* Clinton: Press of W.J. Coulter for The Club, 1902. "Social Organizations" pamphlet and ephemera box, Clinton Historical Society (Holder Memorial), Clinton, Massachusetts.

**Rosen, Jody.** "'Oh! You Kid!' How a sexed-up viral hit from the summer of '09—1909— changed American Pop Music Forever." *Slate* (June 2, 2014). www.slate.com/articles/arts/culturebox/2014/06/sex_and_pop_the_forgotten_1909_ hit_that_introduced_adultery_to_american.html (accessed October 1, 2019).

**"Russia's Reasons:** Prof. J.C. Powys Tells Large Audience Why That Country is in the War." *Clinton Daily Item.* September 28, 1915: 1.

**St. Andrew's Mutual Benefit Society (Clinton, Massachusetts).** *Celebration of the 137th Anniversary of the Birth of Robert Burns. Grand Concert and Ball of the St. Andrew's M.B. Society, Town Hall, Clinton ...* (printed program containing order of dances and menu). Clinton: Martin Printing Co. for The Society, 1896. "Social Organizations" pamphlet and ephemera box, Clinton Historical Society (Holder Memorial), Clinton, Massachusetts.

**"St. Andrew's Society."** *Wikipedia.* https://en.wikipedia.org/wiki/Saint_Andrew%27s_Society (accessed December 21, 2019).

**Scotland.** *1881 Scotland Census. Ancestry.*

**Scott, Anne Firor.** *Natural Allies: Women's Associations in American History.* Urbana; Chicago: University of Illinois Press, 1991.

**"Silent film."** *Wikipedia.* https://en.wikipedia.org/wiki/Silent_film (accessed December 20, 2019).

**Simmons College (Boston, Massachusetts).** *Fourteenth Annual Catalogue, 1915-1916.* Boston: The College, 1915.

## SOURCES

**Smith College (Northampton, Massachusetts).** *Annual Register of the Alumnae Association of Smith College ...* Northampton: The College, 1920.

**Smith College (Northampton, Massachusetts).** Biographical/historical note. "John Tappan Stoddard Papers" (online finding aid). *Smith College Libraries.*
https://findingaids.smith.edu/repositories/4/resources/247
(accessed November 13, 2019).

**Smith College (Northampton, Massachusetts).** *Bulletin of Smith College; Catalogue, 1913-1914.* Northampton: The College, 1913.

**Smith College (Northampton, Massachusetts).** *Bulletin of Smith College; Catalogue, 1914-1915.* Northampton: The College, 1914.

**Smith College (Northampton, Massachusetts).** *Some Special Traditions.*
https://www.smith.edu/about-smith/some-special-traditions
(accessed multiple times in 2019 and 2020).

**Smith College (Northampton,Massachusetts). Class of 1915.** *1915 Class Book* (yearbook). Northampton: The College, 1915.

**Smith College (Northampton, Massachusetts). Class of 1915.** *Smith College Class of 1915: 25th Reunion Report.* [Chestnut Hill, Massachusetts: Elizabeth Dewey Perry], 1940.

**(Smith College periodicals):**

*Smith Alumnae Quarterly.*

*Smith College Monthly.*

*Smith College Weekly.*

**Somerset Club (Clinton, Massachusetts).** Printed program for November 27, 1919 minstrel show. "Clinton Drama Shows" pamphlet and ephemera box, Clinton Historical Society (Holder Memorial), Clinton, Massachusetts.

**"Sound film."** *Wikipedia.*
https://en.wikipedia.org/wiki/Sound_film
(accessed December 20, 2019).

**"Speaks for Suffrage:** Miss Helen Todd Addresses Large Crowd at High and Church Streets. Thursday Night." *Clinton Daily Item.* October 15, 1915: 5.

SOURCES

**Sterling (Massachusetts).** Printed annual school reports for the period around 1915. Conant Public Library, Sterling, Massachusetts.

**Stevens, Ellen K.** "The Associate's Responsibility Toward the Religious Life of Her Girls." *Girls' Friendly Society in America Associates' Record.* Vol. 23, No. 1 (January 1915): 9-11.

**Stevens, Ellen K.** "The First Half Century, 1850-1900." *Clinton Centennial Volume, 1850-1950: The Story of Clinton, Massachusetts, Incorporated March 14, 1850, and the Clinton Centennial Celebration.* Clinton: The Town, copyright 1951. 2-17.

**"Ten Women Registered.** Clinton Now Has Total of 111 Female Voters; Interest in School Question. Democrats Were Busy." *Clinton Daily Item.* February 28, 1916: 1.

*Towns of the Nashaway Plantation.* Hudson, Massachusetts: Lancaster League of Historical Societies, 1976.

**"Union Station (Northampton, Massachusetts)."** *Wikipedia.* https://en.wikipedia.org/wiki/Union_Station_(Northampton,_Massachusetts) (accessed December 17, 2019).

**(United States. Census.)** *US Census Records. HeritageQuest Online.* Records for 1890-1940 consulted.

*U.S. Naturalization Record Indexes, 1791-1992.* Ancestry.

**Weeks Institute (Clinton, Massachusetts).** *The Weeks Institute, Clinton, Massachusetts. Season of 1907 and 1908* (printed schedule of programs). [Clinton: The Institute, 1907.] "Social Organizations" pamphlet and ephemera box, Clinton Historical Society (Holder Memorial), Clinton, Massachusetts.

**Wellesley College (Wellesley, Massachusetts).** *Wellesley College News* (multiple issues 1914-1918 consulted).

**Wellesley College (Wellesley, Massachusetts). Archives.** File of biographical material (1942-1986) relating to Christine L. Beck, Wellesley Class of 1915. Wellesley College Archives, Wellesley, Massachusetts.

**Wellesley College (Wellesley, Massachusetts). Class of 1915.** *Legenda, 1915* (yearbook). Wellesley: The College, 1915.

**Willard, Frances Elizabeth.** *Occupations for Women: A Book of Practical Suggestions for the Material Advancement, the Mental and Physical Development, and the Moral and Spiritual Uplift of Women.* Cooper Union, New York: The Success Co., 1897.

**Williams, Geoff.** "A Glimpse at Your Expenses 100 Years Ago." *U.S. News & World Report.* https://money.usnews.com/money/personal-finance/articles/2015/01/02/a-glimpse-at-your-expenses-100-years-ago (accessed December 2, 2019).

**Women's Anti-Suffrage Association of Massachusetts.** *Anti-Suffrage Essays by Massachusetts Women.* [Boston: J. Haier], 1916.

*The Worcester House Directory and Family Address Book ...* Worcester: Drew Allis Company, 1916.

**"Worthy Hotel."** *Wikipedia.*
https://en.wikipedia.org/wiki/Worthy_Hotel
(accessed December 17, 2019).

## About the Author

**Leslie Perrin Wilson** is a writer on local history for both scholarly and general audiences. A retired special collections curator, she is enthusiastic about primary documentation, particularly the diaries, letters, and narratives that tell the stories of women's lives. She and her husband live in Clinton, Massachusetts, in the house Jennie McLeod occupied for half a century.